Business Ideologies
in the
Reform-Progressive Era,
1880-1914

ALFRED L. THIMM

Business Ideologies
in the
Reform-Progressive Era,
1880-1914

The University of Alabama Press
University, Alabama

To the memory of

HERMAN KROOSS

Friend and Teacher

Library of Congress Cataloging in Publication Data

Thimm, Alfred L.
   The role and opinion of the businessman during
the reform-progressive era (1880-1914)

   Bibliography: p.
   Includes index.
   1. United States—Commerce—History.   2. Busi-
nessmen—United States—History.   3. Big business—
United States—History.   I.   Title.
HF3028.T54   338'.0973   75-17869
ISBN 0-8173-5109-4

PREFACE

Herein, the business opinion and the business ideology that prevailed in the United States during the Reform-Progressive period (1880–1914) are described, analyzed, compared with the actual economic role played by the businessman during this era. "Business opinion" is defined as the point of view toward specific issues taken by business leaders, singly or collectively, in terms of their own immediate experiences and successes. "Business ideology," on the other hand, represents the rationalized class aspirations of business or business segments. The process which so often converted business opinion into ideology is examined, as well as the role played by philosophers, economists, and economic institutions in shaping business ideology.

It is intended to enhance our understanding of current business opinion, ideology, and institutions by tracing their roots and describing their development during a particularly crucial and colorful period of American capitalism. In the light of such historical evidence, the originality and validity of current analyses of contemporary business opinion and behavior can be effectively reassessed. To this end, our study sustains as modern a frame of reference as possible, in order to establish a clear-cut identification that is meaningful for both the time period under investigation and contemporary events.

The heterogeneity of American society makes it very difficult to come to grips with true "business opinion." Since the opinions of the local grocery store owner or small town banker are scarcely recorded, the well-publicized opinions of the big businessmen (industrialists, merchants, bankers, and financiers) and their newspapers and organizations must be taken, of necessity, to represent business opinion, unless there is some evidence of a cleavage between small and large business on any specific issue.

v

Inasmuch as trade associations, the National Association of Manufacturers, the Chamber of Commerce, and other modern collective voices of business hardly played a role in the period under study, political parties, politicians, and journalists that were known to express the business point of view come under close scrutiny, as well as business journals, trade publications, and banking magazines. In comparing business opinion and ideology with the actual role played by business, standard economic and historical sources have been used to evaluate business performance.

CONTENTS

1. Introduction: The Background

The rise of the large business corporation in the late nineteenth and twentieth centuries is one of the major changes in history, comparable to the rise of medieval feudalism or of commercial institutions at the close of the middle ages. . . . Corporate enterprise gradually altered the meaning of property, the circumstances and motivations of economic activity, and the careers and expectations of most citizens.

THOMAS C. COCHRAN, *The American Business System*

The post World War II period in the United States has been characterized by major socioeconomic changes. Under the impetus of the wars against Fascism and Communism, heavy government spending and full employment, prosperity and inflation, virtually every institution has witnessed serious changes.

The business community, especially, has been affected by the dynamics of mid-century America, and the corporate managers, who had already replaced the captains of finance and industry in their boardrooms before World War II, managed to take their place in the imagination of the public in the post World War II period.

This new managerial class promises to become the first truly conservative group in America history since the defeat of the Southern aristocracy and the decline of the Federalists. Steeped in concepts of "service" and "social responsibility," its intellectual spokesmen have even taken a very dim view of that crass, materialistic idea that business is motivated by profits! The "neo-conservative" spokesmen of the managerial class rather maintain that profit is but a measurement of managerial efficiency.

1

Management's *raison d'etre* is the efficient production of goods and services. These new concepts of "service," of "responsibility" to employees, community, and stockholders, even of *noblesse oblige* hardly could help but result in an increasing personal participation of corporate executives in the actual government of the nation.

The conservatism of the new managerial class demands the existence of a continuity in its development and, if not gods, at least a breed of demigods that can be claimed as the forefathers of the organization man. Thus we witness a general attempt, especially by the neo-conservatives Buckley, Kirk, Rossiter, and the editors of Fortune magazine, to portray the American businessman as the standard bearer of conservatism in the United States.

There is little resemblance, however, between the contemporary conservative "organization man" and the businessmen of the Gilded Age, the tycoons of the Progressive Era, or even the grim Cassandras of the New Deal period. Miriam Beard aptly described the revolutionary businessman:

> he was the perpetual parvenu, the everlasting disturber and expander, who had cut himself off from the dark mysteries of blood and soil, the instincts of emotions that sprang from the furrows. He destroyed the fixed, hierarchical and agrarian order of things by introducing temptations and doubts, by outshining the old ruling classes, or overthrowing them in revolution.[1]

Who can see in this picture the corporate executive of the 1960's and '70's?

A study of both business opinion and the actual role played by the businessman in the period 1880 to 1914 should be especially helpful in answering the question whether the modern corporate executive is a legitimate descendant of previous generations of American businessmen or whether there really has been a "managerial revolution." It was precisely during the last decades of the 1800's that business abandoned again the typically bourgeois attitude toward politics it had acquired in the post Civil War period;[2] henceforth the businessman relied no longer on stooges and politicians to run the country, but rather participated openly in national and local politics. In order to appreciate the radicalism of this step we must note the letter of a businessman of a previous generation to his brother. Sam Colt wrote:

> don't for the sake of your own good name think again of being a subordinate officer of government. You had better blow out your brains at once. . . than to hang your ambitions on so low a peg.[3]

The business ideology of a period that turned the Senate into the world's most exclusive millionaire's club should be of great interest to an era in which businessmen not only have played an important role in politics but have been able to rationalize the departments of defense, housing, and transportation.

There are many other reasons why the period 1890 to 1914 should be of particular interest to us. It was above all a period of transition, especially in the business community where the dynamic captains of industry were handing over their reins to the conservative captains of finance. It was a period in which naive egalitarianism clashed with conservative viewpoints, where the secular religion of classical liberalism was being challenged by Progressivism (welfare liberalism).

The analysis of the relationship between official business ideology, business opinion, and the economic and sociological consequences of business development should materially help us in assessing contemporary events. Furthermore, it provides a good test for the Kirk—W. H. Chamberlin—John Chamberlin thesis of American history as a battle between Conservatism and Liberalism, wherein the businessman has essentially represented conservative opinion.[4]

Although it is the purpose of this study to analyze business activity and opinion rather than to label it, some political terms will have to be defined now, since few words have become so meaningless as "conservative" and "liberal." For our purposes we shall distinguish between classical liberalism, welfare liberalism, and Tory-conservatism.

Classical liberalism has been the secular religion of the bourgeoisie, based upon the economics of Smith, Bastiat, and Say, the political philosophy of Hume and J. S. Mill, and above all the "sociology" of Spencer. Empirical and rational, it believes in the perfectability of mankind, provided the "natural laws" of a *laissez faire* economy are permitted to work unfettered in an institutional framework in which personal liberty and property rights are protected above everything else.

Welfare liberalism, a not quite legitimate offspring of classical liberalism, resulted perhaps as much from the concentration of power that characterized the second half of the 19th century as from the patently unequal shares in the country's prosperity that were enjoyed by labor and agriculture. Thus, the empiricism and rationalism of classical liberalism were turned toward the development of legal and institutional reforms that would protect the individual from the concentration of economic power. Since man was innately good, the evil in the world could be banished by rational government intervention.

Conservatism, which since the demise of the Federalists has played only a minor role in American history, depends primarily upon an established ruling class and on an established church for its existence. Bent upon the preservation of time-honored tradition and institutions, and emphasizing the historical continuity of human wisdom and experience, conservatism does not hesitate to entrust a "responsible" government with significant powers to guide the economy and, above all, to protect the weaker members in society from the stronger. Imbued with the concept of service and *noblesse oblige*, a conservative ruling class has historically been less hostile to social legislation than the liberal bourgeoisie. Conservatism recognizes the inherent evil in men, does not look forward toward a Utopia, but at the same time is basically hostile to the greed and materialism of the bourgeoisie. Burke, Carlisle, John Ruskin, Henry Adams, and the contemporaries Kirk and Burnham can be considered as the conservative philosophers who have most effectively influenced the emerging American conservatism.

Traditionalism, unlike true conservatism, possesses no representative philosopher and no uniform political philosophy. Farmers, artisans, small town professionals, small businessmen, especially in service and marketing lines, essentially then the petty bourgeoisie, comprise the bulk of traditionalists. Attached to their received values, mode of living, and technical arts, the traditionalists are hostile to change *qua* change, distrustful of "foreigners,"—who, of course, might include anyone from a different town, class, race, or educational background—and profoundly antiintellectual. During periods of depression or falling prices, they might embrace radical causes—the Nativist parties, Know-Nothingism, the pre-Civil War Republican party, the Farmers Alliance, the populist-progressive movements, the New Deal—while during periods of tranquil prosperity they tend to follow the guidance of the dominant classes and enthusiastically support a Grant, Coolidge, or Eisenhower.[5]

We also find that the traditionalist has little attachment to institutions that are not of his own making but are dear to the Tory-conservative, such as the role of the courts, the constitution, academic freedom, a career civil service, etc. (Note that these are essentially aristocratic institutions, often irreconcilable with egalitarian values.) Frightened by economic or social instability, the traditionalist is as ready to look to the radical right as to the radical left for support. As a matter of fact, the point could be made that until World War I, at least, there was little difference between the radical left or right. Thus, Populism as well as the Nationalist parties of the 80's and 90's were the clearest expressions of the political philosophy of the pauperized petty bourgeoisie. Only in the first half of the twentieth century does the radical petty bourgeoisie begin to divide its allegiance between LaFollette and Huey Long, Truman and McCarthy, the Farmer's Union and the American Legion.

No matter where the traditionalist seeks his political home, however, his political decisions will be motivated by his status consciousness.[6] Especially when his status position is threatened either by depression or rapid technological change, we shall find that the traditionalist's adherence to the *status quo*, or his longing for the *status quo ante*, is prominently expressed by a strident "populism," by an insistence that all facets of public and private life conform to the established traditionalist views held by "the people." Under favorable circumstances, that is, when supported by important segments of either business or labor, the traditionalist may be able to slow up dynamic changes unfavorable to him, or he may even succeed in turning back the clock temporarily. The anti-railroad, anti-trust legislations of the 70's, 80's and 90's, for example, were the consequences of the activities of the traditionalist Grangers and Populists. Similarly, the farm, anti-chain store, fair-trade, and price fixing legislations of the New Deal were designed to keep alive the independent farmer and small businessman.

It is this superficially conservative impact of the traditionalist which prompts many observers to classify him as conservative; and the Republican party, the traditionalist's home in the twentieth century, as a conservative party. One must not overlook, however, the often radical nature of the traditionalist's views. The essentially radical demand for a "direct democracy" is latent among broad segments of the traditionalist petty bourgeoisie, and emerges whenever the tides of populism run high;[7] it is no accident that both George Wallace and the "New Left" see the current system of representative democracy as a device to thwart "the will of the people." This attitude provides the common denominator for the Jacksonian "revolt" and the Bryant, McCarthy, and Wallace movements. We shall, therefore, make a clear distinction between the status-conscious traditionalism of the petty bourgeoisie and Tory conservatism.

2. The Political, Economic and Social Setting of Business in the Progressive Era

> We have not been a people essentially political, literary, meta-
> physical, or religious. Our habits and folkways have not been
> formed only by voting, reading, logic-chopping, or prayer. . . .
> we have been primarily a business people, and business has
> been most important in our lives.
>
> THOMAS C. COCHRAN AND WILLIAM MILLER, *The Age of Enterprise*

In order to study the role and ideology of business in the progressive era, it is important to sketch the major ideological and
economic developments that led to the emergence of business in
the 1880's as the dominant economic and political institution. In
line with the purpose of our analysis, the ideological and economic developments will be handled separately to permit their
proper comparison.

THE IDEOLOGICAL BACKGROUND AND SETTING OF THE PROGRESSIVE ERA

The lack of a feudal tradition, established church, and hereditary ruling class in the United States at the time of the Revolution set the framework for a political development that was,
above all, characterized by the absence of the struggle between
Conservatism and Classical Liberalism that epitomized the Euro-

7

pean history of the 18th and 19th centuries. The American Constitution was primarily a classical liberal document, pledged to the protection of life, liberty, and property, distrustful of government authority. To the extent that the Constitution was a compromise, it reflected the clashing opinions of the radicals—Samuel Adams, Paine, and Henry—and the moderate (agrarian) liberals—Jefferson and Madison. The "anti-democratic" sentiments (by current standards) ascribed to many of the founding fathers by Beard and others were not incompatible with the tenets of classical liberalism, and most certainly were not at all the exclusive property of the conservatives Hamilton and John Adams.[1]

> To secure the public good and private rights against the danger of the propertyless proletarians, and at the same time preserve the spirit and form of popular government was then the great object to which the convention inquiries were directed.[2] (James Madison in a letter to Jefferson)

Perhaps only the Republican-Federalist clash over the economic role of the government lends itself, superficially at least, to a Liberal versus Conservative interpretation in line with the European precepts. The hostility of the classical liberals toward government was a result of their struggles in Europe to obtain political emancipation and to defeat a hostile class. In the United States, the anti-government ideology of liberalism not only resulted from the colonial struggle against governors and the government of the motherland, but also was based on the (agrarian) liberals' belief that a strong government would not benefit them. Thus even the Hamilton-Jefferson dispute, the one instance of conservative-liberal controversy, permits the interpretation that American history, at least until the Civil War, was essentially a struggle between agrarianism and industrialism, rather than between liberalism and conservatism.

In his *Banks and Politics in America*, Bray Hammond emphasizes that the Jacksonians used the terminology of agrarianism only to advance their interests, the interests of the petty-entrepreneur, against the policies of the merchant bankers of New

York and Philadelphia. "Though their cause was a sophisticated one of enterpriser against capitalist, of banker against regulation, and of Wall Street against Chestnut, the language was the same as if they were all back on the farm."[3] Without taking issue with Hammond's sophisticated analysis, it should be stressed that for our purpose the agrarian *terminology* of the Jacksonians, farmers and enterprises alike, is important. The very fact that the middle class of independent mechanics and enterprisers saw in their family enterprise an extension of the family farm is significant because it not only made the Jacksonian "revolt" possible, but also repeatedly found expression in the Bryant uprising, the Progressive movement, the New Deal, and finally the surprise victory of the last Jacksonian, Harry Truman. The fact that businessmen who were neither agrarians nor small independent enterprisers joined Jackson and the Democrats either out of sincere conviction or, more frequently, for opportunistic reasons— as Hammond has shown elsewhere—does not change the agrarian, petty-burgeosie nature of the Jacksonian revolt.

The interpretation of early American history as a struggle between agrarianism and industrialism takes on additional meaning if we take into consideration the rapidity with which the pragmatic businessmen abandoned both the Federalist party as well as their conservative attitude toward a strong and responsible government.[4] From the time of the first Jefferson administration until this very day, the anti-government attitude of the classical liberals has been one of the integral tenets of business ideology —an ideology, however, that the individual businessman has semed exceedingly ready to abandon in practice whenever his interests demanded.

The pre-Civil War strife between agrarian and (eastern) industrialism was characterized too heavily by the clashing and shifting interests of sections, industries, nationalities and personalities to permit any easy labeling. Yet the doctrine and practices of classical liberalism emerged triumphantly from the Civil War, not only as a political philosophy but also as the essence of business ideology. Because of the heroic role of business in the post Civil War era, this business ideology was widely adopted

by the American public; and, until the Great Depression at
least, the vulgarized dogma of classical liberalism have been an
integral part of American folklore.[5]

The victory of the industrial North eliminated the only significant aristocratic class hostile to industrialism and to the mores
of a pecuniary, acquisitive society. It removed the basis for a
"respectable" criticism of capitalism and eliminated all restraints
on its most dynamic, exuberant manifestations. It consummated
the marriage of industrialism and classical liberalism and turned
the agrarianism of the Western farmer into radical, anti-business,
even anti-capitalistic channels.

> (The Civil War) dramatized in a stroke the changes that had
> begun to take place during the preceding twenty or thirty years.
> On one side lay the Golden Day . . . of a well balanced adjust-
> ment of farm and factory . . . an age in which the American
> mind had flourished and had even begun to find itself. When
> the curtain rose on the post-bellum scene, this old America was
> for all practical purposes demolished: industrialism had entered
> overnight, had transformed the practices of agriculture, had
> encouraged a mad exploitation of mineral, oil, natural gas, and
> coal, and had made the unscrupulous master of finance, fat
> with war profits, the central figure of the situation.[6]

The adapting of classical liberalism to the needs of the vic-
torious business class developed an ideology which almost perfectly epitomized the Marxian definition of "ideology" as the
rationalization of the narrow economic self-interests of its adherents. Yet, among the most prominent intellectual spokesmen
of classical liberalism in the post-bellum period, businessmen,
except for Carnegie, are almost completely absent. Herbert
Spencer, though probably unknown to the bulk of American
businessmen, presented in his "Social Darwinism" a philosophy
that confirmed the very image the successful businessman had
already created for himself, assured him of praise for his past
actions, and justified his future aspirations.[7] The business elite
which was familiar with Spencer's views—probably mainly
through secondhand sources—lionized and idolized him as the

spokesman of business ideology, but they did not attempt any original formulation of business opinion of their own.

> I am an ultra and thorough-going American. I believe there is great work to be done here for civilization. What we want are ideas—large, organizing ideas—and I believe there is no other man *whose thoughts are so valuable for our needs as yours are.* (Italics mine.)[8]

Rather than businessmen it was the academician Sumner, the journalist Godkin, the educator Harris, and the economists Wells and Wayland, who elaborated and propagated the Spencerian thesis. With different emphasis and different voices, they all preached the gospel of self-reliance, hard work, frugality, and survival of the fittest. As the occasion demanded, they were also willing to glorify trade and Darwinian "competition" and to damn the coddling of the poor, government "paternalism," idleness, and collective bargaining.

When the technology of large scale production produced oligopolies and greater inequality of wealth and status, the Spencerian doctrine of "survival of the fittest" turned out to be far better fitted to express the business ideology than the sometimes uncomfortable classical liberalism of Smith and the Mills. Spencerism also led to a revival of the Calvinistic concepts of the improvident poor and the deserving rich, one of the most successful justifications of any ruling-class ideology. At the same time, it should be noted, this new business ideology was quite selective in the application of its concepts of individualism, survival of the fittest, and self-help.

> For capital to combine was logical business practice; for labor to combine was dangerous to the American tradition of individual freedom. Industrial leaders who organized capital into vast corporate entities were elevated to a station among history's greatest; labor leaders who thought to organize labor were menacing agitators. Business monopoly was the logical fulfillment of natural economic laws; the closed shop violated the sanctity of freedom of contract. Business in politics ensured that the civil authority would be exercised by the most respected

members of the national community; labor in politics always could be traced to unwholesome alien instigation. To summon the government to protect by force was the American way of life; to call upon the government to uphold the interest of labor was to rattle the saber of class hatred. To aspire to a position where one could fix commodity prices which the consuming community must accept was but a slightly circuitous way of working for social welfare; to attempt to bargain with capital to do nothing more than discuss wages was presumptuous and dangerous invasion of the right of capital. . . . To exalt one's wealth as God-given was to be a Christian; to confuse precept of charity and radical social reform was to blaspheme.[9]

The Economic and Organizational Setting of the Progressive Era

The Civil War presented the American entrepreneur with the unusual opportunity of assuring him an unprecedented high level of demand at the same time that his political and economic enemies were effectively removed from the domestic (Northern) scene. Above all, it was the standardized nature as well as the size of the Army orders that encouraged the businessman to rationalize his operations, enlarge the scope of his organization, and ruthlessly exploit all available resources.

Most noticeable of these (changes) is perhaps to be found in a greatly enlarged grasp of enterprise and increased facility of combination. The great operation of war, the handling of large masses of men, the influence of discipline, the lavish expenditure of unprecedented sums of money, the immense financial operations, the possibilities of effective cooperation were lessons not likely to be lost on men quick to receive and apply all new ideas.[10]

Vigorously competing among themselves, these fantastically optimistic entrepreneurs built a modern communication network during the postwar period while they were almost simultaneously utilizing this same network to carry on their revolutionary enterprises. The unparalleled network of railroads and telegraph lines not only made the modern mass market possible but provided the organizational wherewithal to both populate and satisfy this market. Mainly it was the organizational revolution behind the emerging railroads, meatpacking, and iron and steel empires that radically changed the mode of living of the industrial man. Ironically enough, the very era that put "rugged individualism" on a pedestal set the groundwork for a collective mode of production that ultimately had to result in a mass society and a mass culture unprecedented in modern history.

The "rugged individualism" of the Civil War and post-Civil War era expressed itself mainly through the vigorous battle for the spoils that was being waged by aggressive entrepreneurs of this era. While larger and larger number of laborers worked under ever-increasing monotony and lived in the industrial barracks of the New York, Boston, and Chicago tenement districts,[11] the public—as well as later historians—watched in awe the Olympic battle of the individualistic titans, Huntington, Hill, Harriman, and others.

The battle of the titans had far-reaching economic, political and ideological consequences for the *post bellum* era of industrial capitalism; it created through the resulting merger movement the major problem of the progressive era around which much of our analysis will be centered. It is worthwhile to note immediately the similarity of arguments advanced by the defenders of bigness in the 1890's, 1950's and 1970's. One must, for instance, compare Andrew Carnegie. as quoted below, with Peter Drucker's defense of bigness in his *The New Society*, and Prof. Bork's attack on former Attorney General Mitchell's "reactionary populist" trustbusting in *Fortune*.[12]

As long as the captains of industry acted like the entrepreneurs of the Schumpeterian[13] and Marxian models, innovations and reinvestments of profit increased production, decreased the price level as well as average profits,[14] and drastically changed the complexion of both individual industries and the overall prevailing mode of production.[15] Perhaps the most important result of the post-Civil War "cutthroat" competition was the resulting business instability and social insecurity.

Although nothing could restore the social stability of a pre-industrial or at least semi-industrial era, the leaders of industry could attempt to remove what they believed was the major cause of business fluctuation, unrestricted competition.

It is worthwhile to inquire into the appearance and growth of trusts and learn what environment produced them. Their genesis is as follows: A demand exists for a certain article beyond the capacity of existing works to supply it. Prices are high and profits are tempting. . . . In a short time the supply becomes greater than the demand and . . . prices begin to fall . . . until the best managed and best equipped factory is not able to produce the article at the price at which it may be sold.

Political economy says that here the trouble will end. Goods will not be produced at less than costs. This was true when Adam Smith wrote, but it is not quite true today. . . . As manufacturing is carried on today, in enormous establishments with five or ten millions of dollars of capital invested . . . it costs the manufacturer much less to run at a loss per ton or per yard than to check his production. . . .

(Thus) the article is produced for months and in some cases for years. . . . While continuing to produce may be costly, the manufacturer knows too well that stoppage would be ruin. . . . Anything promising relief is gladly welcomed. . . Combinations, syndicates, trusts, they are willing to try anything. . . . Such is the genesis of 'trusts' in manufactured articles.[16]

The above quotation is an apt expression of the replacement of the classical concepts of "competition" and "the invisible hand" by Spencer's "survival of the fittest." Carnegie's pronouncements could serve as an illustration of the rational strategic behavior of players of an n-person game postulated by von Neumann-Morgenstern.[17] The essential conclusion to be drawn from von Neumann is that under conditions of instability only a coalition can reestablish stability; of course, if the numbers of "players" are very large—that is, if $n \rightarrow \infty$ we have two possibilities:

(a) a stable model, corresponding to the classical concept of competition (e.g. wheat farming), or

(b) an unstable model which, through coalition and elimination reduces itself to an n-person game, n ≦ 10, but in most cases n ≦ 3. In most areas we can easily imagine pay-off conditions of such a nature as to permit each party to follow a minimax strategy, i.e. to reach a stable equilibrium by following policies similar to those formed by Carnegie's trusts and combinations without any overt collusion taking place.

Carnegie, however, was fully at odds with the business ideology of the post-World War I and World War II period which stresses that

(1) monopolies (in business but not in labor) have been eliminated through the Sherman Act, and

(2) all business organizations, General Motors as well as the corner drug store, are regulated by "competition," "the law of supply and demand," "the dollar vote of the housewife," etc.

Post-World War II ideology is best expressed in a statement prepared by the Economics Principles Commission of the National Association of Manufacturers, "The basic distinguishing feature of competition is whether there are at least two suppliers of a market who make independent decisions on the prices and conditions at which they will offer their goods and services," while monopoly exists "whenever there is one seller of a given article or service." Having thus defined oligopoly out of existence, the N.A.M. economists still claim for their "simple, commonsense" definition of competition, all the consequences the theories of the classical and neo-classical schools ascribe to price competition: "[Competition] tends to assure that goods and services will be produced and distributed at the lowest possible cost, . . . profits will be held to a minimum," and the optimum allocation of resources will occur.[18]

This return of the post-World War II business ideology to a pre-Carnegie, pre-Spencer viewpoint is noteworthy and shall occupy us again when we examine the uniqueness of the businessman of the progressive era.

The impact on business organization of business fluctuations, vigorous technological innovations, a falling price level, and frequent unemployment should have been revolutionary, but actually little is known about the mode of physical production and business transactions in the era of industrial capitalism. We have of course, *Poor's History of the Railroads and Canals of the United States* (1860) as well as his later Manuals; however, the organizational activities and administrative development of the railroads were not representative of their times but more akin to the development of a managerial bureaucracy under the finance capital of the Gilded Age.[19] For background information we must rely on scattered bits such as appeared in the *Scientific American,* the *Proceedings* of the American Society of Mechanical Engineers, the *North American Review, The Nation,* and *Forum.* From these we can draw a tentative sketch of business organization in the era of industrial capitalism.

Entrepreneurial thinking as well as intra-firm activity was influenced by three major psychological-technological factors:

(1) *The Spirit of the Frontier.* Explorations and appropriations of new lands, innovations of new techniques, exploitations of mines and forests impressed upon the mind of the 19th century entrepreneur a belief in the unlimited extent of national resources and a mental attitude favorable to extensive exploitation of resources and wasteful modes of production.

[The American] was the world's most successful farmer, but his cultivation was gargantuan rather than intensive . . . the construction of the transcontinentals was one of the greatest engineering feats of modern history, but the American's railway tracks, like his roads, had to be rebuilt every few years. . . . It was easier to skim the cream off the soil, the forests, the mines— or business investments—and go on to something new.[20]

Mining and railroad construction became the "typical" enterprises of the 19th century; methods that were individually profitable, though frequently socially wasteful, became accepted as standard operating procedures.

William Channing commented thus on this development:

The openings of vast prospects of wealth to the multitude of men has stirred up a fierce competition, a wild spirit of speculation, a feverish insatiable cupidity, under which fraud, bankruptcy, distrust, distress had fearfully multiplied.[21]

Charles Francis Adams was even more explicit:

(The post war years) have witnessed some of the most remarkable examples of organized lawlessness, under the forms of law, which mankind has yet had an opportunity to study. . . . This has been particularly the case as regards those controlling the rapidly developed railroad interests. These modern potentates have declared war, negotiated peace, reduced courts, legislatures and sovereign States to an unqualified obedience to their will.[22]

(2) *The 'Instinct' of Productiveness.* The *Zeitgeist* of the industrial capitalism was essentially one of productiveness. Employer and employees alike were mainly interested in production and took great pride in their roles of producers *qua* producers.[23] Next to his monetary income, his role in the production process determined most the status of the individual. The technological and organizational development of industrial capitalism, however, undermined the ability of the worker to identify himself as an individual producer, and thus laid the foundations for the development of industrial unionism.

(3) *Specialization.* Industrial capitalism introduced a remarkable degree of specialization into the organization of the business enterprise. This specialization took two forms, specialization of the employer and specialization of the employee. The employer discontinued being a generalist who felt at home in any type of mercantile enterprise. In the post-bellum period he developed into a specialist "who put all his eggs in one basket and then watched the basket."[24]

The employees in turn were subjected to ever-increasing "systematization" and standardization. Labor-saving devices were introduced, and the transformation of artisans and craftsmen into machine tenders was significantly stepped up.[25]

The three factors mentioned above changed considerably the organization of business enterprises as well as the role of employers and employees. Especially the intra-firm relations between labor and employer were affected, as Carnegie was one of the first to point out:

> It is very unfortunate that the irresistible tendency of our age, which draws manufacturing into immense establishments, . . . renders it impossible for employers . . . to obtain that intimate acquaintance with employee which, under the old system of manufacturing in very small establishments, made the relation of master and man more pleasing to both. . . .
>
> Thus the employees become more like human machines, as it were, to the employer, and the employer becomes almost a myth to his men. From every point of view this is a most regrettable result, yet it is one for which I see no remedy. The free play of economic laws is forcing the manufacturer of all articles of general consumption more and more into the hands of a few enormous concerns, that their cost to the consumer may be less.[26]

Bishop Potter came to a similar conclusion in a pastoral letter.

> A nation whose wealth . . . [is] in the hands of people who fancy that day after day . . . they can sit down to eat and drink and rise up to play, careless of those who earn the dividends that they spend and pay the rents of the tenement-houses that they own, but too often never visit or inspect, has but one doom before it, and that the worst. . . . When capitalists and employers of labor have forever dismissed the fallacy, which may be true enough in the domain of political economy, but is essentially false in the domain of religion, that labor and the laborer are alike, a commodity, to be bought and sold, employed or dismissed, paid or underpaid, as the market shall decree; when the interest of workmen and master shall have been owned by both as one, and the share of the laboring man shall be something more than a mere wage; . . . when the well-being of our fellow-men, their homes and food, their pleasure and their higher morale . . . shall be seen to be matters concerning which we may not dare to say 'Am I my brother's keeper?' then . . .

may we hope to heal those grave social divisions concerning which there need to be among us, as with Israel of old, "great searchings of heart."[27]

Whatever the actual condition may have been, the folklore in the pre- and immediate post-Civil War period still liked to draw a picture that emphasized the community of interest of labor and employer, and saw in every journeyman a potential entrepreneur and master. Once the effects of the increased scale of operations reduced the importance and significance of the individual employee, his loss of status, individuality and, above all, social mobility had to change his attitude toward the boss.

If he (labor) ever were a free agent . . . the day is passed. Through agencies constantly augmenting and extending, he is, 'cabin'd, cribb'd, confin'd, bound in' to a narrowing circle of possible efforts. Divorced from the land and from the tools of production, he can live only by accepting such wages and conditions as are offered him.[28]

The employers quickly became aware of the changed attitude of their workers, but they were unable either to explain or ameliorate it.[29] As far as any attempts were made to search for the cause of the changed labor-employer relationship, attention seems to have been placed either on the bogus "union leaders" or on economic conditions. Austin Corbin, President of the Reading Railraad, presented bluntly the opinion of his class in the *North American Review*. It is collective bargaining, he held, that breaks up individual bargaining and destroys employer-employee relationships. The employer must protect the good, individual members of the unions who are (mis) led by bad leaders, i.e. the professional labor organizer, who, of course, is but a "foreign importation," who practices his trade only to collect dues.

When it is known—as the writer of this article knows—that a large majority of the membership of these unions is composed of men who are there, not because they want to be, but solely because of their fear of peril to their employment or of suffering personal violence, . . . it would seem to be the duty of employers and of law makers alike to devise some means whereby those workmen who desire to own their own time, and to be masters of themselves may be adequately protected. . . . Some employers have endeavored to accomplish this. They employ no new men who are members of any of the labor unions; applicants are required to promise not to join any while retaining their employment, those who prefer the unions are required to quit the service, and promotions are entirely confined to those of undoubted loyalty to their employer and his policy.[30]

The letters to the editors columns (special correspondence) of *The Nation, North American Review,* and *Forum* during the last fifteen years of the 19th century indicate freely that Mr. Corbin expressed the deepfelt sentiments of many businessmen, including "master-mechanics" and "journeymen-artisans." On the more sophisticated level of government commissions and economic studies, the wage-price relationship was held responsible for the development of a "labor problem."

There were some businessmen however, such as the banker Henry Clews, who just couldn't see that a structural change had occurred in the industrial organization of society:

There appears to be an idea, in certain quarters that the modern concentration of capital into large masses has made it necessary for workmen also to organize themselves into large bodies sinking their individual rights and liberties and selling their labor *en masse.* For my part, I am unable to see the force of this reasoning. . . . It seems to assume that large employers of labor have more power to depress wages than smaller ones. . . . In order to concede the assumption we must suppose that large employers can cease to be competitors for labor. . . . But this can never happen; for capitalists will always produce to the fullest extent compatible with an average rate of profit [note: this is, of course, a thoroughly Marxian concept] and this ensures the largest possible demand for labor, and, therefore, the highest possible rate of wages. . . .

The workingmen are taken care of by the natural laws of

trade far more perfectly than they can be by any artificial arrangement.[31]

Thus the increasing gap between wages and prices as well as the increasing earning differentials between unskilled and skilled labor were mentioned as the possible root of the problem.[32] No one seemed to consider that in a period of rampant individualism, a drastic reduction of the role which a large segment of the society could play as individuals would have to have far-reaching repercussions. Industrial capitalism laid the seeds for the development of the new collective concepts of Labor, Capital, Consumer, etc., that were to dominate the 20th century. The importance of this postbellum event is difficult to overemphasize. The constant growth of individualism since the Protestant Revolution reached its culmination, and its end, in the America of the 1870's, 1880's. Although individualism still remains the keyword of the folklore of the 20th century, the factory replaces the manor as the center of collective production, and Madison Avenue replaces the Church as the source of guidance and entertainment.

Standardization and specialization affected also the training, recruitment, and advancement of the employees within the organization. Division of labor made cheap *ad hoc* training possible, encouraged an increase in the use of unskilled women and children, and brought a decline in the number of formal and lengthy apprenticeships.[33] But the demands of a complex technology required a breadth of technical knowledge that neither the old-line journeyman nor the employer possessed. This forced an expansion in the number, scope, and enrollment of engineering schools, and even the federal government began to subsidize the training of technicians through the Land Grant Act of 1862. Prior to the Civil War, only three civilian engineering colleges existed in the United States: Brown, R.P.I., and M.I.T. The number of engineering students increased from 50 in 1830 to 1,195 in 1890.

The engineer was the first staff expert of any significance to enter the business organization. Although there was a great need for the services of the engineer, the businessman displayed from the very first a rather ambivalent, if not hostile, attitude toward the expert.[34] Employers most certainly did not welcome the emergence of a new type of employee, whose knowledge they couldn't match, whose independence (at least during periods of prosperity) seemed to threaten their role as the master of the enterprise, and whose livelihood did not depend on any particular mode of technological or economic organization.

The structural changes in the internal organization of the firm were, like the concentration of capital, a direct result of the technology of large-scale production. Although the trust issue seemed to have had a greater noticeable impact upon the public attitude towards business and upon business opinion itself, the consequences of the "organizational revolution"—the emergence of a new midddle class of white-collar employees and the development of strong labor unions—might very well have been the paramount consequence of the rise of the giant business enterprise. The new middle class and the unions in turn reinforced the purely technological trend toward mass production by establishing conditions that made the "marketing revolution" feasible. Although in the following chapter we shall deal mainly with the economic and ideological consequence of "trusts and combinations," we shall see that the public and business attitudes on this issue were shaped by the social impact of bigness as well as by its economic consequences.

3. The Dawn of the Progressive Era

The function of entrepreneurs is to reform or revolutionize the pattern of production by exploiting an invention, or, more generally, an untried technological possibility for producing a new commodity or producing an old one in a new way, by opening up a new outlet for products, by reorganizing industry and so on. . . . To undertake such new things is difficult and constitutes a distinct economic function, first, because they lie outside of the routine tasks which everybody understands and, secondly, because the environment resists in many ways that vary, according to social conditions, from simple refusal either to finance or buy a new thing, to physical attack on the man who tries to produce it. To act with confidence beyond the range of familiar beacons and to overcome that resistance requires aptitudes . . . that define the entrepreneurial type as well as the entrepreneurial function.

JOSEPH SCHUMPETER, *Capitalism, Socialism and Democracy*

Politically, ideologically, and culturally, the most significant aspect of the period from the Civil War to 1900 was the development of a new plutocracy whose rule was, seemingly, completely uncontested until the early 80's, and only periodically circumscribed by motley coalitions in the last two decades of the 19th century. The ruling group of the pre-Civil War period —small entrepreneurs, landed gentry, mercantilistic money lenders and speculators—was intensely political-minded and considered itself very openly and class-consciously as the ruling class.[1] Political activity was then an honorific activity, intimately tied to a sense of *noblesse oblige,* responsibility, and service. The artisans, farmer-yeomen, and mechanics ordinarily were

wont to leave politics to their "betters" but effectively retained
a veto, especially in economic affairs, and occasionally, as in the
Jacksonian revolution, became one of the principal elements of
a broad coalition that took over the country. At all times, however, the existence of social and economic class conflicts prevented the ideology of the ruling groups from becoming the
dominant national folklore.[2] In the post-Civil War period, however, the farmers and artisans lost their "veto power" and industrial capitalism succeeded in having its class ideology turned
into a national ideology. Modern communication theory gives
us an excellent explanation for the total acceptance of business
ideology by the public at that time. Communication channels
free from "noise," i.e. impedance to communication, will transmit
excellently even weak signals. On the other hand the occurrence
of even slight "noise" will require a much stronger transmitter
to obtain the same results without ever being able to silence the
noise completely. In the immediate post-Civil War period the
absence of any effective anti-business ideology made the complete
acceptance of business values by the country (North) possible.
In the 80's and 90's the anti-business philosophy of the Grangers,
Populists, and Progressives set up sufficient "noise" in the communication channels to weaken, or at least threaten to weaken,
the status of the businessman in the eyes of the public, although
the power of the business class, i.e. the transmitter, certainly was
not weakened.

The position of the industrialists was strengthened by the cap-
ture of the political parties, the identification of the agrarian
class enemy as the national enemy, and, last but not least, the
development of commercial media of mass communications beholden to the business point of view. It was above all business's
successful and impressive role as a producer during and after
the Civil War. however, that caught the imagination of the
country and enthroned the captains of industry as the cultural
heroes of the public.

Men are moved by many impulses and driven by many instinctive dispositions. Among these abiding dispositions are a

strong bent to admire and defer to persons of achievement and distinction, as well as a workman-like disposition to find merit in any work that serves the common good.

Men like to believe that the personages whom they admire by force of conventional routine . . . somehow contribute . . . to the natural well being at large.[3]

The lack of "countervailing" political power, together with the economic consequences of large scale production—i.e. the declining average cost curve—and the psychological characteristics[4] of the entrepreneur combined to create such a concentration of economic and political power that it threatened the economic survival and cultural status of important segments of the population. It was on this particular issue that the agrarians once more were able to revive the old veto-coalition of the pre-Civil War period and did once more attempt to halt the encroachments of the captains of industry.

Although the economic consequences of monopoly as well as their methods of organizing them aroused the primary and immediate opposition of farmers and small business owners, it was the revolutionary impact of the technology, organization, and rate of innovation of the new great corporations upon society that created the misgivings of essentially traditionalist segments of the population and ultimately led to the "progressive" coalition.

It is interesting to note in this context that most of the famous capitans of industry, who best exemplified the "rags to riches" routine of the 1870's and 1880's, came from the petty-bourgeoisie background of farming and small business. Thus, although they revolutionized the production process and consequently society, they retained in their own behavior most of the values and beliefs of the traditionalists. Vanderbilt, Rockefeller, and later on Ford are, of course, the outstanding examples of this development. Perhaps we have here one of the reasons why the American businessman has been able to combine social traditionalism with his revolutionary impact on the production process.

The monopoly-trust issue provided, however, the emotional impetus for the development of an anti-big-business movement.

The term "monopoly" is used in this instance with the meaning given it by the "anti-monopoly" writers of the 1880's, such as Ghent or Lloyd. It refers to the vertical or horizontal domination of an industry or region by a single firm or combination of firms. If we except the Standard Oil Company, the terms oligopoly or oligopsony would, of course, be more fitting. However, until this very day these terms have remained the sole possession of the economists, while popular discussion, even of a sophisticated nature, continues to refer to large scale enterprises which are able to determine prices administratively and possess huge economic and political power as "monopolies." The following definition of monopoly by Judge Barrett, although quite inconcise, can, therefore, be used as an example of the popular notion that is denoted by the term "monopoly":

> [A monopoly is] any combination the tendency of which is to prevent competition in its broad and general sense, and to control and thus at will enhance prices to the detriment of the public. . . . Nor need it be permanent or complete. It is enough that it may be even temporarily and partially successful. The question in the end is, does it inevitably tend to public injury?[5]

CAUSES AND ECONOMIC CONSEQUENCES OF TRUSTS AND COMBINATIONS

The development of the post-Civil War "plutocracy" was not merely the result of the increasing prosperity and importance of the business community, but rather a direct consequence of the changes in the organization, size, and structure of the individual firm. Although this development should have become quite noticeable in the decade before the outbreak of the Civil War, it seems that it was primarily the spectacular business empires of the Vanderbilts, Rockefellers, and Carnegies that, during the late 70's and 80's, awakened business and public to the realization that an economic and political revolution was taking place. In trying to assess this revolution, both public and business opinion concerned itself mainly with the symptoms of declining price competition and monopolistic practices rather than with the technological cause, the economics of large scale production. Hence, the internal growth of business organization during this period was generally neglected in the ensuing discussion while its concomitants—trusts, pooling agreements, and industrial concentration— received unqualified attention.[6]

The public reaction to the specter of increasing concentration of economic power as well as the historical, legal, and economic analyses of this phenomenon frequently failed to distinguish between the rather distinct factors that were responsible for this development.[7] It was left for Carnegie to point out, in a fascinating lead article in the *North American Review*, at least a few of the basic factors involved.[8] Although he failed to recognize the all-important consequences of a falling average cost curve, he did make the following distinctions:

> (i) "Consolidation" as a result of a high break-even point and cost rigidities. Under such circumstances the company is forced to attempt to stabilize sales, prices, and operating conditions if it is to operate profitably, and
> (ii) "Consolidation" as an attempt to eliminate competition in certain areas where it is essentially wasteful, especially in the field of transportation,[9] and
> (iii) The growth of the Standard Oil Company, a very special case which occurred because it was "managed in harmony with the laws which control business."[10]

In the latter part of his article Carnegie seemed to repudiate the view that competition could be wasteful; specifically he looked toward competition to break up combinations, "presidential (i.e. gentlemen) agreements," etc. The notion of the wastefulness of competition, widely held among both defenders and opponents of business (Beach, Wells, Veblen, Marx) was, of course, incompatible with Carnegie's overall philosophy of the "survival of the fittest."

It is also noteworthy that Carnegie, in his discussion of the Standard Oil Company, referred to the increased efficiency and lower price that can and in this case did result from increased size of operations. Again he did not realize, however, how this economic factor would stabilize the organization and assure it of an existence even without Rockefeller.

Carnegie's analysis of the causes of concentration is, hence, both an excellent example of his understanding of economic forces and a clear demonstration of the power of the business ideology to prevent its foremost exponent from drawing the obvious conclusions from his own analysis.

Apparently neither Carnegie nor the professional economists who wrestled with the trust problem realized that as long as economies of large scale production, management, and marketing prevailed in certain strategic industries, competition of either the neo-classical or Spencerian version could not prevail.[11] Even if we consider that large scale enterprises are only motivated by considerations of technical efficiency, industries whose production functions are characterized by a decreasing average cost curve either must witness the growth of the financially strongest firm to the point where it will dominate the industry—and only extra-economic consideration may prevent it from becoming substantially "the" industry—or, in case there exist a number of firms of reasonably equal strength, an oligopolistic equilibrium will have to develop, such as must have given the 19th century observer all the indication of a combination in restraint of trade. Although oligopolistic equilibria were actually characterized by more or less overt monopolistic agreements during the 1880's, modern game and monopolistic-competition theory show that overt collusion is not an essential or important feature of such a situation.

This view was, of course, completely foreign to both business and public, and a good deal of the trust controversy during the 1880's raged around the various devices that would reduce competition by agreement. The ideological nature of this controversy will be considered below; at this point it is worth nothing that, as in so many "public debates," the essential point of the problem, namely the economic and technological consequences of large scale production, was never touched upon. As a matter of fact, there were few expressions of business opinion—or business criticism—that displayed the insight of Carnegie's above-mentioned article.

An exception to this statement is provided by the *Banker's Magazine*. In the 1890's and 1900's this excellent and sophisticated magazine became a vigorous spokesman for the Gary-Perkins wing of the new professional management; but even in the preceding era of industrial capitalism, discerning analyses of business problems appeared in this magazine that foreshadowed its later views. For example, in a comparatively unnoticed editorial, "The Formation of Trusts,"[12] a guest editor—the banker, William Woodward—held that trusts are "mainly and originally" due to excessive competition and low profits. The public, basically, does not really care about trusts as long as prices are not raised. "For years," he continued,

> the newspapers have described the atrocities perpetrated by the (Standard Oil) Company, and yet they have never been able to excite enough interest among the public to lead to any serious action, (because) . . . the company has sold an honest product . . . at a reasonable figure. . . .
>
> Whether, therefore, these trust companies shall prove to be bad or good, turns wholly on the question of their policy toward the public.[13]

The discrepancy between economic theory and business behavior was pointed out a few months earlier in another editorial. Commenting upon the Anti-Trust laws to be passed "for effect upon the popular vote," the Banker's Magazine displays clearly its lack of enthusiasm for the natural-right doctrines in economics:

> The laws of trade, like those of nature, are supposed to be immutable and unchangeable. The two cornerstones (of classical dogma are) . . . that Competition is the life of trade and that Supply and Demand regulate price. Yet the advocates and apologists of the . . . new American school of industrial science known as Trusts, seem to entirely ignore the doctrines of the founders, (but) claim that combination is the life of trade and that Supply and Demand are no longer able to regulate prices, so as to return a profit to the producer.[14]

As we shall see below, business opinion reflected both Carnegie's and later on *Banker's Magazine's* attitude towards trusts, though frequently at a highly unsophisticated level.

Two significant additional factors that promoted economic concentration but that were cited neither by Carnegie nor by *Banker's Magazine* should be mentioned. The first is the role the investment bankers played in furthering the growth of trusts and reducing competition. Huge promotional profits (Morgan's group made a profit of $62 million in the United States Steel merger, for instance), as well as the opportunity to gain control of enterprises and "stabilize" markets provided a keen incentive for the bankers to promote mergers even in areas where the previously mentioned factors did not operate.[15] This development, however, did not become fully significant until after the crisis of 1893, did not reach its peak until the first decade of the 20th century, and will only be mentioned in passing at this time.

The second significant factor promoting economic concentration was the organizing role played by the "captains of industry." Schumpeter's and Veblen's somewhat overly romantic interpretations of the role of the business leader seem to have overshadowed the real contribution made by Rockefeller, Carnegie, Gould, Vanderbilt, and Harriman. It was their prodigious organizing and manipulative skill within the technological framework of large scale production that produced the giant, often predatory, business organization.[16] It was this organizing capacity that seemed to have been the one factor the colorful robber barons had in common! The "real" captains of industry who possessed Veblen's instincts of workmanship and idle curiosity and performed Schumpeter's role of innovator belonged to a previous generation. They were men like Matthew Baldwin, the locomotive builder; like Robert Hoe, the manufacturer and inventor of rotary presses; like Colt and his superintendent Root, who perfected mass production and advanced industrial engineering more than any other man, before or after; like Singer, Howe, Wheeler, and Wilson, the inventors and manufacturers of mass-produced sewing machines; like McCormick, the reaper manufacturer, Case, the threshing machine producer, and Studebaker, the wagon manufacturer. These true "captains of industry" were all technically extremely competent men, unlike the more glamorous industrialists of the Gilded Age who, with the exception of Hill, did not include a single engineer. It was the genius of Rockefeller and Carnegie, however, that they were able to surround themselves with competent technicians, and by combining engineering, financing, and marketing skills could exploit the opportunities that the economies of large scale production provided!

Because the monopolistic practices in many industries took on such features of chicanery as pooling,[17] rebate agreements, short and long haul pricing, wholesale bribery of legislatures, city councils, and judges, the popular resentment was primarily directed against specific culprits such as the railroads, Standard Oil, or the Meat Trust, rather than against large scale business itself. It would be a mistake, therefore, to consider the decreased acceptance of important tenets of business ideology as well as the reawakening anti-business, or at least anti-big-business coalitions, as the result of a huge, uniform reaction to trustification and monopoly profits.[18]

No matter, however, what the economic and technological forces were that reduced competition and swelled the size and number of corporations—the foremost collectivistic institutions of this period—the reaction among widely differing segments of the populaton to this trend created criticism of certain business practices as well as specific corporations, businessmen, and even such untouchable tenets of business ideology as "competition" itself.

Different aspects of monopoly affected different segments of the population. The result was a widespread but inarticulate criticism and hostility towards specific aspects of corporate activities rather than a coherent, uniform, purposive anti-bigness, anti-business sentiment. Typical of the disinterest in monopolies *qua* monopolies is the complete lack of interest with which the public and the press witnessed the deliberation and passage of the Sherman Act. While the passage of the Interstate Commerce Act—a measure against a special group, the railroads—was accompanied by a heavy flood of petitions and letters descending upon Congress, the Sherman Act proceedings went on almost unnoticed by public, press, or even social science publications. During the period 1899-1901 *The North American Review* had exactly one article on trusts (Carnegie's), *Harper* two, and the *Nation* seven. Professor John D. Clark found that in 1888 all periodicals in the United States, as listed in the Library of Congress, had twelve articles on trusts, seventeen in 1889 and seven in 1890.[19]

THE MARKETING REVOLUTION

The emerging phenomenon of large scale production was accompanied by the development of regional and national homogeneous markets in the place of differentiated local ones. New marketing procedures made the optimum exploitation of mass production feasible, and mass production in turn changed the tastes, customs and social composition of society to provide a further impetus towards large scale production. The "plutocracy" that dominated America in the Gilded Age was as much a product of large scale marketing as of large scale production. As a matter of fact the successful combination of large scale production, management, and marketing was America's most successful contribution to Western Civilization. It produced a mass market, a highly egalitarian mass society and, ultimately, the transition of a production-oriented culture to a consumption-conscious society.

The "marketing revolution" was, like most revolutions, essentially an evolutionary process that started with the early assembly lines and railroads of the 1850's and gained additional impetus from the "New Economics" and the "population explosion" of the post World War II years. The department store and the chain store are charter members of the marketing revolution, and by the 1870's most of the early pioneers had become fully established in the major cities. R.H. Macy and Company started in New York City in 1858, at about the same time as the Atlantic and Pacific Tea Company and at the same time as Jordan Marsh

Company opened in Boston. Wanamaker's opened its doors in 1861 in Philadelphia, Houghton and Dutton in 1877 in Boston, and Woolworth in 1878 in New York City. It was the department store that introduced the fixed-price system, an innovation equally necessary for large-scale retailing and large-scale production. The development of urban rapid-transit systems in turn broadened and unified the market and thus made additional expansion in production feasible, and large scale advertising profitable. Large scale advertising increased the propensity to consume and almost certainly established mass-taste and mass consumption standards. The giant corporate retailer introduced division of labor and the employment of staff specialists into the marketing area, thereby broadening the basis of the new middle class and in turn enlarging the mass-market and mass-production potential.

No evolutionary social or technological process ever seems to have progressed at an even rate of growth; and the Civil War, the merger period of the 1890's, and the post-war periods of the 1920's and the 1940's each witnessed a quantitative change in the marketing methods sufficiently pronounced to justify treating it as a qualitative change.

The production-conscious entrepreneurs of pre-Civil War and Civil War days were generally unconcerned about the development of new marketing methods. In the immediate post-Civil War period, furthermore, there was a high demand for goods, and industry set out to satisfy it as rapidly as possible. After the demand had been satisfied the production rate did not subside, however. We have already seen how Carnegie wondered at this phenomenon of continued production at a loss! The drive to compete for a declining demand had to result, under the technological condition of a declining cost curve, in increasing integration and rationalization of industry. The more successfully the individual companies captured a relatively increasing slice of an absolutely decreasing market, the larger were the numbers of unsuccessful factories that ultimately failed, since they operated at an increasing loss, at an ever decreasing level of capacity.

While it is true that iron is a dollar or two lower than last

year, and that the cost of labor has also been reduced, your
committee is confident that there is not a manufacturer present
who can truthfully say he can afford to reduce the prices of his
goods. . . . *It is a chronic case of too many stoves and not
enough people to buy them.*[20]

Similarly, the match syndicate combined thirty-one manufacturers of matches in the United States and closed all but
thirteen; the anthracite mines in Pennsylvania operated at 80%
capacity; the whiskey industry operated around 40% capacity,
and the iron industry at less than 50%.[21]

The decline in business activity during most of the 1870's and
1880's, and especially during the first six years of the 1880's,
prompted a much discussed and widely noticed flight into pools
and combinations to avoid "ruinous" competition and to provide
price stability. The *Banker's Magazine* commented thus on this
development:

> The aggregation of individual interests into one company has
> been occasioned in most instances by heavy losses resulting from
> competition. . . . It will be found in studyying this subject that
> in times of depression, when competition is keenest and profits
> are lowest . . . that the desire to form these combinations
> springs up and grows the most rankly.[22]

The Commercial and Financial Chronicle approved of this
trend even more wholeheartedly:

> It is recognized now that (the pool) is a measure of self-
> protection, designed simply to avoid the evils of reckless com-
> petition. . . . It is important to bear in mind that . . . the secur-
> ing of fair remunerative rates constitutes the main object of the
> pool.[23]

However, the increasing attention paid to marketing as an
enterprise function was another less publicized but at least
equally important consequence of both the business decline and
the technology of large scale production. Huge capital investments and high break-even points introduce, as was previously

observed, capital rigidity. Thus survival rather than immediate profits, a secure market position rather than market domination, become the goals of the business organization. The efficient utilization of the integrated production mechanism as well as specialization, high overhead costs, and heavy capital investment require an uninterrupted flow of production and a stable level of demand. At the very least, a level of demand sufficient to cover the fixed costs must be established; but this very necessity can and will induce competing firms, especially during a period of declining effective aggregate demand, to suffer any price decrease provided this minimum demand can be maintained.

Frequently, however, the establishment of new productive capacity, or the full utilization of the existing one, must depend upon the marketing organization's ability to establish a firm, non-fluctuating core-demand that will permit an efficient level of minimum production. Thus, the technological prerequisite of core-demand requires a greater reliance of the production departments on the marketing staff. Production and marketing become now continuous and well integrated operations. It is not an accident, therefore, that the decline in price competition and the consequent development of non-price competition coincided with the emergence of marketing as an important aspect of business enterprise. The need for continuous production and the development of a firm core-demand make an inflexible, non-competitive price necessary.[24] At the same time product differentiation, advertising, and sales promotion not only help to establish an artificially delineated market, but they also provide a milder form of competition in which success or failure ordinarily do not mean either market domination or bankruptcy, but rather, at worst, a change in the respective "market penetration of a firm; at best, an increased industry demand with no relative changes.

Combinations, syndicates, and trusts that could combine economies of large scale management and marketing with economies of production were the obvious ways of obtaining a market position that would permit the formulation of long run policies.

> These three influences—a standard product, very large capital, and popular trademarks—seem to have been particularly powerful in bringing about the most successful combinations. . . . Experience further showed that when expensive advertising was necessary to popularize special brands and trade marks, combinations had an advantage over smaller concerns.[25]

The power of the Standard Oil Company, for instance, the most famous of all trusts, was essentially based upon its highly efficient distribution system. Similarly, Carnegie, aside from his organizing ability, contributed to the success of his enterprise mainly by his skills as a salesman and creator of an efficient sales organization. The Consolidated Tobacco Company, on the other hand, relied exclusively on unfair marketing devices such as imitation of competitors' brands, intimidations of dealers and jobbers, abortive boycotting drives, etc., to destroy competitors' sales organizations and to build its own. The McCormick Harvesting Machine Company was as famous for its far-flung dealer organization as for its reapers. The intention to extend this dealer organization abroad and expand the export trade was one of the motives that brought about the organization of the International Harvester Company. One can see, therefore, that the development of an ingenious, dynamic marketing system, though associated with the monopolies of the 80's and 90's, was essentially an autonomous result of the technological revolution of the post-Civil War period.

The impact of the increased marketing consciousness of the business organization on society cannot be overestimated. Most importantly, it was a factor in developing the non-price competition of advertising, product differentiation, and sales promotion, and in reducing price competition at the same time. The substitution of non-price competition for price competition solved a dilemma for the individual businessman, who had felt compelled to praise "competition" in the abstract as the backbone of the immutable laws of economics, while deploring its practice in his own field since the days of Adam Smith. With the replacement of price by non-price competition, he could now distinguish between "vulgar," "chaotic," "cut-throat," and "un-American" price competition and "clean-cut," "friendly," "above-board" non-price competition. Hence, even a member of a pool or a modern trade association who "cooperates" with member firms by abiding by explicit or implicit price, wage, and production standards can sincerely refer to his "competitors" who through displays or sales promotion attempt to attract "his" customers.

Senator Platt, for instance, a Republican stalwart and friend of business, did not find that pooling reduced competition. "What is a pool?" he asked. "It is simply an agreement between competing companies to apportion the competitive business; that and nothing more."[26]

Similarly, Judge Gary distinguished explicitly between various kinds of competition. "I do not think that competition is invariably a public benefaction; for it may be carried on to such a degree as to become a general evil."[27]

Just in case, however, labor might come to make this same distinction between "cut-throat" and "cooperative" competition, the writer Arthur J. Eddy distinguished between:

1. Consolidations—partnerships, corporations, trusts—(formed) to more effectively compete by lowering costs and prices. *This is the only cooperative movement the direct object of which is to serve the consumer* by giving him what he wants at lower prices. . . .
2. *Unions* of labor and unions—to lessen competition and advance prices.[28]

The emerging notion of "orderly" non-price competition in an overall framework of limited cooperation and "live and let live" attitude is, therefore, a peculiar—though of course not exclusive—development of the increased importance of the marketing function.

The increased marketing consciousness of the business organization also produced employees and officers who became increasingly separated from the production process; it opened the door for the replacement, or at least the threat of replacement, of the production-directed captains of industry by the consumption-directed captains of marketing. The number of people whose livelihood was no longer dependent upon impersonal skill or impersonal production relationships but rather on their manipulative skills, on their ability to sell their personality to others, begins to increase at an exponential rate.[29] More important than even the numerical increase is the organizational proximity in which the consumption-directed marketing man and the production-directed industrialist (laborer, mechanic or employer) find themselves. Surely selling, retailing, wholesaling, and even advertising were nothing new—though it is rather questionable whether the old Yankee traders and merchants had much in common, sociologically or psychologically, with the members of the marketing fraternity of later capitalistic periods[30]—but the integration of marketing and production organization into one corporation was a significant innovation. Even today, eighty or ninety years after Rockefeller created his giant distribution system, management and industrial engineering texts are full of caveats about the production-sales relationship, the lack of communication between engineering and sales functions, and the hostility between the production-directed line and the consumption-directed marketing staff.

During the 1880's and 1890's we can attribute the decline of the aggressive, production-conscious, utilitarian, and individualistic spirit of the captains of industry to the increased importance of marketing and the marketing organization in their firms. It is impossible to separate this trend from the phenomena of absentee ownership, bureaucracy, and professionalized management, introduced into industry on a small scale in the immediate post-Civil War era and increasingly in the Progressive Era. Rather it seems that the marketing revolution prepared the ground for the victory of the captains of finance and was in turn strengthened by it. An organized, conscious sales effort, accompanied by embryonic "public relations" attempts, is the first step toward curbing the aggressive individualism and competitiveness of the industrialists. A sales campaign essentially implies that the entrepreneur will no longer rely primarily on producing the cheapest and best product but rather will depend on an organized sales effort to sell his goods. It implies also a greater willingness to conform, at least outwardly, to popular opinion, or at least to give evidence of caring sufficiently about popular opinion to make a conscious effort to guide and influence it. Under finance capitalism these tendencies become much more significant, but it is important to note that they were already implicit in the marketing revolution of the post-Civil War period.

The development of non-price competition and marketing consciousness, however, cannot be ascribed exclusively to the technological advances in communication, transportation, and mass production. The basically one-class structure of the American nation during the middle of the 19th century and the high geographic and social mobility of the individual American created a highly dynamic society in which new consumption patterns could be readily established. The lack of tradition and established modes of living, furthermore, could and did create the phenomenon of competitive consumption, as soon as an increased level of production was able to provide a surplus. Without the social and geographical characteristics of the American landscape, the marketing revolution might very well have taken a different course. In turn we can assume that the marketing revolution emphasized even further the consumption consciousness of the American people. Thus, mass production, the marketing revolution, and the national characteristics of the Americans continued to shape each other's development.

4. The Impact of "Bigness" on Business and the Community

> Every combination in business . . . prevents competition between the persons combined; and in proportion as the business is widely and successfully conducted, its interference with the competition of others increases. The larger the business, the greater the number of persons and the amount of capital engaged in it, the greater is the power of those who conduct it over production and prices.
>
> S.C.T. Dodd, Solicitor of the Standard Oil Company

> A trust is somethin' for an honest, ploddin' uncombined manufacturer to sell out to.
>
> Mr. Dooley

The development of the giant corporation and the decline of price competition had a far-reaching, direct economic impact on the small businessman, and a secondary but no less significant one upon practically all other segments of the population. Concentration of economic power does not necessarily mean the elimination of small business, nor even a decline in the number of small businesses, although contemporary business ideology seems to spend a good deal of money and effort to defend itself against this imaginary charge.[1]

The business ideology of the post-Civil War period was little concerned with this fact, however. It was more concerned with the charge that big business was beyond the control of the

40

market forces and must, therefore, be either regulated by the government or reduced in size.[2] Even an unsophisticated business community and an uninformed public—and I do not mean to imply that the business community *was* unsophisticated and that the public *was* uninformed—had to realize the political implications of such charges in the light of America's historical attachment to the *laissez-faire* doctrines, and the very strong contemporary and politically realistic support for this established philosophy among the "Agrarians" of both parties.

> I suppose that nine men out of ten would tell a stranger that . . . the government . . . interfered little, and would ascribe the prosperity of the country to this non-interference as well as to the self-reliant spirit of the people. So far as there can be said to be any theory on the subject in a land which gets on without theories, *laissez aller* is the orthodox and accepted doctrine in the sphere of . . . legislation.
>
> Nevertheless the belief is groundless. The new democracies of America are just as eager for state interference as the democracy of England, and try their experiments with even more light-hearted promptitude. . . .
>
> Thus it has come to pass that, though the Americans conceive themselves to be devoted to *laissez-faire* in theory, . . . they have grown . . . accustomed . . . to carry the action of the state into ever-widening fields.[3]

It was only natural, therefore, for businessmen to deny vehemently that any structural change had taken place in the economy that might require an "agonizing reappraisal" of the existing political philosophy. At the same time, the average individual businessman, especially the small businessman, was no fonder of competition during the 1880's than he was during the life and time of Adam Smith. Lastly, the truly individualistic captains of industry, who were consciously competing, i.e. warring against each other, meant by "competition" an entirely different thing than the economists of the 1880's or 1970's.

The comparatively new phenomena of trusts and giant enterprises deepened the age-old practical misgivings of the individual businessman towards the concept of "competition" and, in addition, created many new contradictory opinions among the business community and its intellectual spokesmen. There existed roughly three different and often conflicting opinions about the role of competition and the significance, causes, and consequences of trusts and giant corporations. The fact that one and the same businessman, or business group, may have held all three opinions at the same time, has long been an object of scorn and derision to historians and economists. Although, undoubtedly, the intellectual business spokesmen may have been frequently hypocritical in espousing the type of ideological argument most fitting for a particular purpose, we shall see that the individual businessman has held—until this day—several mutually conflicting ideological beliefs in perfectly good faith.

THE VIEW OF THE UNIMPORTANCE OF SIZE

This strand of the business ideology, frequently advanced on a sophisticated level before legislative investigation committees or in quality magazines, holds that the size of a business organization is quite unimportant. The natural laws of "competition" and "supply and demand" always prevail (at least in the long run) regardless of size.

> We have had our age of "consolidation" and "watered stock" . . . [now] the fashion is for "Trusts" which in turn no doubt give place to some new panacea. . . . The great laws of the economic world, like all laws affecting society, being the genuine outgrowth of human nature, alone remain unchanged through all these changes. Whenever consolidations, or syndicates or Trusts endeavor to circumvent these, it always has been found that after the collision there is nothing left of the panaceas while the great laws continue to grind out their irresistible consequences as before.[4]

Mr. F. B. Thurber, a former anti-monopolist, who became an executive of the Sugar Trust, had this to say before the Lexow committee:

A combination of capital in any line temporarily exacts a liberal profit; immediately capital flows into that channel, another combination is formed, and competition ensues on a scale and operates with an intensity far beyond anything that is possible on a smaller scale, resulting in the breaking down of the combination and the decline of profits to a minimum.[5]

The Commercial and Financial Chronicle was, as we shall see below, a strong defender of trusts and a volatile opponent of "unrestrained" competition. However, and this again is quite typical, it rejoined the ranks of the classical liberals and paid its obeisance before the altar of the immutable market forces whenever it dealth with labor unions:

Because the principles governing trade and finance were never before applied to a new country of vast resources . . . and because on that account transgressions of economic law do not bring swift retribution, there has been for a long time a growing indifference to them (the economic laws), causing it to be even more difficult to make those principles have any practical force among the many who gather wisdom only by experience. . . . Hence it is that we see today so many intelligent workingmen joining in on the part of labor against capital. . . . This contest has already gone so far that our industries are sensibly feeling it, foreshadowing another general depression.[6]

The prospects of government regulation, similarly, never failed to provoke business spokesmen to express complete faith in the omnipotent market forces that made regulation unnecessary. Henry Wood, who was a steady though unimaginative contributor to *Gunton's Magazine*—a shrill "house organ" and apologist for the Standard Oil Company in particular and for the trusts and combinations in general[7]—commented thus in *Forum*:

Attempts to regulate rates, prices, and hours by statute are not only useless but harmful. Natural, elastic, and self-regulative principles cannot be displaced by artificial and unyielding legislative metes and bounds, without causing derangement. The true function of legislation is not in the compulsory making of new contracts, but in the enforcement of existing agreements that have been voluntarily entered into. In the final results, the behests of legislation, when they come in conflict with natural laws are not much more successful than are similar attempts by private or corporate combination.[8]

Aside from Carnegie, however, the academic economists, Taussig, Walker, Laughlin, Clark and Bowen, who had a vested interest in the viability of the classical model (Mark Bastiat) were the most prominent and respected spokesmen of the viewpoint that size was economically unimportant.[9]

The views of the above economists are best exemplified by J.B. Clark's essay in which he took issue with J.B. Ghent's *Our Benevolent Feudalism.* "The trust magnate has no baronial power because he is paid his price for a service rendered." The continuation of the Capitalistic system, Clark continued, is by itself proof that it has no qualities which could be considered "feudal." Even though trusts may rob some groups there is no physical subjugation and hence no feudalism. "Trusts have reduced the number of competitors, but competition still survives and wages are thus gauged by the productive efficiency of the laborers. Competition is forever asserting itself . . . [and is sufficient] to restrict the power of great corporations."[10] Undoubtedly, most businessmen were completely unaware of the existence of these *laissez-faire* economists, and equally many businessmen were completely unconcerned with the ideological controversies that raged in the pages of *Harper's, Scribner's, Forum, Arena, North American Review,* and *Nation.* Still it is the intellectual that formulates the class ideology, and the "practical" businessman, "sturdy" farmer, and "honest" workingman that turn the theories of an alien economist or philosopher into deeply felt and thoughtlessly mouthed platitudes.

Interestingly enough, the academician's view of the prevalence of competition regardless of size became approximately fifty years later the "official" view of the National Association of Manufacturers in the post-World II era[11] and the widely and vigorously presented official view of corporation officials, attorneys, and the Supreme Court judges in the early 1900's. For instance, Charles M. Schwab, President of United States Steel, testifying before the Industrial Commission in 1901, insisted that the steel price was determined by the law of supply and demand.[12] The President of the Cambria Steel Company, as quoted by Supreme Court Justice Buffington in his decision, showed that "his and other companies in the steel business feel that the (U.S.) Steel Corporation has no power, even if it disposes, to monopolize, restrain or stop their business."[12a]

At the same time the view of the unimportance of size was apparently least popular among the most effective defenders of bigness (Perkins, Wells, Beach, Gunton, *The Tribune, Banker's Magazine, Commercial and Financial Chronicle*) and even its academic authors slowly began to distinguish between bigness *per se* and "artificial" monopolies.

> In a historical movement like the development of consolidations, concentration and monopoly, there may be a first stage when it is new and people are alarmed by the prospective threat it presents. There may come [then] a stage when people find the world going on much the same as before in spite of the presence of the new factors, and their emphasis is toned down to a secondary qualification *on a system built around the old factors. . . .*
>
> Later still may come a stage at which the old factors have really developed their power, perhaps to the point of dethroning the older forces from their dominant position. The students *may be forced to shift their emphasis.*[13]

Carnegie, the neo-classical economists, and the professional apologists relied on classical concepts to show that trusts could never become monopolies. At the same time the patricians, the conservative non-business elements in the middle class, as well as business groups opposed to protectionism or threatened by monopolies, used the tenets of Ricardo and the value system of classical liberalism to attack the trusts. Godkin, Horace White, and Lloyd became the spokesmen for this group which alarmed C.E. Perkins, president of the Chicago, Burlington and Ohio, sufficiently to charge that thanks to articles like Lloyd's in the popular monthlies the ignorance on transportation and monopolies was as dense among businessmen, lawyers, and legislators as among farmers. The only way to counteract the ignorance, he wrote, is to reply in the same journals, rather than to write for farmers' organs and the like, for the readers of the former are the influential interests, the property interest. Once they could be made to see that the "let alone" policy was the best, "then we shall have a great many helping to educate the voters, men who are now dead set the other way."[14]

The View of the "New Economics"

The use of classical economics by the "respectable" propertied classes as a device to attack monopolies led the apologists of trusts to set forth a different line of arguments. They held that (a) competition was wasteful, (b) bigness was efficient, and (c) a "New Economy" was developinig and the old laws, but for the concept of the survival of the fittest, were no longer applicable.

The first two points, at least, were explicit in Carnegie's N.A.R. article on trusts.[15] John D. Rockefeller subscribed to all three when he said:

> This (the combination) movement was the origin of the whole system of modern economic administration. It has revolutionized the way of doing business all over the world. The time was ripe for it. It had to come, though all we saw at that moment was the need to save ourselves from wasteful conditions. . . . The day of combination is here to stay. Individualism has gone never to return.[16]

The efficiency and order of integrated operations seem to have been their major justification in Rockefeller's eyes. Referring to his non-integrated competitors, he states: "They had not the means to build pipe lines, bulk ships, tank wagons; they couldn't have their agents all over the country; couldn't manufacture their own acid, bungs (etc.). . . . They couldn't have their own pur-

chasing agents, as we did, taking advantage of large buying."[17]
Senator Platt, in the same vein, questioned the assumption

> that all competition is beneficent to the country and that every
> advance in price is an injury to the whole country. The great cor-
> porations of this country, the great monopolies of this country
> are every one of them built up on the graves of weaker competi-
> tors that have been forced to their death by remorseless compe-
> tition.[18]

Thus the "natural laws" of the "invisible hand" are being
seriously questioned. Competition can now be good ("clean,"
"American," beneficial") or bad ("un-Christian," "cut-throat,"
"vicious," "un-American," "wasteful").

The Report of the Committee of the New York State Senate
on Trusts (1889) again laid special stress on the evils of competition.

> Combination rarely exists except as the result of excessive
> competition. . . . In the natural condition of affairs the law of
> supply and demand primarily fixes the reasonable and natural
> price of every commodity. But under the stimulus of *excessive
> competition* new elements, good and bad enter the picture, and
> each rival . . . with rapacious ingenuity lessens the cost to the
> consumer below the natural and reasonable price. . . . But the
> cheapness of the price is temporary only, for each producer ex-
> pects when his competitor is driven off to be able to fix the
> price, and, *for a while at least,* to oblige the public to pay a sum
> in excess of that which, in its normal operation would be re-
> quired by the law of supply and demand.
>
> Combination to increase the price is often the very way of
> escape sought from this state of affairs. (The trusts) prove be-
> yond question or doubt that combination grows out of, and is
> a natural development of competition.
>
> . . . while the trust is full of danger *it is not of necessity a
> monopoly* nor inconsistent with public advantage within cer-
> tain reasonable limits. (Italics mine.)[19]

It was left, however, for the pamphleteer Beach and the
respected economist Wells to present the most sophisticated

defense of trusts. Beach stressed the productiveness of trusts and the wastefulness of competition.

> A trust . . . instead of being a cause, is a result of lower prices, overproduction, and diminished profits. . . . It is entered into because the parties to the agreement believe that they can in that way . . . eliminate or control competition, maintain . . . prices, check overproduction and make money more easily.
>
> Prior to the year 1880 . . . manufacturers in this country . . . found a market for as much of their product as they could furnish at an adequate profit; but since then the selling price of almost every one of the articles of commerce has declined from 16 . . . to 50%. The manufacturer was at the same time confronted with organized and aggressive combinations of laboring men so that . . . he has been compelled to pay almost the same price for labor.
>
> Competition, as business is now conducted, costs the public a million of dollars, where monopoly, *such as it is possible under modern conditions* can extort a penny. . . . The slightest reflection enables . . . us to understand that when two men employ themselves in doing what one man alone can do, there is a waste of energy for which . . . at least the consumer of those products must in some way or another pay.[20]

Mr. Beach continued, "Another cause of combination [was] the organized and aggressive combinations of laboring man," which is entirely uncontrolled, while trusts will always be controlled through free entry:

> Whenever profit grows excessive by reason of an increase of selling price . . . outside capital will come in or the trust will disintegrate.
>
> No truth is any truer than this; and it makes an end of the objection that trusts in those United States . . . are or can be monopolies.[21]

In the same month Wells wrote in the *Popular Science Monthly*.

> Society has practically abandoned—and from the very necessity of the case has got to abandon, unless it proposes to war

against progress and civilization—the prohibition of industrial concentration and combinations. The world demands abundance of commodities . . . and experience shows that it can have them only by the employment of great capital on the most extensive scale.

In his *Recent Economic Changes* (D. Appleton & Company, New York, 1889), Wells strayed even further from the primrose path of classical American economics. Disturbed by the fact that large-scale firms would continue to operate even though operating at a loss, he concluded reluctantly that industrial overproduction is not only possible but may even become chronic, and combinations were thus the only feasible solution. In a similar vein George Gunton wrote in the January 1889 issue of the *Political Science Quarterly*: "The only economic and social interest the community can possibly have in either the diffusion or concentration of capital is that it shall be employed as to produce considerable wealth most cheaply. . . . [Trusts are] raising the plane of competition and minimizing profits." In the same issue Professor E. B. Andrew pointed out, however, that in the period 1861–72 when trusts were still quite unimportant, the price level fell 10.9%; in the period 1873–81, when trusts became strong, the price level dropped 74%; and lastly during 1882–87, the heyday of trusts, the price level fell only 2.3%

Messrs. Gunton and Wells showed a good deal of perception in their writings, anticipating in many ways views later advanced by J.K. Galbraith in his *Affluent Society* and *The New Industrial State*.

Interestingly enough, the business spokesman who most enthusiastically welcomed the rise of combinations displayed fully the American businessman's propensity to find roaring radicals firmly entrenched in Washington. In 1889, under the administration of President Harrison and a stalwart Republican Congress, Beach bemoaned the fate of the businessman:

Let those who cry 'monopoly' loudest consider that capitalists never have less irresponsible power than they have today, that

monopoly was never so shorn of its strength . . . and that mere
wealth never counted for so little.[22]

The editor of the *Commercial and Financial Chronicle* clearly
believed that "creeping socialism" or the welfare state had already arrived in 1887, a year in which the notorious radical
Cleveland held sway in Washington.

A political philosopher, seeking in the current history of
America for evidences of the tendencies of our time, would find
abundant reason for thinking that men are losing something of
their individual independence, and looking more and more to
the community to protect them in what they term their right. . . .
The most promising and significant movement [in this tendency
is] . . . the great and increasing demands of "labor" for new protective laws. It is a good theory and a sound theory . . . that
every man has a right to dispose of all his labor . . . that an employer has an equal right to employ whom . . . he wishes, and
that terms of employment and wages are simply and wholly
matters of agreement between the employer and each person
employed.

Of course, continued the *Commercial and Financial Chronicle,*

we have long ago become accustomed to a very different rule
of practice and one runs a fine risk of being set down as old
fogyish who ventures to express a preference for the old rule
as more just and more becoming for a people who think they are
free.[23]

The businessman's manic-depressive fluctuations between
Rotarian self-congratulations and "this is the end of Western
civilization" depressions seems to have occurred most frequently
among the intellectual spear-bearers of the business community,
and especially among the business journals such as the *Chronicle.*
We shall see shortly, however, that other strands of business
ideology shared this characteristic manic-depressive evaluation
of the businessman's fate.

SURVIVAL OF THE FITTEST

While intellectuals of the business world as well as economists, attorneys, and journalists attempted to justify the way of trusts to men by subtle arguments, the bulk of the monopolists and trust officers were blithely unconcerned about the public attitude towards them, provided it did not interfere with their plans. Supremely confident that they were the wave of the future, they relied implicitly as well as explicitly upon the Spencerian concept of the "natural law" of survival of the fittest whenever they deemed to justify their action.

Vanderbilt explained before the Hepburn Committee, "They [the Standard Oil crowd] are very shrewd men. I don't believe that by any legislative enactment or anything else, through any of the states or all of the states, you can keep such men down. You can't do it! They will be on top all the time. You see if they are not."[24]

Carnegie commented admiringly on Pullman's successful mergers, "Pullman monopolized everything. It was well that it should be so. The man had arisen who could manage and the tools belonged to him."[25]

Blaine, the Robert Taft of the 1880's and 1890's, exclaimed in a speech attacking Cleveland's and the Democrats' concern with trusts: ". . . well, I shall not discuss trusts this afternoon. I shall not venture to say that they (are) altogether advantageous or disadvantageous. They are *largely private affairs* with which neither President Cleveland nor any private citizen has any particular right to interfere."[26]

The nickel monopolist Wharton angrily rejected the insinuation that the success of his "protected" trust was due to the tariff: "I have supported and aided the Government more than it has supported and aided me. . . . I am one of the men who create and maintain the prosperity of the nation and who enable it to survive even the affliction of wrong-headed and cranky legislators."[27]

James Hilll, who fully shared Wharton's concept that "we" made prosperity, "we'" made the country, asserted that "the fortunes of railroad companies are determined by the law of the survival of the fittest."

George Hearst, upon joining his fellow business tycoons in the most exclusive "Millionaire's Club," the United States Senate, epitomized the views of its members:

> I do not know much about books; I have not read very much; but I have travelled a good deal and observed men and things and I have made up my mind after all my experience that the members of the Senate are the survivors of the fittest.[28]

The captains of industry, such as Hill, Wharton, Carnegie, etc., can well be exempted from Brooks Adams' dictum that the Industrial Revolution had raised "a timid social stratum to the position of a ruling caste. A social stratum which had never worn the sword, which had always been overridden by soldiers, and which regarded violence with the horror born of fear."[29] The Hills, Fricks, and Whartons most certainly did not dread violence, but rather revelled in overcoming opposition and hardships. Their "we built America" was one expression of this supreme self-confidence and swagger.

These supermen could, of course, not be bothered with mere man-made laws, and W. T. Harris, United States Commissioner of Education, exclaimed admiringly:

> Captains of industry depend on higher education to keep themselves out of jail, for great business combinations involve and must adopt legal precautions to avoid civil and criminal liabilities.[30]

It was left, however, for the academician Youman to epitomize this line of thought:

> Social forces cannot be created by enactment and when dealing with the production, distributing and commercial activities of the community, legislation can do little more than interfere with their natural causes.[31]

Neither the aggressive captains of finance nor their admiring ideologues were able to keep from claiming for their model of biological competition the benefits which, according to the classical economists, accrue to a market economy from price competition. At the very least, "free entry" and competition among capital were to provide that automatic regulation which was necessary if government regulation was to be avoided. The economist, Franklin Giddings, advanced the view that fear of competition rather than competition keeps prices down, but that in the long run the classical doctrines still prevail since the fear of potential competitors entering the market will control combinations.[32] In a lengthy review the *Commercial and Financial Chronicle* agreed fully with Gidding's description of this process, but did not accept his view that "modern competition" did not modify Ricardo's theory.

> It (Ricardo's theory) was not merely that competition made prices right on average, but that it might be trusted to steady prices. The former effect, with some limitations, still continues. The latter does not. . . . The competition of investors still tends to limit profits, but the competition of sellers no longer stops merely because prices fall below cost of production.[33]

Interestingly, the *Chronicle* rejected in the same review Clark's concept of the emergence of the manager as the dominant factor in production. It held, rather, that capital employs the manager, and that, therefore, the manager is not an independent factor of production.

POPULAR REACTION TO TRUSTS

The social and psychological consequences of trustification, the marketing revolution, and the closing of the frontier have generally been neglected over the analysis of the political reaction. Not only were the old Calvinistic values of self-help, individualism, and frugality threatened by the growth of large scale organization, the Christian values of the community were deeply shocked by the tales of corruption and conspiracy that the various legislative investigation committees uncovered. Generally we find a forgetfulness, cynicism, and unwillingness to testify among the corporate executives which compares with the contemporary court performance of members of the Mafia or "New Left." Quoting haphazardly we find that the vice-president of the New York Central "would not remember having signed a rebate agreement with the South Improvement Company."[34] At the same investigation the quibbling and cynicism of the South Improvement Company executives prompted the chairman to exclaim: "During the whole examination there has not been a direct answer given to a question. I wish to say to you that such equivocation is unworthy of you."[35] The Committee of Commerce, a Congressional committee to investigate the South Improvement Company, discontinued its investigation suddenly, after eliciting sensational testimony and prompting the dissolution of the company through its publicity. The committee permitted principal witnesses to refuse to testify, without taking recourse to the Fifth Amendment, or to produce records.[36] The secretary of the pipe line company, American Transfer Company, questioned about his organization replied, "I don't know anything about the organization," although he distributed yearly dividends of $3,093,750 on $100,000 of capital.[37] It was, however, before the bar of the Hepburn Committee that the Standard Oil gang for the first time made famous the phrase "I refuse to answer on the advice of counsel." Generally it was impossible to get direct answers to the simplest questions:

Hepburn: You are a member of the firm of Charles Pratt and Company, are you not?
Henry Rogers: Yes, sir.
Hepburn: That firm is one of the Standard Oil's affiliated firms, is it not?
Rogers: I don't know that I understand your question.
Hepburn: You ship under the Standard Oil rates, do you not?
Rogers: I really don't know whether we do or not. (!!!)
Hepburn: Are you a member of the Standard Oil Company?
Rogers: If I was, I think that is a personal question.[38]

The laurels for consistent use of the Fifth Amendment go to

William Rockefeller, however. Asked who were on the board of directors with him, he replied:

> "I decline to answer on advice of counsel."
> "On the ground that the answer will incriminate you?"
> "I decline to answer on the advice of counsel."
> "Or is it that the answer will subject you to some forfeiture?"
> "I decline to answer on the advice of counsel."
> "Do you decline on the ground that the answer will disgrace you?"
> "I decline to answer on the advice of counsel."[39]

The trusts were an immediate and real threat to both the survival of the small entrepreneur (be it the independent oil producer or the small farmer) and the upward mobility of independent artisans and farmers. It was out of this deep-set feeling of moral shock and angry frustration that the populist revolution finally developed. Although the petty-bourgeoisie did not revolt until the 1890's, it was the 1880's that prepared this development.

Typical of the events that raised anti-trust sentiments was "the Strike of the Millionaires against Miners" which the radical pamphleteer, Demarest Lloyd, brought to the attention of the public in his addresses and newspaper stories.

> The gentlemen of many millions, sitting under brilliantly illuminated Christmas trees in joyous mansions in Chicago, Erie, St. Paul, New York, by a click of the telegraphy, made a present of mid-winter disemployment to one-third of 'their' town . . . [and threatened to keep the mines closed] until the grass grew in the streets.[40]

It would be a mistake, however, to assume that the popular resentment against the trusts resulted in an articulate anti-trust philosophy or prompted serious proposals for general anti-trust legislation. The periodicals and newspapers of the period provide little evidence for the Cochran-Beard thesis that the Sherman Act was the result of a strong popular outcry against the monopolies. It seems much more likely that the skilled politicians in both houses of Congress were aware of the growing but inarticulate hostility of widely differing segments of the public against a business reality that conflicted with the Calvinistic ethos of the upper-mddle class and the Boston-Philadelphia aristocracy, and with the classical liberalism of intellectuals and academicians. The Sherman Act, passed without excitement, little discussion, and hardly a trace of public response, seemed to have been a subconscious attempt to pacify this subterranean discontent. If we note the enthusiasm with which business spokesmen have ever since cited the Sherman Act as a proof of the absence of business monopolies, the above interpretation of the passage of the Sherman Act becomes quite convincing. In the words of Senator Platt:

> The conduct of the Senate has not been in the line of honest preparation of a bill to prohibit and punish trusts. It has been in the line of getting some bill with that title that we might go to the country with.[41]

The Sherman Act, at any rate, did not and could not halt the trend towards bigness, mergers, and combinations, and the foundation was laid for the reform movement that would ultimately culminate in the New Deal. Perhaps nothing is as indicative of the popular attitude towards the trusts during the early nineties as Grover Cleveland's message to Congress, December 7, 1896:

> [A] topic in which our people rightfully take a deep interest [is] the existence of trusts and other huge aggregations of capital the object of which is to secure the monopoly of . . . trade . . . and to stifle wholesome competition. When these are defended, it is usually on the ground that though they increase profit they also reduce prices. . . . [Even if prices should sometimes decrease] such occasional results fall far short of compensating the palpable evils charged to the account of trusts and monopolies. *Their tendency is to crush out individual independence and to hinder or prevent the free use of human faculties and the full development of human character.* Through them the farmer, the artisan, and the small trader is in danger of

dislodgement from the proud position of being his own master, watchful of all that touches his country's prosperity, in which he has an individual lot, . . . to be relegated to the level of a mere appurtenance to a great machine, with little free will, with no duty but that of passive obedience, and with little hope or opportunity of rising in the scale of responsible and helpful citizenship.

To the instinctive belief that such is the inevitable trend of trusts and monopolies is due the widespread and deep-seated popular aversion in which they are held and the not unreasonable insistence that, *whatever may be their incidental economic* advantages, their general effect upon personal character, prospects and usfulness can not be otherwise than injurious.[42]

It is most noteworthy that the classical-liberal Cleveland did not base his ringing condemnation of trusts upon their failure to maintain price competition. While academic economists in the 1880's, 1890's, and 1970's had been essentially concerned with the question whether oligopolies maximize or fail to maximize national welfare, Cleveland attacked the trust problem mainly in terms of its implication for the political and personal freedom of the individual. It is on this basis only that the populist and progressive movements can be fully understood, and it is on this basis that the final evaluation of business activity will be attempted in this study.

5. Social Darwinism, the Pseudoscience of Industrial Capitalism

In every society, however egalitarian in principle, inherited advantages quickly set in motion the process of building up a ruling class, even if the new ruling class has not the additional asset of being able in part to build on the foundations of the old. And so it happened in the industrial society of the nineteenth century; and the story of the industrious errand-boy who became the managing director and of the lazy son of the managing director who became an errand-boy was soon an agreeable myth which took little or no account of the facts of life, But, when this myth was exploded, it carried away with it whatever moral justification had existed for the non-intervention of the state in a society where industry and intelligence were automatically rewarded and idleness and folly automatically punished.

EDWARD HALLETT CARR, *The New Society*

The inability of the business community to develop a uniform attitude toward trusts and competition was but a reflection of the dynamic forces that changed the structure of American industry. Virtual business unanimity on the questions of labor unions and government regulation disguised the fact that the philosophy of classical liberalism had become an inadequate vehicle for the furtherance of business, at least big business, aspirations. There was no room in the classical model for either the "total war" that comprised the "competition" of the aggressive and individualistic robber barons or the pooling agreements of independent businessmen, threatened by the logic of a decreasing average cost curve. Beach was probably right when he said:

> It still remains true that the substantial commercial classes of the people, the men who know the most about the practical difficulties of the present business situation, have not seen the menace in trusts that some other sorts of people have pretended to see.[1]

To the successful tycoon, however, the trusts could be both a result of competition and a tool to avoid future competition. He could, therefore, devote himself to competing (warring) against other predatory interests, while protecting himself against hostile raids by strengthening his empire. Carnegie expressed official big-business ideology—if not opinion—when he professed that

> The more successful the trust, the surer (competition through free entry) . . . is to sprout. Every victory is a defeat. Every factory that the trust buys is the sure creator of another one, and so on ad infinitum, until the bubble bursts.[2]

It was the inability of classical liberalism to serve these conflicting business interests that provided the need for a new philosophy that could serve as the basis of business opinion. Even a robber baron needs a philosophy that permits him to rationalize his actions, and until this day the American businessman has always wanted to be loved as well as to be rich. Hence even a Jay Gould could defy an inquiring Senator by exclaiming, "*We* have made the country rich, *we* have developed the country," putting himself thereby in the niche that folklore and business ideology had prepared for the successful captain of industry.

The Spencerian philosophy admirably supplied the need for a new philosophy that could translate the political-economic aspirations of the business community into a logical system, without departing, superficially at least, too far from established beliefs. This latter fact was especially important because not only had the old ideology gained widespread acceptance among non-business groups, but also the intellectual defenders of the business system had built up strong "vested interests" in the classical strain of the business ideology.

The doctrine of Social Darwinim gave the businessman an opportunity to replace the precise classical concept of price-competition with the vague political notion of biological competition. This Spencerian competition is well defined in the following statement:

> The conduct of trade consists in a multitude of acts varying in their ethical quality. *Competition is a state of war.* . . . Price cutting and rebating, collecting information of the trade of competitors, the operation of companies under other names to obviate prejudice or secure an advantage . . . are all methods of competition."[3]

The term "competition," thus, remained in the vocabulary of the business ideologues, together with its assigned role of autonomously regulating the economy in the best feasible way.

The struggle for the survival of the fittest made poverty a desirable condition as a training ground for future tycoons. Social Darwinism not only emphasized the elasticity of American society but also replaced successfully the somewhat bothersome egalitarian notions inherent in the agrarian tradition of Jefferson and Jackson, the experience of the Yankee settlers, and the writings of John Stuart Mill. Poverty, which the optimistic Smith hoped to see abolished and which the pessimistic Ricardo regarded as an unavoidable evil, became now a necessary condition for future growth.[4] Carnegie presented this view clearly:

> It is the fashion nowadays to bewail poverty as an evil, to pity the young man who is not born with a silver spoon in his mouth; but I heartily subscribe to President Garfield's doctrine, that "The richest heritage a young man can be born to is poverty." I make no idle prediction when I say that it is from that class from whom the good and the great will spring. It is not from the sons of millionaires . . . that the world receives its teachers, its investors . . . or even its men of affairs. It is from the cottage

of the poor that all these spring. We can scarcely read one among the few "immortal names that were not born to die" . . . who had not the advantage of being cradled, nursed, and reared in the stimulating school of poverty. There is nothing so enervating, nothing so deadly in its effect upon the qualities which lead to the highest achievement, moral or intellectual, as hereditary wealth. . . .

Should (a son of a wealthy man) prove an exception to his fellows, and become a citizen living a life creditable to himself and useful to the state . . . I bow before him with profound reverence; for one who overcomes the seductive temptations which surround hereditary wealth is of the "salt of the earth" and entitled to double honor.[5]

Henry Clews similarly recommended poverty as the best possible start in life:

Science . . . has made rapid strides, but . . . has never yet found the method of dispensing with toil of both brain and muscles in the incipient stages of accumulating wealth.

The few who are born to wealth hardly need to be considered. The accumlators among those are comparatively few. . . . Most frequently before the third generation has enjoyed its share . . . they are recklessly distributed to the millions.

The law of distribution affords one of the most remarkable examples of the irony of fate. . . . No benevolent institution could do the scattering abroad of this surplus wealth in a more equitable manner.[6]

The glorification of poverty and the substitution of biological competition for price competition were the immediate and obvious contributions Social Darwinism could make to business ideology. Especially in non-economic issues do we find that the business ideology rested over and over again on Spencerian doctrines, which seemed tailor-made to represent business opinion. As the editor of the *Outlook* noted at a later date:

[Spencer's influence] has been less the influence of an original thinker than of an unconscious exponent of the thought currents

of his time. He has expressed the *Zeitgeist* and in expressing it
has helped to develop it.[7]

Before we explore the specific manifestations of this *Zeitgeist,*
a close look at the development of the Spencerian philosophy
is necessary for a full understanding of its implications.

THE DEVELOPMENT OF SOCIAL DARWINISM
IN ITS AMERICAN SETTING

The immediate post Civil War period found an American
business community whose opinions and beliefs were essentially
non-differentiated from that of the American people as a whole.
Classical liberalism and the Calvinistic virtues, the *mythos* of
competition and *Poor Richard's Almanac,* provided the framework for the American folklore, shared equally by artisans,
merchants, and manufacturers. The great economic and political success of the thriving and frequently ruthless industrialists,
however, exposed the latter to attacks and criticisms, based upon
the very tenets of classical liberalism and Calvinism. Concentration of economic and political power, conscious attempts to avoid
price competition, unscrupulous and unsavory means to obtain
economic and political goals, increasingly conspicuous consumption and crass display of power were all attacked as flagrant
violations of the "American way."

Social Darwinism presented a unique opportunity to rationalize the most criticized activities of the business community,
without demanding a significant change in the opinions held by
the individual businessman. It was, of course, the ideal ideology.

> The fortunate (man) is seldom satisfied with the fact of being
> fortunate. Beyond this, he needs to know that he has a *right* to
> his good fortune. He wants to be convinced that he 'deserves' it,
> and above all, that he deserves it in comparison with others. He
> wishes to be allowed the belief that the less fortunate also mere-
> ly experience their due. Good fortune thus wants to be 'legiti-
> mate' fortune. . . .
> Strata in solid possession of social honor and power usually
> tend to fashion their status-legend in such a way as to claim a

special and intrinsic quality of their own, usually a quality of blood.[8]

Rooted in the American cultural heritage, Social Darwinism modified some basic concepts—such as competition and the cult of the average—just sufficiently to bring them in line with the ideological requirements without demanding the introduction of new symbolism. How smoothly Spencerian doctrine and neo-classical thought could be merged in a completely sincere manner was shown by the *Nation* editorials. Commenting, for instance, upon the "Economic Aspect of Cooperation," the editor wrote:

> The fundamental principle upon which the whole fabric of the science [economic] rests, [is], namely, that men in their industrial operations are governed in the main by consideration of self-interest; the other a principle less distinctly formulated but not less fundamental, that natural selection operates upon men as well as upon inferior animals. To discredit those doctrines seems to be the aim . . . of the so-called economic writing of the time.[9]

The acceptance of the philosophy of Social Darwinism by the business community, however, does mean, above all, the beginning of the development of a differentiated class ideology. The success of the business community in impressing the concepts of Social Darwinism on broad non-business strata disguises the fact that henceforth "competition," "democracy," "free market," and *"laissez-faire"* will mean different things to the industrialists, to the small merchants, to the farmers, and to the economists. The sometimes specious inability of the contemporary business-man to understand the economist's use of the term (pure) competition rests on the peculiar meaning this word took on under Social Darwinism—a meaning which was entirely different from the one Adam Smith had in mind when he built his market system around it.

The, at least superficially, serviceability of the "scientific" Spencerian doctrine[10] as the perfect business ideology seemed to have prevented businessmen as well as scholars[11] from discovering the essential radical nature of the new philosophy. It is this very radical nature of Social Darwinism, however, that gave the American business community its peculiar characteristic and destiny.

As already noted, post-bellum business operated under extremely favorable political circumstances; the individual businessman, therefore, hardly could be blamed for embracing a philosophy that not only promised to be helpful in maintaining this *status quo*, but also rationalized any departures from Jeffersonian capitalism that might have troubled a truly "conservative" businessman; but mere preference for the maintenance of a favorable *status quo* is most assuredly not an expression of a conservative philosophy.

Conservatism, as pointed out in chapter one, means above all an awareness of mankind's continuity of thought and a reverence for tradition and custom. The intellectual discoveries and material needs of the contemporary individual are weighed in the context of the historical wisdom of the past and the potential achievements of the future. Just as the individual is thus related to his forefathers and descendants over time, his contemporary individuality is limited by his "belonging" to a caste, class, or nation which evaluates his action in line with well established and "long-tried" principles. The importance of status and tradition in a conservative philosophy tends to reduce social mobility and discounts purely materialistic motivations.

Conservative philosophies—above all in England and the Germanic countries—contain, in addition, strong sentiments of *noblesse oblige* and the obligations of Christian charity. Although we can find occasionally an agnostic or atheist among outstanding conservatives, the belief in a supernatural power—if not in an established church—can also almost invariably be considered as the *sine qua non* of conservative thought. Equally important, at least in Anglo-Saxon conservative thought, is the tradition of academic and intellectual freedom in the universities and professional and literary societies.[12] Along with this tradition of intellectual freedom for the educated, and perhaps because of it, lies a deep pessimism about the perfectibility of men and an inordinate reliance on tradition and institutions to hold in check men's inherent and unchangeable propensity for evil. It is essentially this latter point that most blatantly distinguishes conservative thought from liberal utopian predilections in general and Social Darwinism in particular.

Primarily it was Darwin's humbling of men's conceit that laid the truly revolutionary basis—revolutionary in Ortega y Gasset's exacting definition of this term—of Social Darwinism, and placed him along with Copernicus and Freud among the most succesful destroyers of established comfortable beliefs. Whether the philosophical implications of Darwin's *Origin of Species* and *The Descent of Man* were quite obvious to either Sumner or Spencer is doubtful—I especially wonder about Spencer—but Spencer, at least, was fully aware of the scientific basis Darwin's evolutionary theory would provide for his already established positivist philosophy. Before becoming acquainted with Darwin, Spencer had been looking to physics, and especially to the Joule-Kelvin principle of the conservation of energy, for a *post hoc* scientific foundation of his synthetic positivism. Luckily for him, Darwin's evolutionary theory presented him with less esoteric means to display his concept of a self-contained universe of constantly changing but quantitatively constant matter and energy.

Darwin's semantically pleasing concepts of "continuous evolution" and "survival of the fittest" enabled Spencer to transfer his cosmological tools from biology into sociology without ever having to convince a single soul that such a transfer was justifiable.

The application of models and tools useful in the natural science to the so-called social sciences was, of course, nothing new by itself. The concepts of Newtonian physics were mirrored in neo-classical economics, and Lamarck's pre-Darwinian biology had undoubtedly influenced the early German geopolitical scholars. Spencer's slavish application of Darwinian theory to a theory of human development is, however, noteworthy for the heroic premise he makes implicitly. By applying

Newtonian concepts to economic theories, the classical economists presumed that the universal laws that plainly applied to the universe also applied to man's economic effort. Spencer, and, of course, Comte before him, made the much more sweeping and radical assumptions that (1) man was but an animal, and (2) that the biological laws of development applied not only to the genetic evolution of man, but also the the social and cultural institutions of man. Comte noted this point quite clearly:

> La philosophie positive est toujours caractériseé . . . par la subordination nécessaire et rationelle de la conception de l'homme a celle du monde. Quelle que soit l'incompatibilité fondamentale manifestée . . . entre ces deux philosophies [i.e. theology or idealism and positivism]; par l'ensemble de leur dévelopment succesif, elle n'a point, an effet, d'autre origine essentielle . . . que, cette simple difference d'ordre entre ces deux notions égalements indispensable . . . L'étude directe du monde exterieur a pu seule . . . produir et developer la grande notion de lois de la nature, fondement indispensable de toute philosophie positive, et qui, par suite de son extension graduelle, et continue à des phènomènes de moins et moins reguliers, et de la société dernier terme de son entière gènéralisation.[13]

This very application of evolutionary biological principles to human institutions not only challenged established thought but also deprecated all past endeavor, institutions, and customs. Man's development now consisted essentially of overcoming and rejecting the handicap of the past. In a paragrgaph that epitomizes liberal American thought, Sumner expresses clearly the radical nature of Social Darwinism:

> In the Middle Ages men were united by custom and prescription . . . These ties endured as long as life lasted . . . In our modern state . . . the social structure is based on contract, and status is of the least importance. Contract, however, is rational . . . A contract relation is based on a sufficient reason, not on customer prescription. . . . It endures only so long as the reason for it endures. In a state based on contract, sentiment

is out of place in any public or common affairs. . . . The senti-
mentalists among us always seize upon the survivals of the old
order. They want to save them and restore them. . . . That life
once held more poetry and romance is true enough. But it
seems impossible that anyone . . . should doubt that we have
gained immeasurably, and that our further gains lie in going
forward, not in going backward.[14]

By the logic of biological development every generation constituted, therefore, an advance over its predecessors, and consequently contemporary society had little use for emotional and
sentimental ties to the "unscientific" and superstitious institutions of preceding generations.[15]

"All is well since all grows better" became my motto. . . .
[Man] had risen to the higher forms [from the lower]. Nor is
there any conceivable end to his march to perfection.[16]

The high regard with which everything "new" is received in
the American business society is undoubtedly traceable to this
aspect of Social Darwinism. Although the National Association
of Manufacturers will pay its homage to the founding fathers
and the Constitution, the American businessman has rarely
shown excessive concern for venerable institutions, customs, or
natural resources that conflicted with his profit motive. Typical
of this pragmatism—and anti-intellectualism—was Carnegie's
article "How to Win Fortune" that appeared in the *New York
Tribune* and was reprinted with great approval by *The Bulletin
of the American Iron and Steel Association:*

The total absence of the college graduate (among the presidents, vice presidents, and officers) in every department of
affairs should be deeply weighed. . . . Nor is this surprising.
The prize takers have too many years the start of the graduate.
. . . While the college student has been learning a little about
the barbarous and petty squabbles of a far-distant past, or trying
to master languages which are dead—such knowledge as seems
adapted for life upon another planet than this, as far as business
affairs are concerned—the future captain of industry is hotly

engaged in the school of experience, obtaining the very knowledge required for his future triumphs.[17]

This lack of reverence for history and traditional institutions not of his own making, which is so noticeable in the American businessman, had the ironic result that until recently the American left, and especially the aristocratic leadership of the left from Jefferson to the Roosevelts to J.F. Kennedy, had been most concerned with the preservation of traditional customs and institutions and the conservation of resources and obsolete classes (such as the small farmer, artisan, or small buinessman).

Social Darwinism and Business Ideology

If the evolutionary basis of Social Darwinism provided the long-run materialistic, secular, and anti-historical context of the post-bellum business opinion, the biological concept of the survival of the fittest provided the immediately applicable, pragmatic frame of reference. It was probably this single feature of pseudo-Darwinism which was most readily accepted by the American businessman. Not only did the concept of the survival of the fittest reinforce the old Calvinistic belief in the deserving rich and the undeserving poor, but by approving the end results it banished all uncomfortable questions about the means used to gain riches.[18] Moreover, the doctrines of Social Darwinism enabled the businessman to characterize the reform elements as either good-natured but visionary cranks "who never met a payroll," or as lazy but cunning and dangerous agitators who attempted to use the gullible public for their own ends.

> The country is just now producing a number of preachers, teachers, and speakers who are hinting more or less broadly through anti-poverty societies and otherwise at ways for getting rich without work. That has always been the dream of a large class in every community, and as it is not hard to interest the vicious, the ignorant and the lazy, as well as cranks of all degrees, in such a scheme, it is no wonder that a crowd should be easily secured by those who but half conceal so tempting a bait.[19]

The demand for protective labor legislation evoked this plaintive note from the *Commercial and Financial Chronicle,* couched in the terminology of Spencerism:

> A political philosopher, seeking in the current history of America for evidence of the tendencies of our time, would find abundant reason for thinking that men are losing something of their individual independence, and looking more and more to the community to protect them in what they term their "rights."[20]

American Industries, the official publication of the National Association of Manufacturers, quoted in a commendatory editorial Morgan's attitude toward reform:

> The only thing which Mr. Morgan seems to have learned during his somewhat successful career is that it pays to mind one's own business. . . . When asked what might be done in the way of remedial legislation to solve the problems of industry, Mr. Morgan said, "It is an admirable work to do but is beyond me."[21]

In the same year the National Association of Manufacturers summed up its attitude toward reform: "There are a great many ways of making people good, but you cannot do it by law."

Similarly, such troublesome issues as the avoidance of competition, the establishment of tariffs, the bribing of legislators, and the deceiving of the public—business conduct which moralists, economists, and reformers from Adam Smith to J.B. Clark and from Jefferson to Godkin have found so very objectionable—could now be defended. Statements by reform elements that "labor has as much right as capital" in the running of an enterprise were bluntly countered by the *Commercial and Financial Chronicle:*

> The prevalence of the existing system [where capital controls labor] is no mere accident. It is a result of the survival of the fittest. The fact of its survival is to a great extent its justification.[22]

The survival of the fittest through "free competition" merely meant the utilization of every means whereby a competitor—that is, anyone whose activities could be considered potentially dangerous—could be overcome. The pragmatic, utilitarian nature of Spencerian "competition" was well defined by Rockefeller in a Sunday school talk:

> The growth of large business is merely a survival of the fittest. . . . The American Beauty Rose can be produced only by sacrificing the early buds which grow up around it. This is not an evil tendency in business. It is merely the working out of a law of nature and a law of God.[23]

Vanderbilt in a previously quoted remark made even clearer what he, at least, understood under "competition" and the "survival of the fittest":

> I don't believe that by any legislative enactment or anything else, through any of the States or all of the States, you can keep such men [the Standard Oil crowd] down. You can't do it. They will be on top all the time. You see if they are not.

Carnegie, in his famous article in the *North American Review* of 1889, made essentially the same point Vanderbilt made, only on a more literate level.

> While the law [of competition] may be sometimes hard for the individual, it is best for the race, because it insures the survival of the fittest in every department. We accept and welcome, therefore, as conditions to which we must accommodate ourselves, great inequality of environment, the concentration of business . . . in the hands of a few, and the law of competition between these, as being not only beneficial, but essential for the future of the race.[24]

The principle of conservation of energy that served as Spencer's model for a biological "equilibrium of mechanism" made any type of government interference both harmful and useless, contrary to the doctrines—from Smith to von Hayek—that welcomed government interference *to maintain* competition. It is quite doubtful whether, for instance, Rockefeller was overly familiar with Spencerian doctrine. His comments on early attempts—later successful—to regulate the packers was, however, reflected in the Spencerian spirit:

> I know none of the men in the beef trade. I never dealt with them. . . . But it is safe to assume from the proportion of their industry that they are sound business men. And it is safe to assume too, that no business could have been built to such proportions on such false principles or by such unsound methods as they are charged with.[25]

The ironmonger Hewitt was equally blunt: "The invasion of government into the domain of industry must be met with uncompromising opposition."[26] The organ of the Iron and Steel Association, *The Bulletin*, was a consistent foe of the Interstate Commerce Act and federal railroad regulation. Though fanatically devoted to the defense of the "protective system," is doubted

> the wisdom of substituting Congressional rules for running railroads in the place of rules and policies which the self-interest of stockholders and the exactions of competition are sure to enforce.[27]

Beyond vindicating the ways of the monopolists and demonstrating the futility of government regulation, the term "competition" takes on an additional ideological meaning in the context of Social Darwinism. If there is struggle for survival—i.e. "competition"—firms must continually enter and leave the market. Those enterprises which are firmly established at any point in time thus not only prove *ipso facto* that they are the most efficient producers, but at the same time by hailing the struggle for survival they clearly indicate that they are willing to give up their place to their betters whenever they should appear. The very fact that these betters do *not* appear is only additional evidence that the Rockefellers, Vanderbilts, and Carnegies *are* the best; otherwise they could not possibly stay on top.

Business developed a strikingly similar attitude in its relation with labor. The very fact that business had superior bargaining power was held to be *prima facie* evidence of its moral superiority. The testimony of Thomas Wickes, Pullman Company executive, before the United States Strike Commission is an excellent example of both business attitude toward Labor as well as the implicit Spencerian basis for these views.[28]

Commissioner KERNAN: Has the company had any policy with reference to labor unions among its help?—Ans.: No; we have never objected to unions except in one instance. I presume that there are quite a number of unions in our shops now. . . .

Commissioner KERNAN: What is the basis of your objection to that union?—Ans.: Our objection to that was that we would not treat with our men as members of the American Railway Union, and we would not treat with them as members of any union. We treat with them as individuals and as men.
Commissioner KERNAN: That is, each man as an individual, do you mean that?—Ans.: Yes, sir.

Commissioner KERNAN: Don't you think, Mr. Wickes, that it would give the corporation a very great advantage over those men if it could take them up one at a time and discuss the question with him? With the ability that you have got, for instance, where do you think the man would stand in such a discussion?—Ans.: The man has got probably more ability than I have.

Commissioner KERNAN: You think that it would be fair to your men for each one of them to come before you and take up the question of his grievances and attempt to maintain his end of the discussion, do you?—Ans.: I think so, yes. If he is not able to do that, that is his misfortune.

Commissioner KERNAN: Don't you think that the fact that you represent a vast concentration of capital, and are selected for that because of your ability to represent it, entitles him if he pleases to unite with all of the men of his craft and select the ablest one they have got to represent the cause?—Ans.: As a union?

Commissioner KERNAN: As a union.—Ans.: *They have the*

right; yes, sir. We have the right to say whether we will receive them or not.

Commissioner KERNAN: Do you think you have any right to refuse to recognize that right in treating with the men?—Ans.: Yes, sir; if we chose to.

Commissioner KERNAN: If you chose to. It is your policy to do that?—Ans.: Yes, sir.

Commissioner KERNAN: Then you think that you have the right to refuse to recognize a union of the men designed for the purpose of presenting, through the ablest of their members, to your company the grievances which all complain of or which any complain of?—Ans.: That is the policy of the company; yes, sir. If we were to receive these men as representatives of the unions they could probably force us to pay any wages which they saw fit, and get the Pullman company in the same shape that some of the railroads are by making concessions which ought not to be made.

Commissioner KERNAN: Don't you think that the opposite policy, to wit, that all your dealings with the men, as individuals, in case you were one who sought to abuse your power, might enable you to pay to the men, on the other hand, just what you saw fit?—Ans.: *Well, of course a man in an official position, if he is arbitrary and unfair, could work a great deal of injustice to the man; no doubt about that. But then it is a man's privilege to go to work somewhere else.*

Commissioner KERNAN: Don't you recognize as to many men after they have become settled in a place at work of that kind, that really that privilege does not amount to much?—Ans.: We find that the best men usually come to the front; the best of our men don't give us any trouble with unions or anything else. It is only the inferior men—that is, the least competent—that give us the trouble as a general thing.

Commissioner KERNAN: *As a rule, then, the least competent men make the most trouble, do they?—Ans.: Yes, sir; if these gentlemen allow themselves to be led by incompetent men that is their misfortune.* (Italics mine).

It is this new meaning of the term "competition" that business spokesmen have had in mind when speaking of competition.

The inability of economists to "communicate" with businessmen is frequently due to their ignorance of business ideology. In the case of certain business economists, such as Hazlitt or Lutz, their "doublethink" habit of using the term "competition" in its Spencerian context but ascribing to it the consequences of Adam Smith's free market mechanism cannot be attributed to ignorance. Eclecticism, however, is a characteristic of all ideologies that has a long and rich history. A classical example is an article in *The Bulletin* of the American Iron and Steel Association that illustrates how business interests can be expressed in the terminology of Social Darwinism *and* classical liberalism, even if both doctrines seem to be completely at odds with the position taken. Defending tariffs on pig iron—an incident of government interference which is in line with "natural development" rather than opposed to it—against the attacks of New England iron manufacturers, *The Bulletin* editorialized under the title, "The Survival of the Fittest":

> We are sorry for the Norway Iron Company and for those other [eastern] mills and furnaces that before long must follow their example. Vast stores of [western] iron and fuel are now . . . in the midst or alongside of flourishing consuming and producing communities, who necessarily wage a friendly [!] but deadly commercial warfare upon less favored sections. The competition that comes by reason of free trading in the United States [!!!] is reducing, and necessarily must generally reduce, the price of all manufactured articles, and those who can make the cheapest will stay—the rest must go. The treasurer (of Norway Iron Company) says that if the duty could be taken off of his *raw material*, pig iron, they could continue to run, despite Western competition. While we are sorry that 500 men should be thrown out of employment by the closing of those works, we are glad enough that the thousands . . . of hardy men who dig the ores and coal have the chance of doing all this work in this country rather than England should have the opportunity of supplying us. It is a fundamental rule that the many must be protected even if a few suffer.[29]

Admittedly, the above is an extreme case of rationalizing

business interests in the cloak of respectable doctrines. It has been chosen, however, to indicate how easily the most outrageous aspirations of vested interests can be defended by reference to the survival of the fittest.

The explicitly pragmatic, utilitarian, and amoral content of the doctrine of the survival of the fittest introduced, therefore, a further radical anti-conservative aspect into the content of American business opinion. In the old Protestant-Calvinistic ethics, success in life was the result of virtue, and failure the consequence of laziness and sin; the possibility that a man might obtain riches in life by unethical, un-Christian means was just not considered feasible. This is far different, however, from a struggle for the survival of the fittest in which the end justifies the means! The complete disavowal of any ethical responsibility for the victims of competition in business ideology is again a direct result of the strain of Social Darwinism in American business opinion. In commenting on the Homestead Strike, the *Detroit News* wrote:

> The great employers of labor, whether they be corporations or individuals, are in no way responsible for the abundance of it or for its cheapness, and it is the supreme point of folly to demand or expect that they shall pay more for it than the lowest price at which it is offered. It is not human nature for them to do so, and there is no law or power on earth that can make them do so.[30]

Henry Clews, whose prolific utterances always seemed to express the prevailing cant in business opinion, expressed the stern Darwinian concept of the struggle for survival in the language of classical economics:

> What this country needs . . . is the same competition in the labor market as is found in all manufacturing markets. Competition will out-maneuver in the end all the generals who are leading the Knights of Labor. Competition alone will prove the only pacifier of labor dissatisfaction and uprising [!] All American citizens, therefore . . . should unite in encouraging the European surplus population to flock to our shores to bring

about the true remedy for our present labor evils.[31]

It is quite interesting, and typical of the ambivalent position of business opinion, that *The Bulletin* quoted Clews' comment with great approval. At the same time this journal consistently—especially during the years 1889 and 1890—showed great concern over the influx of foreign, especially non-Germanic, labor and even called upon Congress to halt foreign immigration to protect the American working man.

> The present Congress should lose no time after it assembles in December in passing stringent laws providing against any further importation of unskilled foreign labor which has been brought here in great numbers. . . . We assure Republican leaders that here is a great evil which has seriously affected the welfare of their party. We allude to it because the Protective policy is everywhere blamed with encouraging the importation of this 'raw material.'[32]

This attitude of the organ of the Iron and Steel Institute is even more remarkable if we consider that the Carnegies and Fricks were one of the major importers and employers of the new Slavic and Italian immigrants. Another indication that class opinions and class ideologies are rarely consistent and logical models.

Not until Leninism and Nazism do we meet another equally amoral philosophy. That Nietzsche, who significantly influenced both Nazism and Lenin-Stalinism, was an ardent advocate of the gospel of Social Darwinism is, therefore, not surprising.

Social Darwinism, at any rate, supplied the American business community with an anti-Christian, irreligious, materialistic rationale which frequent past and contemporary references aligning Christianity with capitalism cannot quite disguise. Spencer and Sumner were agnostics at best, while Ingersoll, the outstanding atheist of his period, was also a leading Spencerian and prominent Republican whose views on social and economic topics were similar to that of the pious Rockefeller or Clews.

Carnegie, Spencer's apostle among the captains of industry, wrote in his autobiography:

> I remember that light came as in a flood and all was clear. Not only had I got rid of theology and the supernatural, but I had found the truth of evolution.[33]

Sumner, an honest radical whose views happened to be frequently comforting to the ruling class, recognized clearly the "brave New World" utilitarianism of Social Darwinism: "The *mores* of the twentieth century," he exclaimed, "will not be tinged by humanitarianism as those of the last hundred years."[34]

Sumner's completely relativistic approach to values, rights, and duties prompted this statement: "There can be no rights against Nature except to get out of her whatever we can, which is only the fact of the struggle for existence stated over again."[35]

The rather "sophisticated" approach towards religion which was not uncommon among business leaders who had accepted the philosophy of Social Darwinism did not keep them from supporting organized religion in an openly cynical manner. James Hill, a nominal Protestant, gave a million dollars to a Roman Catholic seminary in the same spirit with which he bribed political bosses:

> Look at the millions of foreigners pouring into this country to whom the Roman Catholic Church presents the only authority that they either fear or respect. What will be their social view, their political action, their moral status if that single controlling force should be removed.[36]

The Calvinistic-Protestant tradition, however, was very strong, and many American businessmen resembled Rockefeller and Clews in their acceptance of Social Darwinism; that is, complete acceptance of the "law" of the survival of the fittest in the realm of economics and sociology, and a rejection of evolutionary doctrines in the area of religion and cosmology.

Rockefeller, for instance, managed to combine his espousal of Darwinian "competition" with a fundamentalist religious belief that even disapproved of Doctor Harper's "rationalistic" views, while Henry Clews excelled all his life in blithely combining Spencer's materialism with fundamentalist Calvinism. Such a comfortable though highly irrational eclecticism has probably been more typical in establishing the prevailing business opinion than Carnegie's or Ingersoll's materialism or Hill's agnostic cynicism. It certainly explains the strain in contemporary business ideology in which hedonism, Calvinism, and Darwinism seem to be freely mixed *á discretion.*

SOCIAL DARWINISM AND THE STATE

The Darwinian "struggle for existence" would permit nature, if unimpeded, to select the best competitor; over aeons this would produce a change in human nature, which would slowly approach perfection.[37] Attempts at precipitous reforms were, therefore, not only useless—you can't improve on nature—but might even prevent nature from carrying on its selective duties most efficiently. Youmans expressed this sentiment clearly:

> Social forces cannot be created by enactment, and when dealing with the production, distributing, and commercial activities of the community, legislation can do little more than interfere with their natural courses.[38]

W. T. Harris, later United States Commissioner of Education, carried the evolutionary gospel to its logical conclusion:

> Help the poor and unfortunate to help themselves, and elevate them towards human perfection and the divine ideal. . . . [But] adopt all the cunning devices that social science has invented, and you cannot be sure that direct or indirect help of the poor does not undermine their self respect and weaken their independence.[39]

Since reform was, therefore, both useless and dangerous, the possible agent of reform, the state, could contribute to common welfare by completely removing itself from the battlefield of the "struggle for existence." This was essentially nothing new, as the classical liberals well knew, but Social Darwinism provided new "scientific" support for the *dicta* of the classical economists. Under the influence of Social Darwinism, an almost anarchistic attitude towards the state was fostered among American businessmen, which took on an emotional connotation that had been absent in classical *laissez faire* philosophy, and that reappears today in the attitude and the antics of the New Left at our universities.

It was this anarchistic, anti-reform aspect of Social Darwinism that prompted Hofstadter to refer to this philosophy as conservative, though he modified this statement somewhat by calling it a "progressive conservatism." The preceding analysis demonstrated, I hope, how very radical this philosophy really was, if we apply to it the yardsticks of political science. Whether we shall call a philosophy that put the bitch-goddess "success" on its throne "progressive" is, however, purely a matter of taste.[40] On the other hand it can be considered that the irreverent anti-authoritarian doctrines of Social Darwinism emphasized the social, materialistic impulses of the American businessman and prevented the development of a conservative but politically and socially responsible business class. The emptiness of the social life of the successful businessmen since the Civil War and the insecurity and mass boredom experienced by an economically successful nation since 1946 are, at least partially, a consequence of the success of the doctrine of Social Darwinism.

6. The Businessman
in Politics (1870-1896)

A party is in one sense a joint stock company in which those who contribute the most direct the action and management of the concern.

WILLIAM H. SEWARD

Corruption dominates the ballot-box; the Legislature, the Congress, and touches even the ermine of the bench. Our homes [are] covered with mortgages, the land [is] concentrating in the hands of the capitalists. The urban workmen are denied the rights of organization for self-protection; imported pauperized labor beats down their wages; a hireling standing army, unrecognized by our laws, is established to shoot them down, and they are rapidly degenerating into European conditions.

IGNATIUS DONNELLY AT THE POPULIST PARTY CONVENTION, 1892

An adequate study of the businessman in politics must be preceded by a short analysis of the existing political configuration of the period under study. American politics and political parties, lacking the nice ideological and class structure of their British counterparts, are amorphous, complex, and ambivalent.[1] During the post-Civil War period, however, the complexity of the composition of the American parties almost defeats any attempts at merely categorizing and labeling them. Political historians confront us with two views: The Cochran-Bryce thesis[2] that pictures the two major parties essentially as profit-seeking enterprises ("the business of politics") that sell favors to the highest bidders and the Charles Beard concept, upheld by his student Goldman and by Binkley and Schlesinger, that the political parties essentially represented conflicting economic and geographic interests.[3] In addition to these two scholarly theses, there exists, of course, the folklore that the Republican party was the party of capital and the monopolists, while the Democratic party was the party of reform.[4]

An analysis which takes the businessman and living institutions as its starting point can reconcile all three points of view. First, it should be emphasized that we should not speak about Republican and Democratic parties as if they were cohesive, well-integrated parties. For example, consider that the election of 1892 saw the radical, Peter Altgeld, and the conservative Cleveland both run and win on the Democratic ticket. Then, as now, the two major parties were essentially a loose coalition of independent state parties with each state party being much more interested in control of county, state, and judicial offices than in Presidential victories.[5] These coalitions, however, were tied together not only by materialistic self-interests and hopes for the rewards of federal office, but also by the mystique and folklore a going institution exerts. Thus a Blaine and even a Conkling cannot incessantly wave the "bloody shirt" and appeal to the memory of Lincoln without associating themselves, at least in part, with the ideological forces that maintained the Army of the Republic and produced a Lincoln. To ignore the metaphysical powers of institutions is the mistake of those that interpret institutions and ideologies solely in terms of their economic and technological foundations. While institutions may be the result of these materalistic forces, once emerged they take on very real meaning and introduce a strong non-materialistic and frequently non-rational element into the economic and political scene.

American politics, like a Shakespearean play, is thus played on (at least) two levels, and the period under discussion particularly demands a multi-level analysis. On the higher level we find the conflict of opposing—sometimes speciously opposing—ideologies and class interests. It is on this level and within this framework that Presidents, Senators, and the judiciary are elected, and within this context party and national policies are laid down.

On the lower level we find the machines of the different state parties, interested solely in survival which, at least in the period under consideration, means patronage (state and federal) and illicit gains through corrupt practices. The House of Representatives constitutes, perhaps, a third level, separate from the pit and the balcony. The only instrument of national government directly elected by the people, we find it frequently more responsive to the short run (class or sectional) interests of the voters than interested in long run ideological battles.[6] The several levels of political action are, of course, not immunized from each other. During periods of prosperity, complacency, or supremacy of business, the interests, mode of behavior, and outlook of the machine politician (business politicians) infiltrate the higher levels; conversely, during periods of intense ideological and economic strife, we find that Tammany Hall may adopt the vocabulary of a Sockless Simpson or a Reuther without, incidentally, halting the decline machines seem to suffer during such times.[7]

In addition to the several distinct levels at which the political activity of this period must be studied, we must also note the complex climate of opinions and ethical values that permeated American politics. In Beard's "Valley of Democracy" in particular, and in rural small-town America in general, American democracy rested firmly on Anglo-Saxon Protestant ethics. Frugality, self-help, (productive) work, individualism and parochialism were the key words in this Jacksonian philosophy. At the same time we find a strange readiness to acquiesce in corruption, not only among the businessmen and the petty bourgeoisie of the large cities, but also among small-town merchants and farmers. The tradition of the frontiers, the speculative nature of early pioneering and exploring, has introduced a "something for nothing" attitude into the American character; it is in this very attitude that we can find an explanation for the ready acceptance of Spencerism by the public and its absorption into the American folklore. A combination of the pragmatic, speculating frontier spirit with the Spencerian dogma of the "survival of the fittest" is almost bound to create an atmosphere in which corruption, provided it is on a sufficiently large scale, is tolerated, especially if it is successful.

The machine politics of the big cities, especially those of the eastern seaboard, provided a third type of political climate totally different from the two mentioned above. It is not necessary to reassert the important sociological function which was carried out by the Tammany Halls.[8] It is important to emphasize, however, the feudal nature of the boss, the baronial chieftain of these machines. By providing the services of a welfare state, the machine obtained the power inherent in the votes of its adherents in the same manner that the manor obtained the armed services of its vassals. Another extrarational element is thus introduced into American politics. Regardless of the merits of the issues, the vigor of the debate, a certain number of votes are isolated from the issues of their periods, and can be delivered almost at will by the machines.[9]

Lastly, a study of this period must not neglect the forces of class warfare that occasionally made themselves felt. Whatever the significance of the Greenback movement and the strikes and riots of 1877 may have been, they did result in an immediate "united front" of industrialists and low-tariff merchants, monopolists and classical liberals, politicos and reformers. This but emphasizes the thesis presented so far that, at least until 1896, the business ideology reigned supreme in the main stream of American life. Attacks upon business and the profit system were restricted to a few groups, at best vociferous, but numerically, economically, and politically unimportant. If these forces seemed to threaten in any way—and the American businessman has had an enormous talent for discovering revolutionaries under his bed —even as weak an executive as Hayes was able to rally the property-owning *and* property-aspiring classes.

THE CAPTAINS OF INDUSTRY AND THE TWO
MAJOR PARTIES BEFORE 1880

Within this modifying framework of a "multi-level" political activity and three distinct climates of opinion, we can now analyze the political role played by the captains of industry and their relationship with the major parties. We have noted already that the Civil War had satisfied the major demands of the industrialist. The protective tariff, huge land grants to the railroads, and both the Timber and Stone and the Homestead Acts presented an institutional framework in which the aggressive entrepreneur could take the maximum advantage of the opportunities a rapidly growing empire provided. His only political demand was that the present favorable conditions be maintained. The essentially negative attitude of the businessman as well as his absorption in the unprecedented business opportunities precluded any serious active intervention into the political arena, and reduced his political activity to supporting those elements which were most likely to preserve the favorable *status quo.* Since the Republican party was associated with the entire favorable Civil War legislation, the businessman was, of course, willing to show his appreciation. In addition the Republican party—that is, the professional politicians who are the national party, including cabinet members, senators, major office holders, and the judiciary—was in a position both during the Civil War and in the post-war period to do innumerable favors for ambitious and predatory entrepreneurs.

> A United States Senator represented something more than a state, more even than a region. He represented principalities and powers in business.[10]

Strong mutual interests and "business relationship" tied the industrialists to the Republican party. It is, however, in this writer's opinion, misleading to think of the Republican party before the 1880's as owned or even completely dominated by "business interests"; it is a Marxian oversimplification to portray the rule of the "politicos" as a conscious attempt of the capitalists to govern by proxy.[11] Rather there existed an alliance between two distinct and sovereign groups, the professional politicians that made up *the* Republican party, and the industrialists who but wanted to exploit the natural resources and build their empires. Senator Boise Penrose explained the politician-businessman relationship precisely:

> I believe in a division of labor. You send us to Congress; we pass laws under the operation . . . of which you make money; . . . and out of your profits you further contribute to our campaign fund to send us back again to pass more laws to enable you to make more money. It is your duty to help keep us here and our duty to legislate.[12]

Blaine, addressing a dinner given in his honor at Delmonico's, reminded the assembled Goulds, Astors, Mortons, Clews, Havermeyers, etc.:

> That the Republican party is not arrogant nor over-confident when it claims to itself the credit of organizing and maintaining the industrial system which gave to you and your associates in enterprise the equal and just laws which enable you to make this marvelous progress.[13]

The Democratic party received its share—though admittedly a smaller one—of business support. As the traditional home of the free traders it served as the rallying point of those whose interests were injured by the protective tariff. The merchants, financiers, and members of the shipping industry, especially in the big cities of the eastern seaboard, provided the bulk of the financial support the Democratic politicians could rely on. In addition, however, the Democratic party attracted the support of outstanding members of the non-business leisure class, especially lawyers who became the dominant profession in both parties, but also educators, professional men, and members of the old families. Godkin, Henry and Francis Adams, Townsend Martin, Sumner, and Eliot were the typical representatives of this coalition of the old aristocracy and a new leisure class.[14] Only a few members of this new and old leisure class actively entered politics,[15] but it was from these firm adherents to classical liberalism that there developed the most significant opposition to the subsidy hunting of business, the paternalism of the Republican administration, the conspicuous consumption of the *nouveaux riches,* and above all, the fantastic corruption of the governments (federal, state, and city). It was this truly conservative group, which later on was to form the nucleus of the progressive movement, aptly called by Hofstadter "the status revolution," that looked toward the Democratic party to halt the trend toward centralization and paternalistic government support of business. The politicians and the plutocrats in turn reserved their choicest invectives for their enemies of the Right. Roscoe Conkling considered these conservative gentlemen just rival operators: "Their real object is office and plunder," he exclaimed. "When Dr. Johnson defined patriotism as the last refuge of a scoundrel, he was unconscious of the then undeveloped capabilities of the word reform."[16] *The New York Tribune* of September 28, 1877 quotes Conkling again as referring to the critics of the Right as "oracular censors so busy of late in brandishing the rod . . . these men who are playing schoolmaster to the Republican party . . . the man milliners, the dilletanti and *carpet knights* of politics." (Italics in original.) Blaine likened the "stalwart faction" of the Nortons and Conklings to the reformers. Referring to the stalwarts, he called them "bad men, bent on loot and booty, as vicious and detestable as the noisy and pharisaical reformers."

We can now attempt to synthesize the different views of the role of business and the major parties. The leadership and machine in both parties had become fully institutionalized; that is, professional politicians relied upon their manipulative skill to continue their participation in the nation's (or state's or city's) government. The professional politician then, as now, brought both talent for and an enjoyment of politics to his job. Undoubtedly for many it was but a "business," a way to get rich quick.

> The parties of the period after the Civil War were based on patronage, not principle; they divided over spoils not issues. Although American political parties are never celebrated for having sharp differences of principle, the great age of spoilsmen was notable for elevating crass hunger for office to the level of a common credo.[17]

At the same time, however, historians sometimes tend to

forget the institutionalizing impact of the primary tools of politicians, namely ideologies, and thus oversimplify by portraying greed as the sole incentive of post Civil War politics.

We may, therefore, conclude that the directorates of both parties were always eager to obtain the financial support of the businessman—a necessity in order to run the increasingly complex and expensive election campaigns—and individual politicians frequently were more than willing to utilize their strategic position to enrich themselves. At the same time the politicians had to reconcile the demands of business with the established party folklore and the views of its traditional supporters. Thus the Republican politician had to consider the farmers and the homesteaders of the West, the new Germanic settlers in Minnesota and Wisconsin, the small merchants and businessmen of New England, and the Yankee settlements in the West.

The Democratic politicians were in the even more difficult position to reconcile the interests of the remnants of the Jacksonian coalition—the poor Southern whites and the big city workers—with the political philosophy of the classical liberals and the demands of the bankers, merchants, and the emerging new Southern middle class. The fact that the Democratic politicians were able to accomplish this task indicates again that they were more than mere spoilmen;[18] perhaps it even indicates that the party performed successfully the mission of a bona fide American political party, namely to reconcile conflicting class and sectional interests and to attempt to satisfy the demands of its adherents.

During the period of 1865–1881 the politicians seemed to be in firm control of their respective parties. In performing the usual role of politicians—reconciling contending economic and social forces and assuring the survival of their organizations by anticipating popular sentiment—the politicos of the post Civil War era most certainly enriched themselves to an unusual degree, and ultimately presented an obstacle to the reasonably efficient conduct of government and business. There seems, however, to exist little evidence that in the ebullient post-Civil War period either business or the general public particularly objected to corruption in government or even were especially concerned with government.[19] The industrialists supported the Republican party; and a good many bankers and merchants, the Democrats. The high tariff industrialists were ardent Republicans, and the low tariff businessmen were Democrats. Except for the rabid tariff partisans though, few businessmen showed any close emotional attachment to either party. Especially the tycoons of industry and finance seemed to have chosen their sides with a highly rational approach. It was, therefore, not too surprising if even the Cooper-Hewitts would rally around McKinley, or if Wall Street chose to support Cleveland's second campaign, whenever each group thought that the interests of the business community demanded such an ostentatious change in party allegiance. This is how Henry Adams described the election of 1892:

> We are here plunged into politics funnier than words can express. Very great issues are involved. Especially everyone knows that a step towards free trade is inevitable if the Democrats come in. For the first time in twenty-eight years a Democratic administration is almost inevitable. The public is angry and abusive. Everyone takes part. We are all doing our best, and swearing at each other like demons. But the amusing thing is that no one talks about real interests. *By common consent they agree to let these alone. We are afraid to discuss them.* Instead of this the press is engaged in a most amusing dispute whether Mr. Cleveland had an illegitimate child . . . whether Mr. Blaine got paid in railway bonds. . . . Parties are wrecked from top to bottom A great political revolution seems impending Yet, when I am angry, I can do nothing but laugh.[20]

There was really little need for such a change as long as the business ideology continued to dominate popular thinking.[21] The sugar tycoon Havemeyer, most likely, expressed the opinion of a substantial number of sophisticated businessmen and corporations when he explained: "The American Sugar Refining Company has no politics of any kind . . . only the politics of business.[22] Testifying before a special committee of the Senate, Havemeyer furthermore claimed that this "politics of business was the custom of every individual and corporation and firm, trust or whatever you call it."[23]

Asked, before a different committee, whether he ever contributed to State campaign funds he replied:

> We always do that. . . . In the State of New York where the Democratic majority is between 40,000 and 50,000 we throw it their way. In the State of Massachusetts where the Republican party is doubtful, they probably have the call. . . . Wherever there is a dominant party, wherever the majority is very large, that is the party that gets the contribution, because that is the party which controls the local matters.[24]

Senator Allen, chairman of the special committee to investigate the Sugar Trust bribing activity, commented: "Then the Sugar trust is a Democrat in a Democratic State and a Republican in a Republican State."[25] But the Sugar Trust was not the only business that supported both Democrats and Republicans. In the Standard Oil Company the Rockefellers, Flaglers, and Archbolds were important Republican contributors while Henry Payne and his son-in-law Whitney had excellent connections with the Democrats. James Hill contributed to Cleveland in 1884 and to Harrison in 1888,[26] while Gould contributed simultaneously to Blaine and Cleveland. Immediately upon Cleveland's election Gould sent a telegram to remind Cleveland of his "obligation," "Governor Cleveland: I heartily congratulate you on your election. All concede that your administration as Governor has been wise and conservative, and in the large field of President, I feel that you will do still better, and that the vast business interests of the country will be entirely safe in your hands."

Ida Tarbell described the attitude of most of the tycoons when she wrote:

> The Standard men as a body have nothing to do with public affairs, except as it is necessary to manipulate them for the "good of the oil business." . . . Ever since 1872 the organization has appeared in politics only to oppose legislation obviously for the public good.[27]

It was once more left for Jay Gould, though, to epitomize the
political faith of the sophisticated business baron: "I was a
Republican in Republican districts, a Democrat in Democratic
districts. But everywhere I was for Erie," he announced during
the investigation of the Erie Railroad by the New York legislature.[28]

THE BUSINESSMAN ENTERS ACTIVE POLITICS (1880–1896)—
A CASE STUDY OF THE BUSINESSMEN IN THE
CABINETS FROM GRANT TO McKINLEY

From the early 1880's the complexion of American politics
began to change. The old line political bosses either died, or
changed their behavior and outlook,[29] losing a good deal of
power in this process. The business community, which was at
least partially responsible for this change in affairs, filled the
power vacuum either through glamorous captains of industry
at the peak of their careers,[30] or through its representatives who,
however, were also primarily businessmen,[31] or through presidents of powerful business organizations who, without running
for office, took a very serious though most certainly not altru-
istic interest in politics beyond the mere purchase of favors.[32]
This increasing business participation is reflected most accurately
in the composition of the cabinets of the post Civil War presidents.

Grant's cabinets did not include a single *bona fide* captain of
industry. James D. Cameron was, of course, a railroad president
and had many financial interests but he was first and last a politician and owed his "business success" to his father, boss Simon
Cameron, and to his own political role. Significantly, Grant's
cabinet was made up of two distinct types of professional politicians: members of the old pre-war ruling leisure class[33]—such
former Whigs as Hamilton Fish, Elihu Washburn, William Belk-
nap, Alphonso Taft, and Edwards Pierrepont—and the new and
rising class of the post-war "politicos," men of humble background like Zach Chandler, Jacob Cox, George Boutwell, etc.,
to whom politics was a business, a means of obtaining power,

wealth, and prestige. Today with the demise of machine politics, and the institutionalization of the profession of law, politics no longer offers such an easy escape hatch to the underprivileged. Its place has been taken by union politics and union careers, exemplified by such widely differing successes as Reuther or Hoffa. The latter, interestingly enough, is a complete "throwback" to the Camerons and Logans.

Hayes' cabinet did not even contain a pseudo-businessman like Cameron. All ten men who were members of Hayes' cabinet at one time or another were professional politicians (eight were lawyers) primarily of the pre-war, upper class model (Evarts, Devens, Maynard). Garfield's cabinet was similar in composition to Hayes'. It contained no businessmen, only one old-line Whig—William Windom, Secretary of the Treasury, a lawyer of pioneer background—and lots of lawyers.[34] One of them, Lincoln's son, Robert T. Lincoln, the Secretary of War, became an important railroad executive in later years, but he was essentially a corporation lawyer and a bureaucrat, never an entrepreneur.

The period 1880–1884 was a transition period during which the businessman began to take a more active part in politics. Arthur's cabinet already included one banker and a politician-businessman. The banker, Hugh McCulloch, Johnson's old secretary of the Treasury, held the same job in Arthur's government. Henry M. Teller, Secretary of the Interior, was probably a politician and lawyer first, but he had been actively interested in many business ventures and always continued to show sufficient interest in his enterprises to enable us to call him a businessman.

On the surface, at least, Cleveland's first cabinet presented little change from Arthur's. It contained two financiers, Whitney (Secretary of the Navy) and the banker Fairchild (Secretary of the Treasury). Although the rest of his cabinet consisted of professional politicians, it is interesting to note that they belonged uniformly to the pre-Civil War ruling classes.[35]

The big change in the political atmosphere was heralded by the Harrison cabinet. It contained five outstanding entrepreneurs and merchants: Charles Foster, a wealthy small-town businessman; Redfield Proctor, the marble king; Stephen B. Elkins, mine and railroad owner; John Wanamaker, the Philadelphia merchant; Jeremiah Rusk, a banker, a stage-line owner, and a successful governor of Wisconsin. Unlike the businessmen in the Eisenhower cabinet who came to Washington as political novices and returned to their corporations at the first opportunity, Harrison's businessmen had become serious politicians and worked on their "second trade" both before and after their cabinet tenure.

Cleveland's second election meant a return to power of upper-class classical liberals who represented Cleveland's wing of the Democratic party. But among these we find Davis Francis, a merchant and exporter, as Secretary of the Interior; Daniel Lamont, financier and banker, as Secretary of State and Attorney General.

McKinley's cabinet proved that the businessman in politics had come to stay. Its most powerful figure, Mark Hanna, was nominally not a member of the cabinet, but there was little doubt in anyone's mind that McKinley not only owed his political career to Hanna, but that Hanna's advice counted more than that of anyone of McKinley's cabinet members. Mark Hanna was, of course, the very personification of the successful businessman turned politician in order to introduce businesslike methods and the business viewpoint into public affairs. The business viewpoint received further representation by the six major business executives that held cabinet posts in the two McKinley administrations: Lyman Gage, a manufacturer; Russell Alger, the well-known Michigan industrialist and Republican kingpin; James Gary, another manufacturer; Cornelius Bliss, a successful merchant; Ethan Hitchcock, the first plate glass manufacturer in the United States; James Wilson, a merchant, farmer, and effective politician. Incidentally the cozy business-politics alliance that prevailed under McKinley was well illustrated by Hitchcock's contribution to this country's tariff legislation. When the time came to write the plate glass schedule, McKinley called upon his good friend Hitchcock, then Secretary of the

Interior and also the foremost plate glass manufacturer in the country, to do this little job.

The other members of McKinley's cabinet were not just professional politicians with a law degree, but lawyers like Root and Kenna, who mixed politics with a successful corporation law practice. Of the old-style politicians—post Civil War version—only John Sherman was left in McKinley's cabinet, and he owed his sudden eminence as Secretary of State mainly to McKinley's desire to reward Mark Hanna with Sherman's Senate seat. The era of the politicos had come to an end. To appreciate the change fully we must note Arthur's comment on businessmen in politics in 1878: "(Elections are won) when all the men in politics are pleased and satisfied and set to work with enthusiasm for the ticket. They bring out the votes, and if you trusted these elections to businessmen the Democratic party would get in every time."[36]

Equally indicative of the change in the political atmosphere is the conversion in 1882 of Blaine, the professional politician and scorner of upper class amateurs, to Blaine, the spokesman and adulator of the industrialists.[37] In Grant's cabinets the old leisure class shared its rule with the politicos; in McKinley's cabinet the Roots shared the rule with the businessmen. There was little doubt that the politicos were the senior partners in the 1868–1881 period. We shall attempt to analyze below who played the role of the senior partner in the period 1881-1901.

A Caveat. This short introductory account of the changing nature of the political parties should not be interpreted as a belief that the transfer of power from the politicos to the businessmen is considered either desirable or an improvement; if anything, the opposite. Before 1884 the professional politicians served to a certain extent as a countervailing power; their very nature compelled them at least to consider the interests of the non-business classes. The corruption that existed was more of the "mink coat" variety of the 1950's than of the "Teapot Dome" type of the 1920's. The development of the businessman into a captain of politics removed a good deal of this "countervailing power"; ultimately it introduced an element of class warfare into the political life (the campaign of 1896, the Progressive movements) and produced the sharp political issues so dear to the hearts of the political scientists.

THE CAUSES AND CONSEQUENCES OF THE BUSINESSMEN'S ENTRY INTO POLITICS

The increase in the political activity of leading businessmen, characterized by strong business representation in the cabinet, Senate, and party leadership was the result of several diverse factors. The most important one, at least in this writer's opinion, was the fact that the industrialists had developed into a new leisure class, and, prompted by different motives, utilized their newly found leisure to participate actively in governmental affairs. For our present purposes it is not important that probably the majority of the successful industrialists came from middle class and upper class parents.[38] It is much more important that Carnegie's claim that "the millionaires who are in active control started as poor boys and were trained in the sternest but most efficient of all schools—poverty" had become an integral part of the business ideology and was widely accepted as true. Diamond in his *The Reputation of the American Businessman* shows how Cornelius Vanderbilt's death in 1897 brought forth a chorus of speeches and newspaper comments, in which the rags-to-riches line was the central theme. Chauncey M. Depew, the "Senator of the New York Central", expressed the business ideology clearly. "Vanderbilt is a conspicuous example of the products and possibilities of our free and elastic condition . . . the same opportunities which he had before him are equally before every other man." And, at Vanderbilt's funeral: "Beginning in a humble position . . . he rose by his genius . . . to the control of vast enterprises."[39]

It must be added that the emergence of 40% of the business leadership from "lower" classes is not only quite an impressive indication of the social mobility of the period but also sufficient numerically to give the entire business class a new complexion. The pre-Civil War period (business leaders born between 1790–

1819) shows only 37% emerged from the "lower" classes, and only 30% (Mills' figure 29.3%) were of non-bourgeoisie background in the succeeding generation (born 1850–79). After a long period of public and academic acceptance of the Horatio Alger myth, a rather substantial amount of literature has been devoted to the analysis of the social and economic background of business leaders. Although the purposive samples of the various authors differ too much to permit a concise analysis, there exists overwhelming evidence of an amazing social mobility which can only be underemphasized if it is compared to the claims of the Horatio Alger myth. By the standards of any society, past or present, the constant renewal of an upper class by 30 to 40% is very impressive. Only if the actual mobility is measured against the exaggerated claims of the business ideology does it become worthwhile to emphasize that the majority of American businessmen came from a highly select group which most certainly did not consist of poor farmers, workers, and immigrants, and that from the Civil War period on, each successive generation contained a smaller percentage af business leaders of lower class origin. Where Mills still found among the businessmen of the immediate pre- and post-Civil War generations that 37% and 30% respectively had been of lower or lower middle class origin, Miller found at the most only 14% of the business leaders of farm or working class origin during the period 1901–1910.[40] Mabel Newcomer found that during the 1900's roughly 25% of the businessmen in her sample were of farm or working class origin.[41]

The fact that during the 1880–1900 period the 40% of the arrivés included some of the most outstanding, glamorous, and controversial captains of industry was important in the acceptance of Carnegie's "from rags-to-riches" mythology. Aside from Carnegie himself, Pullman, Rockefeller, Armour, Swift, Fisk, Drew, and Gould had come from poor farming and working class families. "Commodore" Vanderbilt, Cooke, Hill, Rogers, Harriman, and Huntington had petty-bourgeois backgrounds at best and started their careers at the bottom. Stanford and George Hearst had an upper or, respectively, middle class background but had been penniless before they started their climb.

We find, therefore, that by the 1880's there existed a group of confident, powerful men who fairly suddenly found themselves in the possession of leisure and power. Moreover, these were truly "men of affairs"—unlike so many members of the "old genteel" classes whom they met at Newport and on 5th Avenue—whose very business activities had forced them into close contact with politicians and government officials.[42] Although later business ideologists refer to this period as the *laissez-faire* era where the businessman was "unfettered" and free from governments supervision, these businessmen were quite eager to obtain government support in the form of subsidies, tariffs, or legislative aid against hostile interests.

A good example of the dependency of the businessman in "the age of laissez-faire" upon the success of his Washingtonian efforts is provided by a letter Huntington wrote to Colton in 1877.

> I think Congress will try very hard to pass some kind of a bill to make us commence paying on what we owe the government. I am striving very hard to get a bill in such shape that we can accept it, as this Washington business will kill me yet if I have to continue the fight from year to year, and then every year the fight grows more and more expensive.[43]

The chronicler of machine politics, G.F. Howe, similarly cites the "unbridled acquisitiveness of the average businessman, for whom by the pressure of the lobby the government was made to serve as an agency to fatten profits."[44]

Senator Aldrich, in a speech before the Tariff Commission, cited not at all disapprovingly that "there was a representative of the sugar interest on the Commission and those interests were carefully looked out for."[45]

The businesslike relationship between the industrialists and various levels of government is perhaps best exemplified by the schedule of "fees" paid by the LaCrosse and Milwaukee Railroad. A government investigation discovered that a total of $872,000 was paid to judges, editors, politicians, including payments for the purchase of:

one governor	$ 50,000
one state comptroller	10,000
one private secretary	5,000
"a certain Smith'	10,000
thirteen Senators	175,000
one first secretary, Senate	10,000
one first secretary, House	5,000[46]

The Report of the United States Pacific Railway Commission, 1887, presented the following data of railroad slush funds, which were used to influence federal legislation in a completely businesslike manner:

Union Pacific & Kansas Pacific	$2,349,554.80
Central Branch	333,661.65
Sioux City and Pacific	37,287.75
Central Pacific	2,361,154.88
	$5,081,659.08[47]

The cost of such business relations were obviously high! It was no wonder, therefore, that Huntington could complain about the "expense" of political activity. The same man who after the Civil War stated that "if you have to pay money to have the right thing done, it is only just and fair to do it," complained in the above-mentioned letter to his friend Colton:

You have no idea how I am annoyed by this Washington business, and I must and will give it up after this session. If we are not hurt this session it will be because we pay much money to prevent it, and you know how hard it is to get it to pay for such purposes.[48]

We can see, therefore, that the businessman had become involved in public affairs, and that once he possessed power and leisure it was only a question of time before he would overcome the American middle-class aversion against active involvement in politics. Quite typical of this is a Harper's editorial on politics that appeared in 1881. Decrying the fact that gentlemen cease being gentlemen once they enter politics, the entire editorial is based on a fictitious observer who exclaims: "I can't imagine how a gentleman . . . can dabble in politics . . . unless he wants something."[49]

If we consider the businessman's self-confidence and optimism, his belief—so typical of Protestant-American thought—that every problem can be solved by a healthy application of "common sense" and business methods, then it is only surprising that he did not participate earlier in politics. Admittedly, though, both American folklore and business ideology belittled the role of politics and emphasized that progress was the result of activities in the market place.

Not surprisingly, the American business leader was only too willing to let himself be thus portrayed as the center of creation. We have already noticed how Wharton considered himself "one of the men who create and maintain the prosperity of the nation. Similarly *Leslie's Illustrated Newspaper* wrote at the occasion of Vanderbilt's death, "An Astor, a Stewart, a Vanderbilt is a blessing . . . each give honorable, remunerative, and permanent employment to an army of men and women.[50]

Bishop Lawrence of Massachusetts expressed the views of a substantial part of the clergy when he wrote:

> In the long run it is only to the man of morality, that wealth comes. We believe in the harmony of God's universe. . . . Godliness is in league with riches.[51]

Henry Clews truly represented the "Wall Street Point of View" when he wrote:

> The wealth accumulators, I contend, are as a rule, the best citizens. In fact, they are the citizens, above all others, who make it possible under our present system to attain the highest enjoyment and development, physical, moral and spiritual, of which mankind thus far is capable.[52]

It was left for Bryce, though, to epitomize the relationship between the business tycoons—specifically the railroad men—and politics:

> These railway kings are among the greatest men, perhaps I may say the greatest men in America. They have wealth, else they could not hold the position. They have fame, for everyone has heard of their achievements; every newspaper chronicles their movements. They have power, more power—that is more opportunity of making their will prevail—than perhaps anyone in political life, except the President and the Speaker, who, after all, hold theirs for four years and two years while the railroad monarch may keep his for life.[53]

We may conclude, therefore, that but for the belief in the sterility of political life—the other side of the Spencerian coin—the American business leader would have already demanded his "rightful" place in the government of *his* country before 1880. But Nicholas Murray Butler told him that:

> Nature's cure for most social and political diseases is better than man's and without the strongest reason the government should withhold its hand from everything that is not, by substantial common consent, a matter of governmental action.[54]

Charles Eliot, paraphrasing Spencer, reminded him that:

> The spontaneous cooperation of men in pursuit of personal benefits will adequately work out the general good, if the state should discharge its plain duties simply of enforcing the sanctity of contract.[55]

Huntington became annoyed when his partner Stanford showed a growing interest in politics *per se*, rather than in politics as a device to further the fortune of the Southern Pacific. Forcing Stanford to resign the presidency of the Southern Pacific, he wrote his stockholders:

> If a man wants to make a business of politics, all well and

good; if he wants to manage a railroad, all well and good; but he can't do both at the same time.[56]

The tendency of the willful politicos to overreach themselves by the beginning of the 80's in levying a tribute upon business that might become excessive and in making uncertain the condition under which business executives had to make decisions, was one of the major factors that prompted business to enter politics more actively. Wasn't the political field just another aspect of the struggle of the survival of the fittest? The fittest in the market place should not have to bargain with useless, unproductive politicians, who even had a tendency to listen to popular demands occasionally and to annoy the captains of industry with investigations and anti-trust prosecutions.

The Northern Securities investigation, for instance, truly perturbed Hill: "It really seems hard when we look back upon what we have done . . . that we should be compelled to fight for our lives against political adventurers who have never done anything but pose and draw a salary."[57]

We have already noted Huntington's exasperation at the costs involved in keeping the grasping Washington politicians in line. John Van Allen, one of the earlier businessmen in politics, expressed the sentiment of many leading businessmen in a letter to John Sherman in 1877:

> There are so many important reforms to be effected that it is needful that especial pains shall be taken in the selection of the President's constitutional advisers . . . no steady application of labor and capital can be hoped for until important reforms are effected, and an administration shall be organized on principles widely different from those which have governed the present one [Hayes'].[58]

Still, fifteen years later, when the civil service reforms supposedly had reduced the power of the predatory politicians, even an Archbold had to resort to installment payments to satisfy Quay, a latter-day "stalwart." "My dear Senator," Archbold wrote, "I will do as you say, provided you finally say you need so much. Please ask for payments as needed from time to time, not all at once. . . . Not because I think we should but because of your enticing ways, I enclose your Certificate of Deposit for $10,000."[59]

Once, however, the businessman had entered politics, either to reform it or to grab the public honor which was his due, or even to guard his interests the better, he casually accepted positions of power and trust. But the business leaders did not enter the Senate *en masse* until the late 80's and they did not obtain significant cabinet representation until Harrison's administration.

The Businessman and Civil Service Reform. Businessmen as a group, as a class, made their first collective and perhaps noblest effort as members of the various reform movements in the seventies. Together with "liberal" intellectuals (Schurz and Godkin), members of the "old" families and the professions, they were active in the "New York Citizens Committee to oust Tweed." Cooper and Hewitt were among the leading Democratic businessmen active in this committee while W.E. Dodge, Sloan, and Constable were representative of the reform (business) Republicans and Tilden, Belmont, and Havemeyer represented a faction of conservative anti-Conkling Republicans.

Until the "stalwarts" on national and local levels had begun to squeeze the businessman until he hurt, the latter had been rather slow in displaying any interest in civil service reform. Although the alternatives of a spoils system or a professional civil service had been an issue in American politics since the days of George Washington, the businessman had not concerned himself with this issue.[60] Until the 1880's, the advocates of a professional civil service—from John Adams to Henry Adams—were chiefly members of the "old families" and Van Buren seemed to have supported the agrarian attitude towards political office, while the Whigs, when in power, used patronage as freely as the Democrats, though they may have given somewhat greater attention to the question of fitness and competency.[62]

By 1879–80, however, the public at large had become impatient with the stalling tactics of the politicians in Congress. Although by 1876 all parties (Republicans, Liberal-Republicans, Democrats) had included a civil-service reform plank in their platforms, Congress showed little interest in implementing it. The elimination of the spoils system and the establishment of a career civil service was the major issue that combined the political-minded elements among the "better classes." For most of these proponents of reform, a career civil service was but a means "to restore" government to the desirable neutral role postulated by classical liberalism. It is doubtful, however, whether Tilden, Havemeyer, Constable, and the other business-men-reformers shared completely Godkin's and Carl Schurz's belief that the elimination of the spoils system was the solution to all the problems that plagued the country.[63] The agitation for civil-service reform did provide, however, an opportunity for respectable and well known business leaders to take an active part in politics, and is therefore noteworthy.

Unfortunately, however, the "respectable" businessmen and the scions of old families frequently acted like wardheelers once they did enter politics. We have already seen that the *Nation* bewailed the tendency of the Hamilton Fishes to act like the O'Briens once they are sent to Albany. Theodore Roosevelt, after promising his "idol" Hewitt to "take off his coat and work for him," decided to accept the Republican nomination for Mayor and oppose Hewitt because, "It is too good a chance for a young man to advertise himself."[64] When two years later (1888) Tammany Hall attempted (successfully) to purge Hewitt, the sterling businessmen of the Union League Club, including Roosevelt, Lodge, and Depew, deserted Hewitt and municipal reform in droves and backed the nominee of the regular New York City Republican organization, whose only distinction from Tammany Hall was, has been, and is, that it does not win elections. Hewitt commented on this development:

> What kind of Pharisees congregate (in the Union League)?
> . . . Mr. Chauncey Depew in his speech to the Union League
> Club urged them . . . to vote for the Republican candidate and
> to vote against me. And yet no man in this community has more
> frequently come into my office and congratulated me upon the

manner in which I have administered it. Besides Mr. Depew
. . . Mr. Roosevelt also paid his respects to the Union League
Club and to me. I think it is a pity that this young gentleman,
who was used as a catspaw two years ago by men with whom
he would not then or now condescend to associate socially, did
not remember that . . . he came to my office and said to me:
"Mr. Hewitt, I feel it is my bounden duty to come and say to
you how much I admire and respect you for the manner in
which you are discharging your duties.[65]

The apt sketch Steffens drew of another business-reform mayor,
William Strong, further illuminates the early ventures of businessmen in politics:

The man the reformers united upon for mayor was William L.
Strong. He was a merchant; he knew nothing of politics and
the politicians knew nothing of him. He was an ideal candi-
date, therefore. He was the good businessman who would
throw out the rascally politicians and give us a good business
administration. For him were the "honest Republicans," the
fine old aristocratic Democrats, . . . the "decent" newspapers. . . .
    (Strong) gave promises that could not be kept because
they were contradictory. I saw enough of it to realize that
reform politics was still politics, only worse; reformers were
not so smooth as the professional politicians, and it seemed
to me that they were not so honest.[66]

Lincoln Steffens epitomized the thinking of the businessmen-
reformers when he quoted their goal: "Down with the boss. Away
with politics and the politicians. Elect to office good businessmen who would give us a business government."

Regardless of the merits of the reform and the achievements
of a career civil service, the major interest it holds for our
analysis is the light it sheds on business and the business
leaders. Civil-service reform or no civil-service reform, a large majority
of the American people have always shared the Jacksonian belief
that any average American could perform any government job.
Surely there wasn't much skill involvel in "pushing a pencil"
and only an inferior person, who couldn't "make out" in a "regu-

lar job" would want a government job in the first place.[67] Even today the government bureaucracy is not held in high regard. The well-paid American civil servant certainly does not possess the status of his British, German, or Austrian counterpart.

The catastrophic defeat of Greeley in '72, and the refusal in '73 of the voter-conscious House even to consider a civil-service reform bill—in spite of Grant's not-so-vehement urging—as well as Cleveland's defeat in 1888, seem to indicate that to many Americans a civil service bureaucracy still smacked of European, Mandarin, or even Imperial government, and most certainly ran counter to the notion of a government whose main task was to enforce contracts and protect property. The *New York Sun* spoke as late as 1889 for a sizeable segment of the population when it wrote:

> Before skipping gayly away to his Dakotan ranch, where in the words of Mr. Joseph Addison, "the zephyrs and the heifers their odoriferous breath compare," Mr. Theodore Roosevelt, the life of the Civil Service Commission, wrote a letter to the Boston *Journal* in praise of the reform into which he is putting so much elbow grease. It is a longer letter than the letters of recommendation and "influence" he sent to the police commissioners of this town, but it isn't half so good. It is difficult for him to be slow, but with such a tedious, spavined old nag as civil-service reform he cannot but fall into a prosing pace. There is nothing new for him to say. Beating a gong in front of a Chinese idol is monotonous work. Mr. Roosevelt's letter is thus, through no fault of his, deeply uninteresting. We cull one little bouquet of assumptions, however, as a specimen of the jauntiness wherewith the Mandarins of the Green go on arguing from premises which ninety-nine hundredths of the American people do not admit:
>
> > "I do not see how any man can watch the effects of the spoils system, both upon the poor unfortunates who suffer from it and the almost equally unfortunate men who deem that they benefit by it, without regarding the whole thing in its entirety as a curse to our institutions.

It is a curse to our public service, and it is a still greater curse to Congress, for it puts a premium upon every Congressman turning spoilsmonger instead of statesman."

Now, to most Americans it seems that the public service is well conducted under the spoils system, and they are satisfied with it. They do not regard it as a curse to our institutions or to Congress, or to anything or anybody except the Civil-service reformers, whom it seems to affect with positive mania. Congressmen curse the civil-service law, not the spoils system. Statesmanship requires an endowment of intellect, courage, experience, and tact. A statesman who keeps his eye on the offices and looks out for his friends is not likely to have his head in the clouds or to suffer from fatty degeneration of the sense of responsibility to his party.[68]

To advance a civil-service reform project under these conditions illustrates not only that some businessmen found the spoils system increasingly expensive and inefficient but also that the American business system had advanced to a point where it could both appreciate the effectiveness of a bureaucratic system and demand the extension of impersonal business practices into the government. Only a business community well on its way towards bureaucratization and class differentiation could take such a step.[69]

In the short run the civic-minded businessmen who supported the civil-service reform movement may have obtained nothing for their troubles but the bitter hostility and contempt of the Blaines, Conklings, and Ingalls. The latter's diatribe against reform is especially noteworthy:

The purification of politics is an iridescent dream. Government is force. Politics is a battle for supremacy. Parties are the armies. The Dacalogue and the golden rule have no place in a political campaign. The object is success. To defeat the antagonist and expel the party in power is the purpose. In war it is lawful to deceive the adversary, to hire Hessians, to purchase mercenaries, to mutilate, to kill, to destroy. The commander who lost a battle through the activity of his moral

nature would be the derision and jest of history. This modern
cant about the corruption of politics is fatiguing in the extreme. It proceeds from the tea-custard and syllabbub dilletan-
tism, the frivolous and desultory sentimentalism of epicenes.[70]

In the long run, however, the civil-service reform vastly increased the power of the business community because it made
the politicians—at least theoretically—totally dependent upon
business campaign contribution for their survival. It prepared
the ground for the businessman, Mark Hanna, to enter politics
and run it in a "business-like thoroughly efficient way." This
did not mean, of course, that politics became less corrupt. Far
from it. It only meant that money raised among businessmen to
either pay the debts of a promising politician or purchase the
vote of the Ohio legislature was actually spent exclusively for
these very purposes, without any leakages to an unworthy and
inefficient middleman.

> When Harriman wrote that the $260,000 which he raised
> for Roosevelt in the closing days of the campaign of 1904 meant
> a change of 50,000 votes, he undoubtedly implied that they
> were bought like so many railroad shares. In the two cam-
> paigns which Mark Hanna conducted so lavishly, doubtless an
> appalling amount of the coin found its way to the pockets of
> venal voters. But even more demoralizing and shocking are the
> secret arrangements of the party managers with large con-
> tributors. They are given, for their money, a first lien upon
> legislation, or are promised that they will be looked after when
> it comes to distribute good things in office.[71]

Thus civil-service reform tended to strengthen the power of the
business community, and by the turn of the century was generally widely supported by business spokesmen.[72]

   The Businessman-Politician and the Iron Law of Oligarchy.
The reform movement was, of course, not the only avenue to
active business participation in politics. Garfield's and Blaine's
heroic efforts to identify themselves with the industrialists turned
many of these industrialists into active and permanent kingpins

of the Republican party.[73] Cleveland's attempt to overthrow the "protective tariff" reinforced this tendency among captains of industry to become captains of (Republican) politics. Note Cleveland's increasingly populist terminology in his third and fourth annual messages to Congress in 1887 and 1888:

> Our present tariff laws, the vicious, inequitable and illogical source of unnecessary taxation, ought to be at once revised and amended. These laws . . . raise the price to consumers of all articles imported . . . but the majority of our citizens, who buy domestic articles of the same class, pay a sum . . . equal to this duty to the home manufacturer.

In his fourth annual message, December 3, 1888, Cleveland must have sounded like a wild revolutionary to the startled business community:

> We discover that the fortunes realized by our manufacturers are no longer solely the reward of sturdy industry and enlightened foresight, but that they result from the discriminating favor of the Government and are largely built upon undue exactions from the masses of our people. The gulf between employers and the employed is constantly widening. . . . Corporations, which should be the carefully restrained creatures of the law and the servants of the people, are fast becoming the people's masters.[74]

Business leaders in Presidential cabinets and the Senate were the most obvious and widely commented on results of the business community's active participation in the political life of its country. Of much greater importance in the long run was the establishment of business leaders and corporations as permanent centers of power in state parties, regional politics, and the Senate. Thus Russell Alger, the Match King, was the power in Michigan, became Governor, Senator, and even attempted to obtain the Republican nomination for President.[75] The Paynes and the Standard Oil Company ran the Republican machine in Indiana and, to a lesser extent, in Ohio. Jim Hill was powerful in both political parties in the Northwest, and Gould and the

New York Central had been influential in Republican politics long before Garfield solicited personally Gould's support. In the first decade of the 19th century William Miller found that fully 30% of all major politicians were businessmen or corporation lawyers.[76]

No longer did the business leaders chiefly restrict themselves to pressure individual politicians for distinct "favors," but rather from the middle 80's on until World War I, in several instances corporations and individual business leaders dominated party machines led by strong politicians, such as the Du Ponts in Delaware, and the Pews and the "Pennsy" in Pennsylvania, and relied upon their own representatives in state legislatures and the Senate to guard their interests.[77] Typical of these so-called business representatives in the Senate were the large number of brilliant corporation lawyers, who, rather than the millionaires, provided the real Senate leadership.[78] It was the Aldriches and the Gormans who were the real Senate leaders, not the ludicrous Hearst, the illiterate Sawyer, or the vain and over-ambitious Alger.

It is, however, again an over-simplification to consider these brilliant lawyer-politicians merely as representatives of big business. Even Aldrich, whom Hofstadter calls "the watchdog of the corporation," was far more than a watchdog or a mere puppet.[79] Similarly, the Senate during this period (1884–1900) should not be considered as only the directorate of American capitalism.[80] Several factors, frequently overlooked by the Beard-Cochran school, kept the Senate from becoming the interlocking directorate of American capitalism. Even if one conceded that the Aldriches and Gormans were initially but the agents of vested interests, the political power which they were able to obtain through their ability as politicians put them soon in a position different from that of a mere agent, a mere representative. The longer and the more illustrious their stay in the Senate became, the more they adopted the outlook and ethics of a politician rather than of a corporation lawyer. As politicians, of course, their own reelection and the electoral success of their respective parties became major considerations.

Michel's "Iron Law of Oligarchy" works, of course, both ways. Not only do labor union leaders and labor legislative representatives cease to be typical workers by the very process that makes them union leaders or M.P.'s; the political representatives of business similarly cease to typify the "average" business tycoon once they begin to advance in their political career, especially in the milieu of American or Anglo-Saxon politics. We can see how the captain of industry who is supposed to have declared but never did, "What's good for General Motors is good for the country," became the politician to whom his old friends in the Chamber of Commerce gave "a pain in the neck." The development of the millionaire and steel baron, Mark Hanna, into boss Hanna is another example. The unique and imaginative Hanna tended to boss the businessman rather than to be bossed by him. (Incidentally, Hanna and "General Motors Wilson" were probably two of the most refreshing characters in American politics.)

The passage of the Interstate Commerce Act and the Sherman Anti-Trust Act is a case in point. Even if the Interstate Commerce Act was "a delusion and a sham . . . an empty menace to the great interests, made to answer the clamor of the ignorant and unreasoning,"[81] and even if, moreover, the Sherman Act represented only an "effort . . . to get some bill headed 'A Bill to Punish Trusts' with which to go to the country,"[82] the fact is that both bills were passed in response to public demand, and both agencies created under the act developed slowly into *bona fide* regulatory agencies. Thus while the "Iron Law of Oligarchy" might make it impossible for a classical, direct democracy to exist in a modern "democratic" mass society, it also seems to preclude the long run political mastery of a single class.

Another factor, which the Beard school of thought tended to overlook, was the influence of the business ideology on both political parties. The concepts of classical liberalism and Spencerian philosophy persuaded many a politician to advocate and advance business interests as the real interests of the country. This was essentially a period of growth, of progress, and in spite of serious business fluctuations the business leaders were still considered the engines of progress. Even Henry Adams wrote in 1883:

> A capitalistic system had been adopted and if it were to be run at all, it must be run by capital and by capitalistic methods, for nothing could surpass the nonsensity of trying to run so complex . . . a machine by southern and western farmers in grotesque alliance with city day laborers, as had been tried in 1800.[83]

Such conservative and honest Senators as Hoar and Edmunds, for instance, the real authors of the Sherman Anti-Trust Act, sided with business and the propertied classes whenever even slightly radical issues were raised by populists or intellectuals, because they truly believed that the country's progress depended upon a secure and confident business community.[84] The Senate's stand on many an issue which, in "the 20/20 hindsight" of an historian, appears as a sell-out to vested interests might very well have been the logical result of the prevailing ideology.

It is well to emphasize again that the influences of "the Iron Law of Oligarchy" and "the powers of the business ideology" are meant only to modify the stark materialistic conclusion of the Beard school of thought. The political power of the captains of industry, used selfishly and greedily, should not be belittled, as it seemed to be the vogue during the 1950's; but it was not quite so commplete, or so conscious and unified, as is implied by Beard, Cochran, Miller, and Josephson.

7. The Role and Ideology of Finance Capitalism— Part One

We have witnessed in modern business the submergence of the individual within the organization, and yet the increase to an extraordinary degree of the power of the individual—of the individual who happens to control the organization. Most men are individuals no longer so far as their business, its activities or its moralities are concerned. There are no units, but fractions; with their individuality and independence of choice in matters of business they have lost also their individual choice within the field of morals.

Woodrow Wilson, before the American Bar Association, 1910

The increased importance of the businessman in politics during the last quarter of the century was symptomatic of far-reaching economic and social changes that took place within the country and even within the business community. The rapid rate of economic expansion reached its peak in the late 90's. Thereafter the rate of capital formation decreased during the decade 1899–1908 as compared with 1889–1898;[1] real wages reversed their post-Civil War upward trend in the late 90's and, after a decline, remained stable until 1920;[2] most importantly, however, the "frontier" vanished.

Hofstadter, in his *The Age of Reform*, p. 52, makes the interesting observation that in the two decades after 1890 more farms were settled than in the preceding decade. I wonder, though, if the current debunkers of the Turner thesis make sufficient allowance for the psychological importance of the frontier?

111

Especially if the actual "safety valve" effect of the frontier was negligible in practice, the widely proclaimed closing of the frontier must have had a substantial impact. Now the disgruntled farmer, mechanic, or tradesman no longer failed to move West out of personal motivations but because there no longer existed a "West"; thus a readjustment in his ideology was called for.

The large corporations continued to increase in size, however, and with the return of prosperity in 1897 the "merger movement" reappeared on the scene, to reach unprecedented heights during the next six years. "Previous to 1897, scarcely any enterprises in the industrial field were capitalized at more than $50 million; thereafter concerns with a capitalization ranging from $100 to $1000 million were not uncommon, though watering of the stock was far more frequent."[3] At any rate, though, the data in Moody's *The Truth About the Trusts* indicates that during the merger movement of 1898–1903 some 300 industrial combinations had been formed. Seventy-eight of these firms controlled at least 50% of the total output in their respective industries.[4] After 1903–04 the merger movement lost its intensity—until the post-World War I era at least—but by then 318 industrial companies owned 5,288 plants, and were capitalized above 7.25 billion dollars.[5]

The 90's thus represented a transition period during which aggressive, expanding industrial capitalism was replaced by finance capitalism. Although in retrospect this change in the basic characteristic of capitalism and the businessman was of the utmost significance, it proceeded in such a gradual manner that only the most astute observers had an inkling of its importance,[6] and even today analyses of capitalistic development frequently fail to distinguish sufficiently between industrial and finance capitalism. The sociologic and economic significance of this change exceeded by far the transition from merchant to industrial capitalist! Merchant and industrialist had two essential features in common, the willingness to take a risk and the propensity to plough back their profits. It is in these two important features of capitalistic activity that finance capitalism differs radically. Marxists, above all, tend to ignore the qualitative change in society that was introduced by the emerging "captains of finance." Even as sophisticated an economist as Paul M. Sweezy fails to distinguish between industrial and finance capitalism and thus impairs greatly the validity of his argument.[7]

THE CAUSES OF FINANCE CAPITALISM

The most significant characteristics of industrial capitalism were the increase in scale of operation of the individual firms and its concomitant development of mass markets and strong monopolistic tendencies.[8] As already observed, the monopolistic developments under industrial capitalism were essentially the results of two dissimilar factors: (1) unlimited ("cutthroat") competition in decreasing cost-curve industries, and (2) conscious attempt by businessmen to avoid "ruinous" price competition either by means of price agreements, combinations, pools, trade associations, etc., or by attempts to dominate the industry through trusts (Standard Oil) or size and efficiency (Carnegie).

In the 1890's, and again in the 1950's and 70's, it became popular to emphasize the "other" and "higher" forms of competition that have been "replacing" the vulgar price competition This is perfectly proper as long as no claims are advanced for the "new competition" which can be satisfied only by price competition. The task of autonomous optimum allocation of resources and maximization of individual welfare can, theoretically, be performed only by a market operating under pure (price) competition.

Competition which relied on pools and price agreements in the 1890's and manifests itself today in reduced down payments, bigger advertising budgets, and promotional extravaganza is undoubtedly more picturesque, but hardly permits "the invisible hand" to perform its rational allocation process. Whether the economic man and pure competition ever existed is in this context completely immaterial; neither is it material whether price competition actually maximizes welfare or not. It is material, however, that classical economists from J.B. Clark to Shorey

Peterson, "new" economists like Galbraith, and business spokesmen from the National Association of Manuafcturers to *Fortune*, have claimed the virtues for "workable competition" which only price competition possesses.[9]

To the extent that these pools and price agreements took place in industries which were not "natural" monopolies or oligopolies, they frequently proved completely inadequate to maintain a pre-arranged price level. While Carnegie and Rockefeller utilized the periodic depressions to strengthen their monopolistic market positions, innumerable other pools and combinations in "increasing cost" industries fell apart at the first signs of reverses in the business cycle.[10] Even in steel, farm machinery, meat packing, and other decreasing cost industries, the dominance of strong corporations and strong personalities did not necessarily assure the existence of a stable equilibrium position. The huge size of the country, the incompleteness of the marketing and communication systems which produced, in several industries at least, autonomous regions, and the aggressive character of the colorful captains of industry who headed the major combinations and trusts—all these factors combined to introduce uncertainty, risks, and violent business fluctuations into the economy and a desire for order and reliable control into the hearts of the property owners, investors and financiers.

It is interesting to note the amount of instability and uncertainty that was introduced into industrial capitalism purely by the personalities of the leading businessmen. As long as the Harrimans, Hills, and Carnegies insisted on displaying their belief in Social Darwinism by vigorous competitive behavior, situations which under modern monopolistic competition or game theory should result in a stable oligopolistic equilibrium provided the setting for vigorous competitive clashes. (The Harriman-Hill and the Gould-Vanderbilt battles are examples.) Apparently modern game theory heroically presupposes a rationality among contemporary executives which was lacking in the 70's, 80's, and 90's. Perhaps it is this historical experience that prompted the judiciary to be so reluctant in accepting the economists' contention that oligopolistic pactices may result from rational market strategy rather than overt collusion.

The formation of huge corporate trusts and consolidations, however, found the investors ready and eager to supply the necessary funds for reorganizations and mergers, although the industrialists were frequently reluctant to use them, and preferred as much as possible to rely on ploughed-back earnings for financing expansions and mergers. Civil War financing, the development of a bondholding class, together with the National Banking Act and the accumulation of large private and corporate savings, presented a framework which, under the impetus of large-scale marketing and merger transactions, readily developed into a modern money market. The increased use of checks, short-term liquid commercial paper, and the flotation of large security issues indicated that American industry had reached the threshold of economic and financial maturity.

England and France, however, had passed this threshold quite some time before, and the European investor was ready to pour his excess capital into American industry, especially if he could be assured that the chronic instability and chaos that had characterized America's rapid economic development was to be replaced by order and stability.[11] Although the American investor did not seem to mind being periodically fleeced by the Drews, Gates, Fisks, and Goulds, the increasingly important financial institutions took a more sophisticated point of view; the investment banks, commercial banks and life insurance companies which had assumed an ever-increasing importance in the money market, completely lacked the "sporting" attitude of the American private investor, and not only objected to the excessive speculation of the Wall Street buccaneers but also tried to protect their interests against the risks engendered by the competitive aggressiveness of the Carnegies, Harrimans, and Huntingtons.[12] The ineffectiveness of pools and combinations in establishing market stability, the wishes of the European investors,[13] and the demand of American financial institutions for "responsible"—i.e., investor-conscious—management combined to press upon the captains of finance the role of establishing order and "community of interest" in industry and finance. D.E. Montgomery, defending this emerging "community of interest" among capitalists in a scholarly article, declared that such a policy

> admits of the pursuit of self-interest but concedes that the force of group opinion tends to limit that pursuit to methods which do not unduly disturb trade. It (the policy) looks upon efficiency as an informed and sustained ability to sell at a reasonable price, and to stand back of the product even after it has been sold. It gives first consideration to the fit, leaving the elimination of the unfit to the effect of the average group price over a period of time.[14]

Montgomery's article represented an unusually explicit attempt to combine the policy of "community of interest" with the Spencerian concept of the "survival of the fittest." It was also completely unrealistic because nothing was further from the intentions of the "group opinion" than an "average price" which would eliminate all those who presumably could not operate under such a price.

The financiers were ideally suited to establish and enforce a "community of interest" policy. Men like Morgan, Baker, and Perkins hated the chaos of price competition. The Spencerian myth had little appeal to their essentially feudal way of thinking. A "just" price, a "fair" share of the market, a stable industry or economy, and steady dividend payments seemed to them proper goals to be approached by "responsible" management. The average businessman, who never had any fondness for price competition in the first place, found little difficulty in bowing to the dictates of finance capitalism and oligopolistic organization and replaced price competition—if he ever practiced it—with cooperation. Unlike the financier, however, the average businessman was still wedded to the ideology of competition in both its classical and Spencerian strains. No matter how strongly he might have attempted to escape competition in practice, the term "competition" was surrounded by prestige and glamor. In its Spencerian connotation it signified that the businessman had reached his place in society through battle with hostile though inferior forces. In its classical context it meant that through competition the public weal was served best by the play of the market forces. Thus, only a few courageous businessmen, chiefly financiers and professional managers of the Gary-Farrell-Perkins-Schwab-Vanderlip school of thought, had the courage to reject —or at least modify—the time-honored concepts of competition. *Iron Age* expressed the sentiments of the emerging professional manager which, however, still paid lip service to Social Darwinism, very much in the manner of Soviet scientists who always insert a reference to the laws of "dialectical materialism":

> While no agreements for the maintenance of prices were made or suggested, it was the expressed belief of all (at a meeting of representatiives of the steel industry in 1907) that (price) maintenance would result in benefit to the manufacturers, to their customers, to the employees, and to business interests in general; that stability of prices if and when reasonable is desirable; that violent fluctuations . . . are to be deplored. It was also remarked that the present disposition to assist one another by the free interchange of views which would ultimately result in the application of the law of the survival of the fittest, *is in accordance with the present state of public sentiment.*"[15]

Judge Gary was one of the first who dropped all pretensions and clearly presented "cooperation as an alternative to" survival of the fittest. He declared that he was motivated in holding his annual dinners by the desire "to prevent if I could, not by agreement but by exhortation, the wide and sudden fluctuation of prices which would be injurious to everyone interested in the business of the iron and steel manufacturers."[16] However, if the manufacturers refused "to assist each other by the friendly interchange of views . . . and resorted to unreasonable and destructive competition . . . they would *compel the application of the law of the survival of the fittest.*"[17] On another occasion Gary explained his concept of the "just price": "I think any of us would rather have the prices of our tailor or our grocer substantially uniform, *assuming that they are fair and reasonable,* than to have the prices very low in time of panic and depression, and then in other times very high and unreasonable."[18]

Most businessmen, however, as we shall see below, continued to rely upon the role of "competition" whenever they had to justify their role in society. Neither in the 1890's nor in the 1970's do businessmen refer to price competition when they talk about competition. Any other seller who potentially could attract the same buyer was a "competitor" even though price and market agreements, cost and production information may have been exchanged among the "competing" firms.

The businessman was, and is, of course completely sincere when he referred to the fellow members of his pool or trade association as his competitors. For example, the American Iron and Steel Institute, commenting upon the phenomenon of uniform prices in the steel industry, claimed that the increase in the "range of available sources of supply from which any user of steel may satisfy his needs without penalty of price increased the freedom of competition among producers."[19] This statement is, of course, amazingly similar to the one made by Roger Blough, chairman of the United States Steel Corporation, before a Congressional committee in 1958. Mr. Blough expressed the sentiment that uniform price frees the buyer from the compulsion to buy from the lowest bidder and thus introduces "real competition" because the buyer has complete freedom of choice in placing his orders.

Though the businessman was sincere and even justified in drawing attention to the many forms of non-price competition, it was intellectually dishonest—consciously on the part of the business ideologists, unconsciously as far as most individual businessmen are concerned—to claim for non-price competition all those consequences that only price competition can achieve in the classical model. For in the classical model, competition—and only price competition—provides the invisible hand that guides the economy to the maximum use of resources. Once price competition is replaced by non-price competition, the price mechanism can no longer achieve the optimum allocation of the factors of production, and the entire system becomes completely indeterminate. In rejecting price competition, the businessman, however, did not reject the notion that competition maximizes welfare, nor did he reject the values of classical liberalism which depended upon the autonomous "invisible hand" to be maintained.

The success with which the captains of finance organized and reorganized the major capital industries depended largely upon the stage of development of these industries and upon the state of the money market. As a heavy industry grows, it needs easy access to the money market for reorganization and expansion purposes, thus giving the banker an increasing voice in its affairs at the expense of its previous owners. The 1890's and 1900's witnessed the rare combination of a favorable money market, prosperity, and a large number of industries of just "the right age" for banker reorganization and domination.[20] There existed, of course, no uniform "at the stroke of midnight" replacement of the industrialists by the financiers. In some of the older industries—for instance, railroads—the bankers had been playing an increasingly important role ever since the 1850's,[21] while, on the other hand, Henry Ford—as perfect a representative of industrial capitalism as Carnegie—did not cease to dominate the automobile industry until the 1920's; the Pews, Kohlers and Du Ponts were similarly "industrial capitalists" who feared bank loans like sin and thus maintained their family empires until the 1950's. The Fords were also able to keep their company free of Wall Street entanglements, though they could not prevent the domination of the industry by General Motors, the creation of the investment bankers.

The dominance of financiers and bankers among Cleveland supporters in the 1892 election, however, as well as Cleveland's policy during his second term, signified the ascendance of finance capitalism as much as the Morgan-inspired organization of General Electric and the reorganization of Westinghouse Electric Company. The blind acceptance by industrial capitalism of the deflationary gold-standard party-line which was laid down by the captains of finance in the 90's indicated—at least to this writer—the onset of intellectual old age among the captains of industry. As things turned out, the bank credit expansion under the McKinley administration, supported by gold discoveries, increased government spending, and the war with Spain brought about the very inflation the business community of 1896 had feared so much. Except for Coin Harvey, and a few others from the underworld of economics, no attempt was made to connect the prosperity of the McKinley years with the inflation that occurred under a "business" administration elected to guarantee a "stable" dollar. We can, therefore, assume that finance capitalism became the dominant institution in the early 90's and reached its first peak of economic and, above all, political power during the McKinley administrations. Carnegie's sale of his empire to Morgan's "Steel Trust" in 1900 signified the end of an era.

CONSOLIDATION UNDER FINANCE CAPITALISM

The major economic task that confronted finance capitalism was to establish order and prevent the chaotic flare-ups of economic warfare that had continuously threatened the economy.[23] The stout insistence of the industrial capitalists on continuing aggressively competitive tactics in oligopolistic situations not only incurred serious capital losses but also was considered responsible for the economic fluctuations of the 70's, 80's and 90's.

Whether this belief was correct or not is entirely immaterial for our purposes. It is sufficient that business ideology did blame "cutthroat" competition for the recurrent depressions. After the organization of United States Steel, John B. Claflin expressed the opinion of his day:

> With a man like Mr. Morgan at the head of a great industry, as against the old plan of many diverse interests in it, production will become more regular . . . and panics caused by overproduction become a thing of the past.[24]

Interestingly enough, a severe critic of Morgan and finance capitalism came to a similar conclusion:

> Buccaneering and ruthless competition created business disturbances, lowered the general level of profit, and upset the

complex relations of corporate business. Stabilization was necessary.[25]

The *New York Tribune* found that Carnegie's expansion plans
—prior to his retirement—meant "plunging the steel industry
into a war which would prove disastrous to some of the weaker
combatants and costly and wearing to the strongest."[26] The
Commercial and Financial Chronicle "proved" convincingly that
panics could no longer occur due to the control imposed by
industrial and financial concentration,[27] and James J. Hill declared that "where great consolidations have been effected there
is no longer any danger of disturbance in trade through the
erratic action of the individual owner."[28]

By stressing the "community of interest" and the "live-and-
let-live" concepts—so strongly at odds with the industrialists'
philosophy of Social Darwinism—the finance capitalists not only
followed a policy in line with their own specific interests, but
a policy that seemed to benefit the entire business class and
thus, by means of the "natural trickling down" of profits, the
entire nation. We shall see later on that there is a considerable
difference between the industrialists' concept of "automatic
though involuntary benefit to society through a struggle for survival of the fittest" and the "trickling down" concept of finance
capitalism. Certainly, the defenders of "finance capitalism" found
it much more difficult to defend gross inequalities in income
distribution. "Wealth concentrated in the hand of the very rich
is not such a public calamity as a great many seem to think.
They must use their money for the 'public good,'" a clergyman
stated.[29] Similarly a financial newspaper found that, "Rich men
are valuable in any community, and they are more and more
disposed to treat their wealth as a public trust."[30]

The "historical mission" of finance capitalism to act as a cata-
lyst in concentrating and "rationalizing" capitalism has been
stressed by writers like Josephson and Corey. This view fits in
nicely with a Marxian approach to history, but even institution-
alists (Veblen, Cochran, Miller) and Christian Socialists seemed
to have shared this opinion. A speaker at the "Christian Social-

ist" convention in 1901 exclaimed: "Someday after the Trusts have, with great labor and difficulty, taken the cart up the top of the long hill, we shall relieve them of their labors. We will say 'this is our cart' and take it.[31]

However, the establishment of stability and "community of interest"[32] among the major business organizations may have been one of the historical achievements of finance capitalism, but it was hardly the major factor that prompted individual financiers in making the specific decisions that brought reorganizations and mergers. Neither was the prospect of increased efficiency a major consideration in merger processes, though it was the one aspect most frequently used to justify industrial combinations and trusts.[33] Interestingly enough, the anti-monopoly elements failed to object to the notion that ever-increasing size and concentration of control will produce ever-increasing efficiency. Although such a view is undoubtedly in line with Marxian theory, the middle class Progressives and Liberals should have attacked this view more strenuously. It was left for Brandeis to point out, convincingly, "that the unit in business may be too large to be efficient, and that "most of the trusts which did not secure monopolistic positions have failed to show marked success as compared with the independent concerns."[35]

The huge promotional and underwriting profits associated with mergers, rationalizations, reorganizations, and stock flotation were in most cases the immediate *short-run* motivations that prompted investment bankers and financiers into action and persuaded the industrialists to sell out to them. The rugged old industrialist, James J. Hill, commented:

> The only serious objections to trusts has been the method of creating them—not for the purpose of manufacturing any particular commodity in the first place, but for the purpose of selling sheaves of printed securities which represent nothing more than good will and prospective profits to promoters.[36]

The economic and political power inherent in bigness *per se* seems to have been the major *long-run* consideration, however.

The growth of corporations and of combinations tends to strengthen the forces which seek to control the machinery of the government and the laws in behalf of special interests . . . the productive forces are the purse-bearers. The businessman, whether alone or in combination with other businessmen, *seeks to shape politics and government in a way conducive to his own prosperity.* As the business of the country has learned the secret of combination, it is gradually subverting the power of the politicians and rendering him subservient to its purposes. That government is not entirely controlled by these interests is due to the fact that business organization has not reached full perfection.[37]

Morgan expressed this idea much more succinctly. "Men owning property should do what they like with it," he insisted, and the concentration of economic power in a few major corporations, allied with each other by interlocking directorships, was most certainly a way to enable a Morgan to do with "his" property as he liked. It is quite doubtful, however, whether Morgan ever considered the small middle class investor as a "man of property." The organization of the General Electric company, United States Steel, A.T. & T., etc., created huge combinations of capital with a widely dispersed ownership and thus a *de facto* separation of ownership and control without the legally questionable "trust" device. Whether this was an additional, consciously considered factor in promoting mergers or not, there is little doubt that finance capitalism quickly began to regard the consequences of stockholder dispersions of great strategic significance and to consider the directors and the *de facto* management of the corporations as the "real" owners, the "real" men of property. Again Morgan expressed the sentiments of the captains of finance:

We don't want financial convulsions and have on thing one day and another thing another day. The policy on which the future of the company depended should be continued. . . . I wanted the stock put so nothing could interfere . . . with the policy we had inaugurated. . . . It was our idea to organize a holding company with a capital so large that no rival corporation could purchase a controlling interest in it and so wrest away the control.[38]

Hill, writing to Lord Mount Stephen in 1901, fully described the freedom of action and reduced uncertainties which the giant corporation bestowed upon its management:

> We could not build a great permanent business, extending across the continent and even across the ocean, on the basis that tomorrow the (freight) rate might be changed, or the party with whom we were working to reach the diifferent points of production had some other interests or some greater interests elsewhere. It was necessary that we should have some reasonable expectation that we could control the permanency of the rate and be able to reach the markets.[39]

The ability of finance capitalism to promote mergers and reorganizations depended, of course, on its ability to sell the shares of the new corporations on an increasingly efficient money market. The successful accomplishment of this task was aided, or perhaps even made possible, by vital changes in the rate of American economic development during the 1890's. The rate of growth of American capital development began to decline with the closing of the frontier and the completion of the major capital investments in the railroad and steel industries.[40] At the same time the supply of domestic (and foreign) capital kept increasing due to the profits of the large business organizations, the increase in population, and, above all, the growth of a prosperous middle class. The wealth estimates for these periods —for whatever they are worth—give the following data: National wealth rose from $43.6 billion in 1880 to $65 billion in 1890, to $88 billion in 1900 and to $186 billion in 1910; national income rose for the period from $7.4 billion to $31.4 billion in 1910.[41]

By channeling the growing supply of savings into financial merger transactions, finance capitalism established itself as the dominant factor in industry during the prosperous period 1896–1903. The panics of 1903 and 1907, and especially the stagnation that followed the panic of 1907, gave conclusive evidence, however, that even a "community-of-interest" and concentrated economic power could not avoid depressions. Fictitious market appreciation of securities proved itself as inadequate a substitute for real investment in the early 1900's as during the 1920's.

THE CONSOLIDATION MOVEMENT IN THE IDEOLOGY OF FINANCE CAPITALISM

Establishing "order" and "community-of-interest of property owners" was the key to both the economic endeavors of finance capitalism and to its ideology. Morgan, who epitomized finance capitalism even more than Carnegie did industrial capitalism, provided the keynote for a policy that professed to protect the interests of the bondholder and, secondly, of the stockholder by fostering a cautious "live and let live" attitude, a complete disavowal of Social Darwinism.

Testifying in the Northern Securities case, Morgan explained freely why he had put a representative of the competing Union Pacific on the board of "his" Burlington railroad: "(It was done) simply to show everybody concerned that J.P. Morgan and Company were acting under what was known as the community-of-interest plan and that we were not going to have a battle in Wall Street."[43]

The "community-of-interest" was nicely expressed by the "coordination" of the Hocking Valley Railroad, the Baltimore and Ohio, and the Chesapeake and Ohio under Morgan's influence. Traffic in coal was now allocated evenly; coal output was restricted—33% below capacity—and prices remained steady and high.[44]

Similarly, even James J. Hill seemed to abandon all ideas of competition and "survival of the fittest." He recognized that the "sole object (of 'coordinating') was to bring together as nearly as possible the general policies of the Northern Pacific and Great Northern, so that both companies would avoid unnecessary expenditures in building new lines or in the operation of existing lines."[45]

Hill's attempt to combine the Chicago, Burlington and Quincy

Railroad with the Great Northern and the Northern Pacific was described by J.G. Pyle as "a big mosaic put together by forces so great, so far above any permanent individual contradiction or interference, that he (Hill) looked upon himself as their servitor."[46]

The anti-competitive elements in the various expressed opinions of leading finace capitalists clashed, of course, vigorously with the established folklore of the value of competition and the rule of the autonomous "invisible hand." The very success of industrial capitalism in establishing its ideology as the "received truths" of the post-Civil War middle and property-owning classes created political and ideological difficulties for finance capitalism. The Populist and Progressive movements were essentially expressions of the demands of the property-owning agrarians or urban middle classes for the reestablishment of a society of independent entrepreneurs. Their demand for federal intervention reflected only their opinion that the "invisible hand" could not operate in a monopolistic economy. "Concentration of wealth and power in a few hands is undesirable, even though the aggregate of wealth and economic power is thereby enhanced."[47]

Theodore Roosevelt, Perkins, and the *New Republic* crowd were, of course, in favor of "regulated" trusts. There is little doubt, however, that in this case at least, the intellectual leaders of the Progressive movement were not representative of their followers. Note the enthusiasm with which the Progressives later on supported the Jeffersonian anti-trust policies of Wilson (to the great disgust of Roosevelt). So far as the "old middle class" supporters of the Progressive movement are concerned, it must not necessarily be assumed that their ardent support of anti-trust legislation signified a great love for price competition. More likely it meant but a plan to oppose the encroachments of the giant corporation; at best, a pious desire for price competition for someone else. In that respect "competition" is the opposite of "inflation." The businessman will honor "competition" in the abstract on the Fourth of July, but will be rather unhappy if it affects his own transactions (as a seller). "Inflation," on the other hand, is intrinsically bad, especially if it demonstrates its presence through price increases in those commodities which our hypothetical businessman has to buy. A persistent and steady price increase among his own goods is rarely met with scorn, however; as a matter of fact, government undertakings which might reduce "his" inflation— such as reduced tariffs, elimination of subsidies, etc.—are bitterly opposed as "unfair."

The ideology of finance capitalism, therefore, had to reconcile the anti-competition and anti-government intervention opinions of the Morgans and Stillmans with the Social Darwinism of the industrial capitalists. In accomplishing this task, the architects of the business opinions of finance capitalism created an ideology which not only was logically inconsistent but also frequently conflicted with the private opinion of important business leaders.[48] The Morgans and Bakers most certainly could not accept the essentially radical cant of "competition," "democracy," and "invisible hand" by which business opinion tried to clothe the economic facts of finance capitalism with the myths of classical liberalism and industrial capitalism. Neither were the individualistic, old-line capitalists, from Russell Sage to Henry Ford, always able to accept the "doube-think" notion that "monopoly is competition," nor were they always ready to surrender willingly to Wall Street. Thus, the ideology of finance capitalism did not represent the thinking of the entire business community, nor, probably, did the sophisticated captains of finance really believe all those sentiments they themselves were publicly expressing. Under finance capitalism, business ideology—the rationalized beliefs of a ruling class—and business opinion were no longer completely synonymous.

How far the more sophisticated elements in finance capitalism had departed from the established beliefs of the business community can be illustrated by an important editorial in the *Bankers Monthly*:

> Competition (occurs), obviously, when supply is steadily in excess of demand; prices must (then) bend downward to the

point where only the strongest can survive. . . . The struggle to live and to sell is competition.

When the boom is on, the mills run full time. When reaction comes . . . men are thrown out of employment. . . . Competition means liberty, it is said, and it is true, but it means liberty to the sweater and the bloodsucker to compete with the employer who wants to pay fair wages. It means, also, liberty to the tricky merchant who fails often, and grows rich, to compete with the merchant who pays his debt.

There is no doubt that one of the causes impelling business into combinations is disgust and revulsion against certain phases of competition.[49]

The intellectual honesty with which the *Bankers' Monthly*, the *Bankers' Magazine*, Perkins, Vanderlip, and a few others generally tried to meet the issues of "combination versus individualism," "competition versus cooperation," "union of capital versus union of labor," was refreshing, though ordinarily not representative of the overall ideology of finance capitalism. Even the above-mentioned group seemed to join in the overall chorus of pronouncements that deprecated the pervasive influence of the bankers (though generally not that of the corporations). The very essence of the public announcements of finance capitalism was the professed belief that Morgan, the monopolists, and the money-trust possessed little real power or, at the very least, that their power was greatly exaggerated by agitators and politicians.

For example, Henry P. Davison, a Morgan partner, stressed before the "Pujo Committee" that his firm drew no advantages from having interlocking directors on various boards of directors.

UNTERMYER: You recognize, do you not, that there is a great advantage in having the entree and the interest in these banks, and representation on the board, or do you think there is no advantage whatever?
DAVISONS   Absolutely no advantage at all.
UNTERMYER: None whatever? You think it is a disadvantage?
DAVISON: At times, not always.[50]

Similarly before the same committee, Morgan insisted that there were no such thing as a money trust:

MORGAN: You cannot make a trust on money.
UNTERMYER: There is no way one man can get a monopoly of money?
MORGAN: No, sir, he cannot. He may have all the money in Christendom, but he cannot do it.
UNTERMYERS   If you owned all the banks of New York with all their resources, would you not come pretty near having a control of credit?
MORGAN: No sir, not at all.[51]

* * * *

UNTERMYER: When a man has got vast powers, such as you have, —you admit you have, do you not?
MORGAN: I do not know it, sir.
UNTERMYER: You don't feel it at all?
MORGAN: No, I do not feel it at all.
UNTERMYER: You do not think you have any power in any department of industry in this country?
MORGAN: I do not.
UNTERMYER: Not the slightest?
MORGAN: Not the slightest.[52]

It is noteworthy though that at the same testimony Morgan did not hide his preference for combinations:

UNTERMYER: You are opposed to competition, are you not?
MORGAN: No, I don't mind competition.
UNTERMYER: You would rather have combination, would you not?
MORGAN: I would rather have combination.[53]

Thus Morgan, Baker, and others publicly emphasized their lack of power and influence. The intellectual defenders of finance capitalism—who, due to the reticence of the finance capitalists, played an unusually important role in expressing the ideology of finance capitalism—had the more difficult task of stressing the benefits which the efficient, large combinations bestowed upon the public and at the same time they had to demonstrate the absence of monopolistic conditions due to the autonomous market forces.

> It is sobering to reflect on the attitudes of professional economists of the period toward the merger movement. Economists as wise as Taussig, as incisive as Fisher, as fond of competition as Clark insisted upon discussing the merger movement largely and exclusively in terms of industrial evolution and the economics of scale. . . . One must regretfully record that in this period Ida Tarbell and Henry Demarest Lloyd did more than the American Economic Association to foster the policy of competition.[54]

The simplest device to belittle the concentration of economic power was, of course, the use of quotation marks whenever the terms "monopolies" and "trusts" were used, and to imply that only politicians and (foreign) agitators were opposed to the large combinations of capital, just as they were opposed to any form of property.

> The signs are abundant that the politicians of both parties will declare war against what they call 'trusts'. . . . The real object of [the Jacksonian] attack [upon the money powers] was accumulated wealth, and that is the object now. . . . Combination on a great scale is [but] the consequence of doing business on a great scale.[55]

The free-lance writer and businessman, George E. Roberts, made the most heroic effort to combine the various divergent sentiments of business ideology in the widely commented upon article "Can There Be a Good Trust?"[56]

Anticipating the line of argument advanced by contemporary business ideologists, he bemoans the "socialist" attack upon the "competitive system" which he quickly redefines as "indeed rivalry, but rivalry in service to the community."[57] Large and small companies are essentially alike in the manner in which they serve both the community and themselves. Carnegie and James Jones (a Senator from Arkansas and the promoter of a cotton-press company) alike "draw their rich rewards out of (the) additional wealth produced by them" or "out of economic savings which [the trust] effects."[58] If Senator Jones' company could have made their organization more efficient by making it "as big as one of the so-called 'trusts' " . . . he (Jones) would have favored doing so.[59]

> The so-called "trusts" of this day are plain corporations like the one in which Senator Jones is interested . . . they have no power or immunity from competition except such as large capital gains . . . so long as it (the trust) pays its dividends out of the economic savings effected by its superior capital no objection can properly or reasonably lie against it.[60]

There still remained the vexing complaint of small-town businessmen about the closing of factories by the trusts. Roberts tried to meet this argument in his last paragraphs by falling back on Say's law.

> Such management of industries (as the shutting down of factories) is advantageous to the community as a whole, even though all the immediate savings be retained by the corporation. There is a gain of wealth to society; and whoever may own it, that wealth becomes a productive factor in the community, and inevitably enters into competition in some line to supply the needs of the community.[61]

It was, however, rare to find such an ambitious attempt to meet in one essay a wide range of attacks upon the combinations of finance capitalism. Hanna's short comment, "trusts are a natural evolution of modern commerce and have come to stay,"[62] was much more typical, as was the comment, "Does anyone propose to do away with competition? Of course not. Then somebody must succeed in it," made by a delegate to a "conference on trusts."[63]

The *Bankers' Monthly*, however, took a less superficial view of the "trust problem," for the benefit of its readers. Its comments are noteworthy not only for their honesty but also for the absence of the notions advanced in the above examples that there was no "real" problem, nor anything "really" new. "The trust problem," the *Bankers' Monthly* declared, editorially,

> is important beyond the present and is ultimately associated
> with the future organization of economic life.
> We are in the midst of another transition period in history.
> We are passing from individual to corporate enterprise neces-
> sarily. We are passing from individualism to centralization. The
> huge business machine, with all its machine ramifications, is
> driving out the small workshop. . . . By combination business
> in most industries is being reduced to a few large units, run by
> a few large units.
> This is an age of commercial giants. . . . There never was a
> time (however) when greater scientific consideration was given
> to the amelioration of the condition of all classes than now.[64]

The most complete and sophisticated defense of the consolidation policy of finance capitalism was contained in a symposium
on "Industrial and Railroad Consolidations,"[65] in the *North
American Review*, which in its excellence and completeness must
be compared with Carnegie's successful presentation of the
ideology of industrial capitalism in the same magazine in 1889.[66]
The importance of the participants and of the opinion expressed
require considerable attention to this ideological *tour de force*.

Russell Sage, the old Wall Street buccaneer and rugged indi-
vidualist, opened with a carefully worded indictment of the
consolidation movements, especially of the stock watering that
accompanied reorganization movements.[67]

> to me, there seems to be something very much like sleight of
> hand in the way in which industries are doubling up in value,
> as at the touch of the magician's wand. Here we have a factory
> —a good, conservative, productive instrument. . . . It falls into
> the hands of the consolidators, and whereas it was worth
> $50,000 yesterday to its owner, it is (now) worth $150,000—
> at least on paper. . . .
> Under these circumstances a "squeeze" seems to me inevi-
> table. The Clearing House is reporting from week to week and
> expansion of loans far beyond anything that was dreamed of
> heretofore. This cannot go on forever; yet from all appearances
> the era of consolidation has only set in.

The great success of the Standard Oil Company is always advanced by the believers in consolidation, whenever the scheme is attacked. It is true that this company has had enormous success, and that it has benefited the community. . . . Through its excellent management . . . it has added many hundreds of millions to the wealth of the country. It has made its owners, the capitalists, very rich, and it has acted well by its employees and by consumers. . . .

But if consolidation has produced all these things, it has also in the case of this company produced a feeling of unrest and disquiet, industrial and political, that threatens to bring serious results. . . . Is it desirable to add institutions that cause such commotion and keep all the newspapers in the land, rightly or wrongly, busy with denunciations? [Conservative men] doubt it. The chief owners of the Standard Oil business have grown so enormously wealthy that, in their individual as well as in their corporate capacity they dominate wherever they choose to go. . . . They can almost compel any man to sell them anything at a price.[68]

The great railroad combinations . . . are based on sounder considerations (i.e. not over-capitalized). . . but they are bad nevertheless. *They are sure to arouse the people.* . . . It is right and proper that the capitalist who invests his money in railroads . . . *should be assured of a reasonable and fair return;* it is right that railroads have an agreement not to cut rates . . . but this should be done in conventions, by meetings, by agreements, *not in the stifling of competition.*[69]

Russell Sage's main argument that monopolies were not necessarily "bad" *per se* but dangerous because of present popular resentment and possibly more dangerous future developments[70] was countered by James J. Hill, who had finally come to terms with finance capitalism. Stressing the efficiency of large-scale operations Hill, consciously or by accident, appealed to the production-oriented old middle class of artisans, independent farmers, and small businessmen by emphasizing the imminent elimination of the unproductive middlemen by the integrated corporation. Hill's article, written in the language of industrial capitalism, made an excellent, Galbraithian case for the mergers and combinations of finance capitalism.

> The new system (corporate consolidation as compared to the old trusts) in force today is neither illegal nor harmful to the community. . . . The old scheme left intact all the corporations it found in existence. In the nature of things no economy in production could be effected. . . . [Under the new system] operating expenses are reduced combining a number of institutions under one management. *Useless officers and unproductive middlemen are cut off.* The systems of purchasing and distriibution are simplified (through vertical integration). . . .
>
> The feeling existing against consolidation is undoubtedly general, but investigation will prove that it is almost invariably unreasonable. . . . There are a few—that is, comparatively few— in the community who can advance good reasons for their opposition. They are the middlemen, and the small competitor who was unable to meet the large concern in the open market. To them consolidation has been a distinct injury. This is apparent, and under our social and business system inevitable. The aim in business, as in politics, is to do the greatest good to the greatest number, and the greatest number is benefited by the consolidation. . . .
>
> All progress is the development of order. A uniform method is the highest form of order. The benefits accruing to the people and the extent of their progress, will be in proportion to the extent of the application of uniform methods to the production of what they require.[71]

Charles Schwab, who during his testimony before the Industrial Commission in 1901, had pictured United States Steel as just another enterprise, fully in the grip of the laws of supply and demand with no advantages incurred by its size, presented an entirely different point of view in his article "What May be Expected in the Steel and Iron Industry," Part III of the symposium.[72] While Hill merely emphasized the efficiency of large-scale operations, Schwab went further and emphasized the wastefulness of classical competition and the ignorance of politicians who opposed the "wave of the future." In his contempt for competition and democratic process, Schwab was quite representative of finance capitalism.

> The larger the output, the smaller relatively is the cost of production. This is a trade axiom. It holds good whether the output consists of *pins* or locomotives. . . . It is the recognition of this principle that has brought about the era of business consolidations in the United States. . . .
>
> Heretofore . . . competition was deemed the life of trade. The more competition the better for all concerned. A few saw the wastefulness of this system, but there seemed apparently nothing better to take its place. . . . [But] the effect of combination was found to be that it cut down the cost of supervision, *the non-productive element of labor;* that it made possible the highest development of mechanical appliances; that it displaced the middleman who . . . was wont to take a big slice of profit, *adding so much to the ultimate cost, without adding anything to value.*
>
> It was such a logical result that the only marvel is the opposition which the combination has had to overcome. . . . That there should be political agitators who oppose the idea, and that there should be newspapers who war against it, is conceivable. Both politicians and newspapers are dependent upon a division of popular sentiment. . . . [But] the men who exclaim against the combination might just as reasonably exclaim against the scheme of carrying the mails on the railroads, instead of by pony express.
>
> Here and there, a combination may have been effected with the idea of increasing the cost to the buyer, but wherever this has been the case the combination has failed. . . . Any industry that is important enough to warrant combination is important enough to attract capital in competition, if it endeavors unfairly to increase the price of its production. A combination, like an individual concern, can only hold its trade provided it gives the best goods at the lowest price consistent with a reasonable profit.[73]

The reader should note how the "wasteful competition," driven out the front door by the combination, is again let in the back door to protect the very same combinations against charges of concentration of arbitrary power. It is not possible that one of the leading bureaucrats of finance capitalism, who was instrumental in creating United States Steel and knew the tremendous combination of financial power that was necessary to accomplish this combination, could have been so naive as to really believe that the possible competition of capital (free entry) was of sufficient consequence to influence, say, the decision-making process of U.S. Steel.

The opinions of Charles Flint, Treasurer of United States Rubber, and F. B. Thurber, President of the United States Export Association and a member of the Sugar Trust, who, like Schwab and Hill, were representatives of the newly developing managerial class employed by the captains of finance to run their industries, were less articulately expressed than Schwab's and Hill's, and did not present anything new. It is interesting, however, to note Flint's belief that the new professional management is less autocratic and more (socially) responsible than the industrial capitalists of old.[74] Flint noticeably, though implicitly, anticipated current sophisticated management opinion that sees in top management a highly trained arbitrator among the conflicting clamor of labor, consumer, and stockholder.[75]

James Logan's "Unintelligent Competition a Large Factor in Making Industrial Consolidation a Necessity" presented a retreat from Schwab's all-out attack on "wasteful" competition.[76] Although Logan's position—General Manager of the United States Envelope Company—marked him also as a member of the emerging managerial class, his views represent a compromise between the anti-competition position of finance capitalism and the industrialist's glorification of competition as instrumental in the survival of the fittest.

> Without doubt, many consolidations have been organized (in order to stamp out competition); but there are many others which have been organized to correct abuses which on account of ignorance and lack of intelligence, have become fastened upon many lines of industry and which threatened their destruction. . . .
>
> Usually one of the first things done by a consolidation is to

revise its price lists . . . [since existing] low prices have been
largely made by ignorant manufacturers, who did not know
what they were doing. When consolidations are effected . . .
more intelligent men take control, men who know what it costs
to manufacture goods.[77]

   Competition is industrial war. . . . [It] means death to some,
harm to all. No monopoly exists [however], because monopoly
means control of the market. It does not follow that competition is keenest where there are the largest number of competitors. In fact the reverse is more often true, for competition
among a great many small firms means primitive ways of
doing business, and the pace is ordinarily slow. But with large
corporations, few in number . . . with modern up-to-date
methods of doing business, competition is being reduced to a
science, and when it has worked itself out the consumer will
get better goods for less money than under present ignorant
[sic] competitive conditions.[78]

Logan's attempt to distinguish between "ignorant," i.e. price
competition, and "scientific," i.e. non-price competition, is ingenious but seems to have been quite representative of business
thinking during this period. It is typical of the businessman's
eternal distinction between price competition—which to him is
not competition but unethical warfare—and non-price competition, that is the various efforts of other sellers to obtain a larger
share of the consumer's dollar. Similarly, Logan's attempt to
prove through a display of sophism that monopolies could not
exist was representative of business thinking and could even be
found in Supreme Court decisions. It is, however, an indication
of the remaining strength of the ideology of industrialism and
classical liberalism that Logan ended his article by epitomizing
the businessman's attitude toward competition, which still was
(and is) to the businessman a strong and perhaps mysterious
force:

   There must always be competition. To stamp it out, were
   such a thing possible, would mean stagnation and death; . . .
   it is no compliment to the intelligence of the businessmen who
   have done so much for the progress of the world to suggest

even that they are so short-sighted as to believe that that pro-
gramme could be carried out. .. . We need competition if we
would grow but it ought to be honest and intelligent competition.[79]

The Secretary of the American Sugar Refining Company,
J. Searles, went even further in presenting the businessman's
view of monopoly and competition. Appearing before the
"Lexow committee" of the New York legislature, he first emphasized how the very size of the Sugar Trust made the Trust
independent of the world's market, and therefore protected
patriotically the interests of the consumer. Asked by Senator
Lexow whether the Sugar Trust was a monopoly and whether,
in general, combinations of capital made labor suffer, he an-
swered:

> There is a law, let me tell you, sir, higher than the State of
> New York. That is the law of supply and demand. No trust
> has ever been yet organized, no corporation has ever been
> created, and there never had been any combination of capital
> of any sort big enough to violate the law. . . . The consumer is
> amply protected by the operation of this law, just as the com-
> bination of capital is held in check by it.

Summary: Although the various statements of the leading
businessmen of the 1900's concerning the role of the large business organization do not portray quite the unanimity of opinion
that seems to have prevailed under industrial capitalism, several
important factors stand out: Opposition to aggressive "wasteful" competition and atomistic enterprise is the essence of
finance capitalism. Admiration for the efficiency of the collectivistic corporation and contempt for the backwardness of individualistic entrepreneurship is shown either quite openly or in
Aesopian language. There is little if any emphasis on the role
of the individual, though in reognition of the popular hostility
toward monopolies, business ideology emphasizes that the "old"
wasteful competition is only replaced by a superior type of
competition; monopolies cannot exist by the very "laws of eco-

nomics" consolidation tries to avoid. Thus, the ideology of
finance capitalism portrays (1) competition as wasteful, to be
replaced by efficient consolidations, (2) the market impotence
of the giant corporations due to the laws of competition, (3)
the absence of any market advantage due to size, and (4) the
elimination of inefficient middlemen by the well-integrated, sci-
entifically managed corporation.

The logical contradiction of points (1) and (2) and of points
(3) and (4) should have weakened the ideology's impact upon
the public. Moreover, it seems difficult to believe that private
business opinion actually accepted the official ideology. Actually, however, there is little evidence for either assumption.
Only in the rare cases when business leaders dealt at length
with the questions of competition and bigness did the various
contradictory elements of the business ideology become noticeable. In the short run, at least, and in context with a particular
issue, class ideologies do not have to withstand the test of
rationality and logic. The business opinion reacted toward such
specific issues as bigness, consolidation, money-trust, income
tax, Presidential powers, conservation, child labor, factory legislation, etc., as its immediate interests demanded. Only in those
instances when serious criticism invalidated a particular business position, or when the business community had to rally the
largest possible part of the property-owning classes around itself, do we find an expression of business opinion sufficiently
lengthy to betray the illogical elements in the business ideology.

Rationality and logical consistency are, of course, qualities
which rarely distinguish class or group ideologies. To the extent
that industrial capitalism developed a comparatively logical and
pseudo-scientific ideology, it only demonstrated its ideological
debt to 18th century classical liberalism and rationalism. The
contradictions and, in several cases, apparently flagrant intellectual dishonesties which characterized the business ideology
of finance capitalism, were, perhaps, only representative of the
difficulties in developing a simple "black and white" class ideology in an increasingly complex world in which "variations of
gray" had become the dominant color. An attempt will be made,

however, in the two successive chapters, to trace several medieval qualities inherent in the philosophies of the leading captains of finance, as well as to point out the transitionary tone of the business opinion of this period. Especially faced with an increasing conflict between reality and ideology were those aspects of business opinion which maintained an essentially "industrial" view of the role of business and the entrepreneur.

8. The Role and Ideology of Finance Capitalism— Part Two

The armored knight practiced an art that required lifelong training and every one of them counted individually by virtue of personal skill and prowess. . . . But social and technological skill undermined and eventually destroyed both the function and the position of this class. . . . Now a similar social process undermines the role . . . and the social position of the capitalist entrepreneur. His role, though less glamorous than that of medieval war lords, also is or was just another form of individual leadership acting by virtue of personal force and personal responsibility for success. His position . . . is threatened as soon as this function in the social process loses its importance, and no less of this is due to the cessation of the social needs it served than if those needs are being served by other, more impersonal methods.

Joseph A. Schumpeter, *Capitalism, Socialism and Democracy*

The consolidation and merger movement of finance capitalism was a chief factor in creating economic and social forces which were to destroy the material foundations of individualism, classical liberalism, and its offspring, the Protestant Ethos of Industrial capitalism.[1] The ideology of industrial capitalism, however, was substantially adopted by finance capitalism, and continued to provide the basis for business opinion in the post-World War II era. Only by 1960 had the discrepancy between ideology and reality become sufficiently great to make the continued formalistic adherence to the values of industrial capitalism ridiculous,

141

if not pathetic. Although, in addressing itself to the public, the institutional spokesman of business (corporate) enterprise may occasionally still rely on the images and vocabulary of the Protestant Ethic, corporate management is guided in its internal policies and procedures by a philosophy which represents a radical departure from the belief and ideology of industrial capitalism. The impact during the 1960's of Riesman's *Lonely Crowd,* William H. Whyte's *The Organization Man,* and Mc-Gregor's *The Human Side of Enterprise* upon middle class and management readers was essentially due to the fact that each group could immediately acknowledge their previously often unnoticed departure from the values of the Protestant Ethic.

It would be, however, completely misleading to draw the inference that we have witnessed an organizational revolution in the post-World War II era, which suddenly replaced the Protestant Ethos with the conformity and mediocrity of corporate collectivism. Far from it. Although the roots of the managerial *evolution* reach to the empires of the captains of industry, it was essentially finance capitalism that replaced dynamic individualism with the collectivism of corporate bureaucracy. If there ever was a revolution, it took place at the turn of the century rather than during the post-World War II era.

It was, therefore, a gradual process that replaced the captains of industry with the professional managers as heads of large business enterprises. Although the professional managers of the banker-controlled combinations departed in motivations and organizational procedures from their predecessors, their interest *vis à vis* the public, labor and government were essentially the same. Since concentrated economic power provided finance capitalism with a potentially extraordinary freedom of action, it was in its interest to avoid the development of any other rival power center such as big labor or big government. The ideology of industrial capitalism provided, of course, the perfect tool for such a policy. As long as the public would accept the basic tenet that even the largest corporation was but a pebble in the tide of powerful, *autonomous* and impersonal forces, no demand for the development of "countervailing powers" could arise. Thus finance capitalism found a ready-made ideology to further its interests as the dominant group in society.

Again it is misleading to assume, however, that the individual financiers and corporate executives held opinions that differed from the official business ideology. Undoubtedly, different sophisticated individuals might have privately acknowledged the increasing divergence between reality and business opinion. The bulk of the business community, however, corporate managers and old-line entrepreneurs alike, tenaciously held to the old beliefs and saw itself as the exponent of rugged individualism and as the aggressive victor in the battle for survival of the fittest.

In specific instances and in decisions pertaining to their own organizations, the behavior of the businessmen would frequently run counter to his professed opinions and beliefs, but it cannot be stressed enough that few ever recognized this and fewer yet ever wanted to recognize it. In addition, of course, there were in the first as well as in the seventh decade of the twentieth century small businessmen and giant entrepreneurs whose lives, thinking and behavior fitted well into the mold of the Protestant Ethos. Rockefeller, whose lifespan covered the periods of industrial and finance capitalism as well as the beginning of managerial capitalism, Hill, Ford, General Wood, Avery, Weir, Henry Kaiser, and others provided contemporary heroes for a business civilization, as well as an all-important reminder that the rewards for aggressive individualism, hard work, risk-taking, and courage were still impressive. Perhaps it was the very continued existence of these captains of industry into the eras of finance and managerial capitalism that masked so successfully both the counter-revolutionary impact of finance capitalism, and the medieval quality in the thinking and philosophy of Morgan, Perkins, Baker, and other outstanding financiers. The rejection by the financiers of the (classical) liberal, individualistic, and frequently democratic and egalitarian aspects of the ethics of industrial capitalism, however, failed to reach public consciousness or, for that matter, even the consciousness of the "second string" financial leaders. Henry Clews, for instance, a bureaucrat and

Wall Street banker, who resembled an industrial entrepreneur as much as a Hollywood cowboy resembles the cattle hands of the Old West, preached rugged individualism and survival of the fittest in word or print while devoting his life's work to the elimination of competition and the creation of bigger and bigger industrial combinations.[2]

The depression of the 1930's brought the public rejection of the values and myths of industrial capitalism. The significant growths and bureaucratization of the major corporations in the twenty-five post-war years of a full-employment economy, together with a collectivization of risk-taking and investment, as well as the autonomous, impersonal nature of research and saving, have prompted today a reappraisal of the old business ideology by corporate management. This reappraisal has, of course, been materially affected by the views of the sophisticated spokesmen of professional management, the Mayos, and Barnards, and their institutional counterparts, *Fortune, Harvard Business Review,* and Harvard's Graduate School of Business Administration. Similarly, the total conquest by the "Progressive" educationists of the university Schools of Education and the state accrediting departments has only in the twenty-five post-war years produced its full results, especially in the suburbias inhabited by the lower and middle levels of corporate management. The combined impact of collectivistic life adjustment, anti-individualism and anti-intellectualism in the schools, with group-think, "group-dynamic," and group-manipulation in the corporations, provided finally the emotional climate in which Riesman and Whyte could chronicle the abandonment of the Protestant Ethic by most segments of the corporate business community.

Today again, as in the days of industrial capitalism, the public and business share the same opinions and beliefs, though in a much less conscious and less publicized way. The institutional spokesmen of business (Chambers of Commerce, National Association of Manufacturers, etc), however, still use the vocabulary and political-economic theories of industrial capitalism to advance the interests of corporate enterprise.[3] Among independent and small-town businessmen and professionals, as well as among the emerging middle classes of minority groups, the loyalty to the ideology of industrial capitalism is not only still strong but is accompanied by a mode of business and private behavior not out of line with the professed opinions and beliefs of these groups. In his *America Comes of Age,* André Siegfried pointed out that the emerging middle class of second and third generation Italian, Jewish, and Irish businessmen presents a caricature of Americanism. They adopted all the materialistic drives and attitudes of American business civilization "without acquiring at the same time the traditional stolid restraint of the Puritan conscience."[4] Siegfried's analysis fits in rather well with Riesman's description of the emerging minority middle classes as the last outpost of "inner-directedness," and also explains the emergence of a Republican majority among Italian, Irish, and Slavic voters during the 1968 and 1972 elections.

It is, however, among the large corporations, the most significant institutions of our time, that a complete departure from the behavior and philosophy of industrial capitalism can be found. In the following pages we shall attempt to show that this departure—Riesman and Whyte notwithstanding—is not a post-World War II phenomenon but is firmly rooted in the emergence of finance capitalism at the turn of the century.

THE PERSONAL CHARACTERISTICS AND OPINIONS OF THE LEADING CAPTAINS OF FINANCE AND THEIR IMPACT UPON BUSINESS IDEOLOGY

Consolidations and their ideological defense (discussed in chapter 6) were, of course, not the only contribution of finance capitalism to the changing economic and political scene. An appraisal of the role and beliefs of finance capitalism, and its impact upon the American scene, must, however, always begin with, and again and again return to, the mergers and consolidations of finance capitalism as both the result and the determinant of its economic, social and political beliefs. It should be emphasized that the 1890's only saw the acceleration of a trend that started well before the Civil War. Turnpike and railroad companies then were already large-scale organizations with all their characteristics, namely a bureaucracy (cf. Poor's comments quoted above) with considerable separation of ownership and control and dependence on finance capital. The change in technology during the second half of the nineteenth century produced a more or less steady growth of the scales of organization and consequent separation of ownership and control. During the 1890's this quantitative change became sufficiently large to constitute a qualitative change, that is, the now observable transition from industrial to finance capitalism.[5]

The large corporation—and its concomitant, oligopoly— was, therefore, not the result of finance capitalism. The increasing separation of ownership and control and the acceleration in the development of the professional manager were essentially the result of the growth in large-scale organization. The device of interlocking directorates, and the emphasis on the community-of-interests were, at least partially, consequences of the economic framework of finance capitalism, in whose interests the professional managers were supposed to run the enterprises.

> If by a 'money trust' is meant an established and well-defined identity and community of interest between a few leaders of finance which has been created and is held together through stock holdings, interlockiing directorates, and other forms of domination over banks, trust companies, railroads . . . and industrial corporations, and which has resulted in a vast and growing concentration of money and credit in the hands of a comparatively few men— your committee has no hesitation in asserting as a result of its investigation that this condition, largely developed within the past five years, exists in this country today.[6]

John Moody commented similarly on the interlocking directorates:

> Viewed as a whole, we find the dominating influences in the Trust to be made up of an intricate network of large and small capitalists, many allied to one another by ties of more or less importance, but all being appendages to or parts of the greater groups, which are themselves dependent on and allied with the

two mammoth Rockefeller and Morgan groups. These two mammoth groups jointly . . . constitute the heart of the business and commercial life of the nation.[7]

The personal characteristics of the Morgans, Bakers, Stillmans, and Vanderlips also played a role in shaping the characteristics of the giant business institutions of this period, more than perhaps a purely materialistic interpretation of history could show. Lewis Corey's *The House of Morgan* provides a classical example of the dilemma Morgan presents for a purely Marxian interpretation of history. On one hand, we find that the development of finance capitalism seems to present a nice corroboration of Marxian theory, and thus Corey presents the consolidations as part of the "inexorable" movement of history. On the other hand, Morgan's strong personality forces Corey to show him, over and over again, as a man possessed of vast powers, willfully employed. This "devil theory" of history, of course, is a direct contradiction of the implicit Marxian basis of his analysis. In his *The Decline of American Capitalism* Corey deals with a period singularly lacking in strong characters, and his interpretation is thus far more consistent, though much less readable. Perhaps a portrayal of Morgan in which he was shown as a man who exploited rather than perpetrated historical changes would have been more accurate.

The abhorrence of "chaos," instability, and even risk-taking by Morgan and other captains of finance has already been commented upon in a previous chapter.[8] Though important in their economic consequences, these attitudes were accompanied by a general corporate-medieval philosophy, a complete repudiation of Social Darwinism, which left, above all, a lasting "Morgan" imprint on the social thought of American corporate management.

The medieval, almost Thomistic philosophical bases of Morgan's beliefs—which were to become quite typical of his class—expressed themselves above all in his insistence that the management of America's business machinery could be trusted only to a few of the "best" people, who guided by a code of right and duty, were to handle their "God-given property" as they saw fit. Before the "Pujo Committee," for instance, Morgan could give no other reasons for his investment in the Guaranty Trust Company than that he believed it to be "the thing to do." Only after much questioning did he add that he didn't want the stock to be dispersed, i.e., fall into bad hands.[9]

There are other parts of Morgan's testimony before the "Pujo Committee" that are of special interest because they showed again and again his medieval assumption of total control and responsibility. At the same time, even Morgan, whose very name had become a byword for "cooperation" and "community-of-interest," never repudiated "competition" completely throughout his testimony but denoted some practices as "competitive."

> UNTERMYER: Do you not think it would be entirely feasible that securities . . . should be sold in competition?
>
> MORGAN: I do not.
>
> UNTERMYER: Do you not think there ought to be some kind of competition for them?
>
> MORGAN: No, I should think not.
>
> UNTERMYER: You think not? There is not, in fact, any competition between the New York Central and J.P. Morgan and Company in the purchase and sale of an issue?
>
> MORGAN: There is very apt to be.
>
> UNTERMYER: When was there ever such a thing?
>
> MORGAN: (Continuing) Because the company may think their securities are worth so much, and we may say that they would not sell for that, that they would sell for less.
>
> UNTERMYER: Then you settle it between you, do you not?
>
> MORGAN: Yes.
>
> UNTERMYER: That is not what I meant by competition. What I meant by competition is this: Do you not think the company should be in a position to have other banking houses compete for these securities and perhaps get a higher price than you might think they are worth?
>
> MORGAN: I do not.[10]

Asked about the bank's role as fiscal agent in a bond issue,

Morgan admitted that it had no real legal responsibility but added these significant words:

> but it assumes something else that is still more important, and that is the moral responsibility which has to be defended as long as you live.[11]

George F. Baer, the president of the Philadelphia and Reading Railroad, epitomized the feudal sentiments of finance capitalism in his famous comment to a Wilkes-Barre resident:

> The rights and interests of the laboring man will be protected and cared for by the Christian men to whom God has given control of the property rights of the country. Pray earnestly that right may triumph, always remembering that the Lord God Omnipotent still reigns.[12]

The *Bankers' Monthly* commented on the unequal distribution of wealth in an editorial which could have been the subject for any medieval sermon:

> No matter how much some people may think Dives ought to be punished for setting a good table, Dives and Lazarus are equally entitled to protection under the law. The law cannot obliterate the natural differences in man. God made man different here, and hereafter we are told the difference will be still more marked. . . .
>
> There are churches and jails; homes of wealth and homes of the friendless. There is too much to eat and too much hunger; too much clothing and too many people in rags; too much coal and too many shivering firesides; and it has been so ever since pasturage grew scarce for the joint flocks of Abraham and Lot.[13]

The sophisticated Elton Mayo, though apparently centuries rather than decades removed from George F. Baer, expressed similarly the feudal, paternalistic attitudes of corporate and finance capitalism. The *noblesse oblige* elements have become more outspoken, but essentially Mayo is concerned with the manipulation of the work force by management who "knows best," whether or not it rules by divine sanction.[14]

George Baker implied that the burden of economic government rested heavily but securely on the shoulders of finance capitalism when he testified that, "In goods hands I don't see that [the concentration of money and credit] would do any harm . . . [and] I don't believe it could get into bad hands."[15] Untermyer questioned Baker sharply on his and the Morgan attempts to buy "into a great many banks." Baker, after a series of evasive answers, which in a less illustrious witness might be called lies, admitted that the concentration of credit had gone far enough:

> UNTERMYER: You think it would be dangerous to go further?
> BAKER: It might not be dangerous, but it still has gone far enough. In good hands I do not see that it would do any harm. If it got into bad hands, it would be very bad.
> UNTERMYER: If it got into bad hands it would wreck the country?
> BAKER: Yes, but I do not believe it could get into bad hands.

This exchange is extremely important. Note there is no longer any outside autonomous force—no competition, or "free entry" —that would automatically restore the equilibrium. Power is consciously concentrated in "responsible" hands! By the grace of God, the Morgans and Bakers will see to it that the country is not wrecked. This is a complete break with the ideology of Social Darwinism.

Accordingly, J.P. Morgan, the prince of finance, expected to be rendered the respect due to a prince. "If we have done anything wrong, send your man to see my man and they can fix it up," he said accusingly to President Roosevelt when the latter initiated an anti-trust suit against the Northern Securities Company.

The above quotations and similar statements by other business leaders were, of course, frequently as indicative of arrogance and a "the public be damned" attitude as of *noblesse oblige* and stewardship. Especially in the first decade of finance capitalism a "healthy" buccaneering attitude was still widespread among corporation executives.

The business leaders of this period were often as unable to distinguish between personal, stockholder, organization, and public interests as are contemporary Teamster leaders, and they were similarly unable to perceive the immorality of any action which ultimately benefited the organization and, of course, its executives.[16] McCall, the president of the New York Life Insurance Company, was quite representative of this group, and in his testimony before the New York State Legislative Insurance Investigation Committee he blandly admitted to:

(1) having paid $50,000 to the Republican campaign fund out of company funds (without any bookkeeping entry);
(2) having distributed $100,000 to lobbyist and slush funds;
(3) having paid $200,000 to "Judge" Hamilton, a well-known "fixer," without any accounting entry showing this disbursement initially.

Later on, the books were "altered" to show some spurious transactions.[17]

The *Nation* commented editorially on McCall's "cavalier" testimony:

[This] is the theory of the benevolent tyrant . . . with which we are squarely confronted. If a company is only big enough, has the adequate number of millions, and impinges upon the interest of the community in endless ways, then its president is entitled to do whatever seems right in his own eyes. . . .

Unfortunately this fallacy of bigness . . . that the reasons which apply to administering hundreds of dollars necessarily fail when it is a question of millions of dollars, overlooks two things. One is the law, the other is morals. . . .

[But] we understand perfectly that the gentlemen who have felt themselves chartered to use corporate funds as they saw fit, indignantly disclaimed bad motives. *Indeed, they seem almost as much oppressed by the sense of their own rectitude as by their own conscious wisdom, power and success.*[18]

Thus, it can be seen that a sense of—frequently only theoretical—stewardship and "divine sanction" took the place of the "survival of the fittest" in the ideology of finance capitalism.

This was accompanied by a preference for the *status quo*—and consequently a decline in innovation and capital investment— and ostentatious consumption which could have satisfied any Bourbon.[19] While there was no starving proletariat to rage against waste and opulence, neither did the business community possess the culture, charm, and sophistication of the original Bourbon society to make their conspicuous consumption acceptable. While the middle class resented the undemocratic, ostentatious airs of the "new" society as a repudiation of America's puritan, egalitarian tradition, the total absence of good taste and good sense antagonized also the patricians and the intellectuals. Henry Adams commented:

> Setting aside the few, like Pierpont Morgan, whose social position had little to do with greater or less wealth . . . scarcely any of the very rich men held any position in society by virtue of his wealth, or could have been elected to any office, or even into a good club.[20]

His brother Charles held a similar opinion.

> I have known, and known tolerable well, a good many "successful" men—"big" financially—men famous during the last half century; and a less interesting crowd I do not care to encounter. Not one that I have ever known would I care to meet again, either in this world or the next; nor is one of them associated in my mind with the idea of humor, thought or refinement. A set of mere money-getters and traders, they were essentially unattractive and uninteresting.[21]

The gauche ostentatiousness of the finance barons, together with the popular fear of the growing economic power of the giant combinations, the disclosures of the insurance investigation, and the corruption issue raised successfully by the muckrakers against the big houses and big parties of the captains of finance, made a reform movement almost inevitable.

Actually, of course, there were other issues more important than the conspicuous consumption of the business tycoons and the corrupting influence on municipal, local, and federal levels exerted by medium and big business.[22] The increased class consciousness engendered by the Populists and the growing union movement, the decline in purchasing power, and the closing of the frontier, all these factors combined to make large segments of the American middle class more concerned with immediate remedies of actual or imagined grievances.[23]

THE EMERGENCE OF "PROGRESSIVE" CAPITALISTS

It was the inevitability of reform, as well as the sense of public responsibility inherent in much of the thinking of the Perkins-Vanderlip wing of finance capitalism, that prompted several outstanding members of the new ruling class to advocate reforms and government regulation of business. George Perkins, Nelson Aldrich, Elihu Root, Frank Vanderlip, and Henry Gant were the representatives of this unorthodox wing of capitalism that not only tended to cooperate with the Progressive movement of Roosevelt but also anticipated the Technocrats of the 1920's, and perhaps even the "successful" cooperation of business and governments in pre-World War II Italy and Germany, and post-World War II Japan. George Perkins expressed the "progressive" views quite clearly:

> The railroads are fast coming under federal control. Our banks are under federal control. The very food we eat is more and more coming under federal regulation and inspection . . . but the creator of these things—business commerce—has been up to today left to shift for itself. . . . It is very difficult for me to see how it is not possible for us to face calmly and sensibly a proper regulation of business. . . . The time is ripe . . . [for] some sort of regulation of interstate and international business.[24]

Perkins proceeded then to develop his plan for the successful (self) regulation of business. He suggested the creation of a commission of "Commerce and Labor," consisting of businessmen, who would

(1) License interstate and international business;

(2) Make license depend upon compliance with federal regulations;

(3) Make public financial reports and activities;

(4) Approve (or disapprove) business practices, (especially capitalization of corporations); and

(5) Punish violators.[25]

William Temple, steel executive and former head of the Steel Association—a "pool"—expressed a very similar opinion before the "Stanley Committee."

> The government must have general supervision of the affairs (of a centralized industry) if necessary, and I think it is desirable, if not necessary, in a corporation of that sort (viz. U.S. Steel). . . . I think there is hardly any extent at which you could stop it (viz. supervision).[26]

However, Temple was opposed to government regulation of banking as a model of federal supervision. Similarly James Farrell, president of U.S. Steel, believed that

> it is important for the government to assume the power of such supervision of corporations engaged in interstate traffic as will result in full and clear publicity of the general operations, their receipts and expenditures and profits and losses. . . .
> When it might appear to the government . . . *that prices in any line of industry are unreasonably high,* they should be empowered to make inquiry into the facts, to call upon manufacturers to disclose their profits, and to . . . indicate to manufacturers their opinion as to the reasonableness of their price.[27]

Judge Gary advocated similar government supervision without price control, at the same hearing:

> THE CHAIRMAN: (Augustus Stanley): Do you think it possible, Judge Gary, to move a concern as stupendous as the U.S. Steel Corporation in a direction of absolute government control without finally landing in government ownership? Can you. . . . stop short of that ultimate goal?
> GARY: I think you can . . . but that has been done with banks,

national banks, and with . . . railroads, more or less. . . .
REP. LITTLETON: Is it your position that cooperation is bound
to take the place of competition?
GARY: It is my position.[28]

During the same testimony Gary defended his famous dinners
as spreading understanding and preventing destructive competition. He was also quite outspoken in condemning Carnegie.

Perkins, the professional manager and politically-minded citizen, was already consciously distinguishing himself from the
ordinary businessman who is only interested in monetary gains:

> I have spent most of my life in . . . corporation work. . . . I
> have not thought of myself as a banker. . . . Therefore I have
> had an exceptional opportunity to look into them and become
> acquainted with such problems [trusts]. . . . And I gradually
> came to believe they are going to be the problems of our time
> in our country, and that they can only be solved by men who
> have had practical experience with them. As I was not especially
> ambitious to become . . . an enormously wealthy man, I thought
> I would be more interested in trying to lend a hand to the
> solution of some of these problems than to go on simply from
> the standpoint of making money the rest of my life.[29]

Theodore Roosevelt soon became the center of attraction of
the "Tory" wing of finance capitalism. Especially Perkins and
Root seemed to have had a great influence on Roosevelt, and
their views of strong though regulated corporations as an essential part of the ruling mechanism of the country fitted well into
his progressive-conservative philosophy. Roosevelt's letter to
Hanna during the anthracite strike of 1902 best exemplified the
thinking of the Roosevelt-Perkins-Root group.

> From every consideration of public policy and of good morals
> (the mine owners) should make some slight concession. . . .
> The attitude of the operators will, beyond a doubt, double
> the burden on us while standing between them and socialist
> action.[30]

Years later Roosevelt referred to his actions during this strike in the following illuminating words: "I was anxious to save the great coal operators and all of the class of big propertied men of which they were members, from the dreadful punishment which their own folly would have brought on them if I had not acted."[31]

The views and motivations of those elements in finance capitalism that were ready to welcome government regulation and reform—either as the lesser of two evils (Hanna) or because of deep personal convictions (Perkins, Root, Knox, Gary, Bacon) —were again well expressed by Roosevelt during the Congressional consideration of the Hepburn bill: "I think they are very short-sighted not to understand that to beat it [the bill] means to increase the danger of the movement for government ownership of railroads."[32]

There was more, of course, to the support that Perkins, Munsey, Root, and others gave to Roosevelt and the Progressive movement than just a cautious hope to stifle criticism of corporate business by introducing innocuous reforms. Perkins, at least, seemed to have recognized that the same technological factors which replaced the independent business with the "efficient trust" would require a strong and efficient "big" government to provide an institutional framework which would permit the corporate organization an optimum long-run operating condition.[33] One of the clearest statements of the Roosevelt-Perkins-Gary approach to large-scale organization and the Sherman Act was advanced by Frank Vanderlip, president of the National City Bank:

> In a situation where transportation has made a single business community continent-broad and where there are available practically unlimited supplies of capital . . . it is inevitable that the economies of large-scale business should become absolutely compelling forces. That is what happened. Natural laws have been at work. Not the machinations of criminally-minded men, but the operations of obvious economic laws, have produced the large business units against which the . . . intense opposition of many people are directed.
>
> The hypothesis upon which the enforcement of the Sherman

law rests is that the remedy for the evils believed to be inherent
in large-scale business is to break up big organizations into
small parts and force a return to the competitive conditions
that existed [before]. . . .

I believe this hypothesis is fundamentally false. I believe
that the economic theories upon which it is based are erroneous.
[However] that there *is* a great economic problem is undeni-
able. There are undoubtedly businessmen who believe that we
are merely in a phase of radical political thought which will in
time pass away. . . . I feel that men who stick to such an attitude are blind . . . I know also that to men *with the inidividu-
alist point of view of a generation ago* the mere suggestion of
anything in the shape of government supervision of business
seems new, radical, unnecessary . . . heretical. For my part,
however, I need no further demonstration of the fact that we
have moved far from that old individualistic view *than to con-
trast the position of the individual of today with the power,
influence and potential capacity of the modern corporation.* . . .

The Sherman law, to me, seems like an attempt at turning
back the hands of the clock. . . . There are many hasty thinkers
who find magic in the word "competition." They lose sight of
the fact that competition carried to its logical conclusion often
causes both competitors to lose money. . . . We see the boom
of competition in sweat shops, and we do not like its accom-
panying results. . . . What we need (are) . . . principles that
should govern legislation. . . . . Those principles . . . lie
in the direction . . . of public supervision. Certainly, however,
business should not be controlled merely because it is large.
And control to a point where the government should fix prices
should only be approached as a last and final resort. . . . I believe
in the proper control of capitalization Such control would
(protect) the . . . investor and public.[34]

Perkins and Vanderlip anticipated some deep currents in
American capitalism that later on resulted in the paternalistic
"scientific" management movement in the twenties, sympathy
for Mussolini's corporate state in the thirties, the "welfare-state"
corporation in the post-World War II period, and the admiration
and acceptance of bigness by the Lilienthal-Galbraith type

"Liberals" in the sixties. The one feature these different events have in common is a conviction that corporate business must play an ever increasing social, economic, and political role.

Although the businessman had, at least since the Civil War, stood as the representative of the established order against the mostly feeble attacks of other groups, it was only during the early 1900's that some corporate managers and financiers tended to become a really "conservative" force. While it may be doubtful whether Burke, Carlyle, and Hobbes were more widely read in the 1900's than in the 1880's, at least some segments of the business community abandoned their essentially nihilistic attitude toward the government of the nation and began to display a responsible, conservative attitude. But despite this development, American business as a whole has been prevented from developing into an essentially conservative group by its ideological adherence to the folklore of industrial capitalism. The political roots of this belief—to be distinguished from its social roots which rested firmly in Protestantism, and especially non-conformism—reached back to the economics of the Manchester liberals and the rationalism of Locke and the Radical Whigs.[35] These, however, were the beliefs and theories of a business class that aggressively fought the power and privilege of a retreating aristocracy! Radical tenets, however, are quite useless to a class that has become the dominant power in society. The inability of the business community—except for a few prominent finance capitalists—to develop a conservative philosophy has, of course, resulted in an almost chronic separation of power and responsibility in American politics. Until 1960, the Republican party had continued to be essentially a nihilistic force that operated as a veto group, rather than the instrument of a political philosophy that strove for power and responsibility, quite unlike the conservative parties in England, Canada, and Australia. Once the professional politicians were either tamed or replaced by the capitans of industry and finance, the Republican party, in line with the atomistic philosophy of industrial capitalism, has refused to act like a government party, even if in power. Unless held in control by a strong President (Theodore Roosevelt) or a strong boss (Mark Hanna), the Republicans have too often preferred to act as the opposition party, and the business community has failed to identify itself consistently with *its* party and *its* government, even if outstanding business leaders were Senators and Governors.

The *de facto* abandonment of much of the ideology of industrial capitalism by the Morgans and Schwabs provided a unique opportunity for business to develop a truly conservative opinion and philosophy in line with economic reality. The inability of the leading businessmen to adjust themselves to the conservative reforms of Roosevelt, or to abandon completely—for their own as well as public communications—the ideology of industrial capitalism, permitted this opportunity to disappear. The schism between business opinion and reality, between business ideology and the actual role played by business became "institutionalized." Not only did the businessman, the cultural hero of his country, continue to act as if "the revolution" were around the corner—as if the government were in the hands of a hostile class—but he also continued to be concerned primarily in protecting his short-run interests rather than establishing a long-run policy. Such a short-run policy may have been quite effective for the eighteenth century businessman, for whom each gain presented a broadened basis for new attacks on the ruling aristocracy. It was short-sighted and dangerous in the nineteenth and twentieth centuries, not only for the businessman himself, but for the entire country. "The orderliness of change depends largely on the skills of the conservatives; if the established leadership group in society can absorb the challengers, change can be orderly and peaceful. If the established groups either resist the challengers too vigorously or do not resist at all, change is likely to be violent and discontinuous and much of the benefits of a broadening society is likely to be lost."[36]

It was this preoccupation with short-run problems that prevented the Republican party from recognizing the long-run consequences and interests of financial and corporate capitalism. It was, however, the continued use of the cant of Social Darwinism by the leading spokesmen of finance capitalism and the

Republican party that gave the latter the appearance of expressing the sentiment of the petty-bourgeoisie, while actually the eastern financial and corporate capitalists have dominated the GOP during much of the twentieth century.

Such a preoccupation with only concrete and immediately recognizable issues by the dominant groups in society would have had to produce near chaos if the economic consequences of finance capitalism had not introduced important long-run forces. The giant corporation produced exactly the kind of continuity, planning, and association of responsibility and power that was absent in the political arena. At the same time, of course, the giant corporation perfected an organization that produced a social environment which completely abandoned the individualistic values of industrial capitalism. It took, however, approximately fifty years before corporate management was even faintly willing to admit that the corporation was not necessarily a hot-house of individualism.

The same American businessman who displayed the greatest flexibility in economic matters and fully developed the legal devices of trusts and corporations in order to adapt himself to the demands of technological change, has shown the utmost rigidity and lack of imagination in the social and political spheres. Paraphrasing Senator Lodge, the businessman dealing with a large political question has been not only ridiculous but frequently outright dangerous, above all to himself. In the more than sixty years since the death of Mark Hanna, the American business community has produced few statesmen or politicians who can compare with Hanna in both vision and effectiveness. Economically successful he was, has been, and is, but the American businessman has generally been a failure politically.

9. The Organizational Revolution

The capitalist process, in much the same way in which it destroyed the framework of feudal society, also undermines its own. . . . The political structure of a nation is profoundly affected by the elimination of a host of small and medium-sized firms the owner-managers of which, together with their dependents, henchmen and connections, count quantitatively at the polls and have a hold on . . . the foreman class that no management of a large unit can ever have; the very foundation of private property and free contracting wears away in a nation in which its most vital, most concrete, most meaningful types disappear from the moral horizon of the people.

JOSEPH A. SCHUMPETER, *Capitalism, Socialism and Democracy*

The giant corporation and its professional management has been the dominant phenomenon of the era of finance capitalism. A product of the technological and economic forces of American capitalism, its development was of course affected by the personalities of the principal business leaders—financiers and corporation executives—of this period. In turn, the corporation affected not only the socioeconomic development of corporate managers and bureaucrats who were to satisfy the peculiar demands of the "organizational revolution."

THE EMERGENCE OF THE MANAGER

The "merger and reorganization" movement of the early 1900's permitted the major financiers to pick the professional management of the major corporations. Corporate management seemed to have had the widest leeway to run the organization as it saw

161

fit, provided the basic policies of finance capitalism were not violated. The true authority relationship between corporate management and finance capitalism is well revealed by another Untermyer-Morgan exchange:

UNTERMYER: Did you name the entire board of directors (of United States Steel)?
MORGAN: No, I think I passed on it.
UNTERMYER: Did you not, as a matter of fact, name the board and pass out a slip of paper containing the names?
MORGAN: I cannot say no one else helped me in it.
UNTERMYER: Did you not only pass on it and approve it, but did you not further select the board and determine who should go on and who should stay off?
MORGAN: No, I probably did the latter.
UNTERMYER: Yes, and having determined who should stay off you necessarily determined who should go on?
MORGAN: I am quite willing to assume the whole responsibility.
UNTERMYER: I want the facts.
MORGAN: *Whoever went on the board went with my approval.*[1]

The Morgan-Gary association was quite representative of the relationship between financiers—i.e., the *de facto* owners—and their professional managers. Gary, the hand-picked chairman of the board, held the same paternalistic, medieval views—especially toward labor relations and price competition—as Morgan, and thus it was quite simple to give him a completely free hand in running United States Steel for the Morgan interests.[2] In 1903 there existed, however, a disagreement between Gary the manager, and Morgan the financier, whether or not to pay a dividend in a poor year. In Gary's decision to oppose the payment of a dividend we can see the beginning of a conflict-of-interest between management and financiers. With Gary's victory, a pronounced step was taken toward the replacement of finance capitalism with its own creation, managerial capitalism.

The corporate executives of other Morgan-controlled enterprises operated very much like U.S. Steel, though perhaps for most managers the smooth and sophisticated Schwab or Corey, rather than the ostentatiously pious Gary, could have served as a prototype.[3] But even the Schwabs and Coreys made attempts to assert their independence during the first decades of the 20th century.

The overall policy which the bankers imposed upon corporate management consisted mainly of a strong effort to minimize risk, uncertainty, and instability. The huge fixed investment, as well as the interest of the holders of the highly watered stock, demanded a policy that would guarantee stable sales, prices, and profits. Since the minimizing of uncertainty facilitates the decision-making process, it can be easily seen that the professional interests of corporate management seemed to coincide with the broader long-run interests of finance capitalism. The very natural aversion of a bureaucracy toward change was therefore strengthened by the basic interests of finance capitalism. Technological innovation, product development, growth through aggressive competition, these dynamic aspects of capitalism were to be avoided, if possible.[4] Within a short time the consequences of this policy made themselves felt, and from 1905 to 1913 the American economy slowly approached economic stagnation. Note, for example, the following data for steel production:

Year	In 1,000 long tons	Steel Production 1870 = 100%	Percentage Rate of Increase (rounded off)
1880	1,247	181.4%	244%
1890	4,277	622.1%	140%
1900	10,188	1,481.9%	150%
1910	26,094	3,795.6%	19%
1913	31,300	4,552.9%	

Source: Adapted from *Historical Statistics of the United States, 1789–1945* (United States Department of Commerce, Bureau of the Census, 1949), p. 187.

"By 1913 savings were mounting faster than new investments in productive enterprises."[5] The decrease in the rate of increase of per capita income coincides roughly with the development of finance capitalism. Thus, from 1869 to 1898 real income increased on a five-year average rate of growth of 14%. From 1898—the first year of the great merger period—to 1918 it dropped to 10%. After 1919 until the outbreak of World War II it had dropped to 3%.[6]

Although panics—except for the purely monetary one of 1907 —were avoided, the labor market remained sluggish through most of the first fifteen years of the twentieth century, and real prosperity did not come to the public as a whole until World War I. Less obvious than these economic consequences, though perhaps in the long run more significant, were the results of two other phenomena: the rapid development of large-scale organizations, and the concomitant separation of ownership and control. Though the roots of these developments lie in the technological advancements of the middle of the nineteenth century, finance capitalism provided the apt institutional framework for the rapid growth of these phenomena.

THE SEPARATION OF OWNERSHIP AND CONTROL

The separation of ownership and control in the business organization had sociological and somewhat delayed political-ideological consequences.

> The modern businessman, whether entrepreneur or mere managing administrator, is of the executive type. From the logic of his position he acquires something of the psychology of the salaried employee working in a bureaucratic organization. Whether a stockholder or not, his will to fight and to hold on is not and cannot be what it was with the man who knew ownership and its responsibilities in the full-blooded sense of those words. His system of values and his conception of duty undergo a profound change. Mere stockholders, of course, have ceased to count at all. . . . Thus the modern corporation, although the product of the capitalist process, socializes the bourgeois mind; it relentlessly narrows the scope of capitalist motivation; not only that, it will eventually kill its roots.[7]

We have already seen that as a consequence of the technological requirements an increase in the scale of organization produced an ever growing army of clerks, supervisors, coordinators, and marketing personnel. With the mounting complexities of industrial enterprises these salaried employees were forced into more and more specialized jobs. Removed from the actual production process in the production-oriented period of industrial captalism, there was at first comparatively little opportunity for job satisfaction, prestige, and advancement open to them. Except for the railroads and the Standard Oil Company[8] the business organizations of industrial capitalism seem to have been slow in developing bureaucratic ladders of advancement. Although a good many captains of industry did start out as salesmen, clerks, or production supervisors, their rise to the top did not take place within one organization, and was the result of speculation and risk-taking rather than the reward for bureaucratic ability. "Top management" consisted therefore primarily of the entrepreneur and his lieutenants. Though the latter frequently possessed a great deal of delegated authority,[9] their relationship with the owner-entrepreneur was essentially an intensely personal one, less formalized than the executive-board of director-banker relationship of the 1900's. As a matter of fact, the formalized relationships of the bureaucratic corporation prompted the public relations man, J.B. Sheridan, to complain:

> We are raising a lot of thoroughly drilled 'yes ma'ams' in the big corporations who have no minds of their own; no opinions. As soon as the old individualists die, and there are not many of them left, I think the corporations will have a lot of trouble in getting good executives. After a man has served twenty to thirty years in one of these monstrous corporations he is not liable to have a mind of his own.[10]

The replacement of the entrepreneur by the investment banker accelerated the change in the status of the bureaucracy. Ford, by the very nature of absentee ownership, to rely on managers as well as on formal written reports, budgets and balance sheets, the various levels of corporate management took on increased importance. It is from this point on that "the internal laws of organization" really made themselves felt. It is also from this point on that the ideological consequences of the separation of ownership and control became more apparent.

Since corporate management—almost by definition—replaces individual effort with emphasis on "teamwork," it is understandable that individualism begins to lose its place in the ideology. Frederick Taylor significantly pointed out that "No great man can hope to compete with a number of ordinary men who have been properly organized so as efficiently to cooperate."[11] *The American Bankers' Magazine* went even further in downgrading individuality. Anticipating most of the sentiments of Whyte's organization man, it wrote:

> [Mr. Sage] is undoubtedly right in that the conditions existing under great combinations of capital tend to repress individual opportunity. If the average American citizen . . . possess[ed] . . . [Mr. Sage's] sagacity he might resent . . . the contradiction of individual opportunity to attain financial prizes.
>
> It is no doubt better for a country when the conditions favor moderate wealth for the largest number of citizens rather than excessive fortunes for a minority and comparative poverty for the remainder. Whether conditions under which the average wealth of the citizen will be improved and exceptional fortunes repressed can be brought about either by methods of business or by law, is doubtful. It is certain that Mr. Sage's exceptional fortune, and other large fortunes, have grown up under the competitive system before trusts and combinations in the modern sense appeared on the financial field. . . . It is too soon to assert that in the long run, after the combination system has been fully developed and perfected in all its details, it will bring about a greater equality in the distribution of wealth than could be hoped for under the competitive system, *but there are many signs that lead to this conclusion. It is highly probable from existing indications that the intense individuality that characterized the average citizen of the United States during the first century of the republic is gradually softening.* This is brought about by the influx of immigrants and the employment of men in large numbers by corporations, and the organization of labor unions. In the early days there were very few organizations,

except very loose political ones, in which the pressure of discipline on the individual was slight. In the service of corporations and in the labor organizations men have been very widely educated to estimate the individual in the belief that he is a mere part of the organization and that his individual rights and ambitions must bow to those of the organization. *The nation is fast becoming a nation of employees. From these employees come those who direct and control the great organizations that furnish employment.* When the period of transition is past and the era of competition has given way to an era when each branch of trade and industry forms a unit controlled under one capitalization, and the people are distributed under various employments under the new system, as they were formerly under the competitive system, what reason is there that discontent should grow into revolution? The people of one period do not rise in their might and overthrow an existing system of employment because it is not the same as one that was known to their forefathers. . . . *In the period of transition from a competitive to a non-competitive system* many evils will be experienced, but probably they will be temporary and will be abrogated by a fuller trial of the same system.[12]

The above editorial seems to express very well the sentiments, if not of finance capitalism, at least of the *Bankers' Magazine*. Consistently friendly to combinations and trusts, this magazine let few opportunities pass to break a lance in the defense of trusts and against "individualism." In an earlier issue of the same magazine the editors made the following remarkable statements, very much in the spirit of Galbraith's "New Industrial State" or Mussolini's "Corporate Society":

The general character of the charges against modern business methods is that they injure the individual in his opportunities to acquire wealth. . . . It is probable that the new business order may reduce the number of great prizes, but that it will increase the opportunity for a larger number to arrive at a competence. . . . [In the new business order] *the interests of all are supposed to be advanced by the absence of competition.* . . . In the long run, the combination will be as beneficial for those who furnish the capital.

It has been the history of the social relations of human beings
that as population becomes more dense, the individual has to
combine with his fellows for mutual protection. The ordinary
laws do not . . . furnish protection and fair play to the poorer
members. Societies are formed to supplement the defects of
the law and to secure its privileges.[13] The help of this society
enables the poor man to obtain the equality of privilege before
the law that the rich man enforces for himself. The unequal
distribution of wealth prevents exact justice being done in
regard to property as well as in regard to personal rights, and
corporations and associations secure to persons of moderate
means an equitable recognition of their rights which they
could not secure as individuals. . . . The trust company is a
wonderful agency by which the accumulated wealth belonging
to persons without the skill necessary to protect and conserve
it can be safely managed. The companies formed for the preservation and management of the shares of affiliated railroads have
for their object the protection of the property rights of the
holder of one share as much as those of the holder of the
controlling interests. . . . The securities companies are intended
to extend this protection and careful management to the securities of the companies involved for the benefit of all holders,
large and small alike.[14]

Except for a rather idealized version of the finance capitalist's
relation with the small stockholder, the above quotation gives
an excellent indication of the sophisticated conclusions drawn
by at least certain segments of finance capitalism from the consequences of separation of ownership and control and corporate
growth. There are numerous quotations from other sources to
indicate that this view was quite widely held.

Financial consolidation is in my judgment a long step forward
to the clearer recognition of industrial cooperation. Trusts,
so-called, carried a destructive aspect until met by this formid-
able front. They sought mainly to sweep away opposing pursuits
and smaller enterprises. But financial consolidations, of which
Mr. Morgan is now the guiding brain and representative leader,
must aim perforce to conserve the interests that build, while
restraining or destroying those that pull down either in rivalry

or from the more predatory spirit alone of "get there." The defeat of competition by consolidation is designed automatically to grind out unneeded middlemen and crash the dangerous speculator. . . . The greed of gain—won, too, with honest toil— is deadly to business. . . . The day of large operations compels both consolidation and conservatism.

Competition is the conflict of small business. It has never won but one thing for civilization, and that was a place for struggle. The holding has been done by cooperation. Just now in the business world it is achieved through the form we call consolidation. *In the world of labor it is gained by organization. The two forms are the constables of security.*[15]

Perkins, testifying before a Congressional committee, stated his belief that the public was beginning to be reconciled to the growth of large-scale organizations:

I think our people realize, perhaps more than we think, the advantages that have come about from doing business on a large scale, through big corporations. I think they feel that a proper distribution of those advantages as between capital, labor and the consumer has not yet been reached. I think that the management of these corporations is becoming alive to the fact, and that there ought to be a more equitable distribution, and that will lead gradually to a change of opinion and a closer organization in our business, if you please perhaps a little nearer a monopolistic situation in time to come, but it has got to be an evolution.[16]

Perkins, more than anyone else perhaps, was aware of how much the thinking of the business group he represented deviated from the ideology of industrial capitalism. Advocating a regulatory commission to pass on future mergers and supervise existing trusts he added:

but we have moved at a tremendous pace (toward government supervision). Your father and mine would not have tolerated for a moment even such a discussion as we have had here today. He would have said that a man's business was his own business, and demanded to be left alone, would he not? Now to move from that point to a point where we admit that we are responsible to other people for what we are doing is a tremendous move.[17]

The opponents of combinations and "cooperation" frequently opposed the giant organizations for the very reason their supporters welcomed them. Especially academic economists stressed the collectivistic nature of modern organizations and anticipated the consequences of separation of ownership and control and of the organizational revolution. Charles Bullock warned:

> The friends of private property and individual enterprise should not forget that awaiting the outcome of our dealings with the trusts stands—socialism. The "billion dollar trust" seems to furnish a practical demonstration of the possibility of organizing the largest industries upon a national scale, and the socialist applauds the efforts of Mr. Morgan and his associates. The concentration of all the railroads into a few groups, controlled by a single set of interests, is a brilliant triumph for the policy of centralization; and for this too, Mr. Morgan has the gratitude of every socialist. The popular discontent caused by the monopolization of one necessary of life for another prepares the soil in a manner ideally perfect for the sowing of socialistic seed.[18]

The above quotation clearly indicates that the decline of individualism was regarded as the direct consequence of the growth of "the combinations of capital and labor." Neither those who welcomed such a development nor those who dreaded it, however, were able to see too clearly the role played by the separation of ownership and control. It is more important, however, for an understanding of the business ideology of capitalism to recognize that only in the more sophisticated periodicals, destined mainly for the eyes of banking and corporate executives, do we find ready admissions that the giant corporation portended the end of individualism and competition as the 19th century knew it.

Whatever willingness might have existed among finance capitalism toward emphasizing the anti-competition, anti-middleman aspects of the corporate combinations during the McKinley-Teddy Roosevelt administration, disappeared in the face of the rising tide of the Progressive-Reform movements. Especially the reappearance of Jeffersonian sentiments during the Wilson administration practically forced the business community to stress its adherence to the Protestant virtues. At any rate, from 1913 until today we no longer find business publications or business spokesmen who are willing to extol the gains in efficiency due to the elimination of middlemen, inefficient small business, competition, individualism or greed.[19]

We have previously referred to the noticeable difference between the (comparatively) private opinions of large segments of the business community and their "official" ideology as one of the peculiarities of finance capitalism at the turn of the century. This discrepancy could have been due to the development of two distinct levels of political discussions which generally accompanies the transition from a limited democracy—restricted to the property-owning, educated classes—to the mass society of a representative democracy with unrestricted suffrage. Rational discussion, in the latter society, is reserved for the top levels of leadership, while the irrational, emotional, manipulative appeals are directed to the primary electorate. Such an interpretation, however, seems more appropriate to British conditions than to American.[20] America has been, in essence, a representative mass democracy since the days of Jackson, and most certainly since the Civil War, but we cannot discover a noticeable cleavage in private business opinion and public business ideology until the 1900's. The more likely though less elegant explanation seems to lie in the anti-big business sentiment that had been developed by the muckrakers, the status revolution of the Progressive movement, and lastly the small business neo-Jeffersonianism of Wilson and the New Freedom. We must note that, for once, the critics of bigness and the advocates and defenders of corporate combinations *agreed* about the descriptive analysis of the prevailing conditions. This did not mean, of course, that the critics of bigness accepted the dogma of the special efficiency of bigness. To

Morgan's statement that "practically all the railroad and industrial development of this country has taken place initially through the medium of the great banking houses," Brandeis replied:

> That statement is entirely unfounded in fact. On the contrary, nearly every such contribution to our comfort and prosperity was "initiated" *without* their aid. The "great banking houses" came into relation with those enterprises, either after success had been attained, or upon "reorganization" after the possibility of success had been demonstrated, but the funds of the hardy pioneers, who had risked their all, were exhausted.[21]

Both sides agreed, however, that indivdualism had been replaced by an economic system of large-scale organization in which there was little room for the middleman, small businessman, or artisan, nor for most forms of competition; except that where *Bankers' Magazine,* Perkins, and Morgan would welcome the decline of wasteful competition, the euthanasia of small business and the inefficient middleman, Brandeis, Bryan, and Wilson would deplore this very development.

The fact that both sides agreed on the description of the economy did not make this analysis necessarily accurate. Especially, the disappearance of the "inefficient" middleman was highly exaggerated. Perhaps the earlier empire builders, such as Hill, Rockefeller, and even Schwab, may have been thinking in terms of increased efficiency through maximum integration. Later on, especially in the post-World War I period, big business seemed less and less concerned with this question. Today it is, for instance, U.S. Steel that insists upon maintaining as anachronistic an institution as a steel wholesaler.

At the same time, however, it was undoubtedly true that the separation of ownership and control had drastically reduced the mass basis of (corporate) capitalism. The technical staff expert, the engineer, the intellectual, on whose services the large organization depends, has no deep-seated loyalty to any given property relationship—a point that is equally recognized by standard Marxian analysis as well as by the neo-Austrians, Schumpeter, Von Mises, and Von Hayek. The technicians were, and still are, mainly influenced by the materialistic consideration of efficiency of production. The artisans, farmers, and independent business-men of the "old" middle class, however, were committed in the early 1900's mainly to the ideological concept of Jeffersonian or industrial capitalism, and were hostile to or at least suspicious of finance capitalism and bigness. Though this class has been sharply reduced in size, little has changed in its ideology.

It is, therefore, of utmost importance for corporate capitalism to convince its scientific and engineering staff that the capitalis-tic production and distribution process is the most efficient sys-tem conceivable. A large-scale breakdown in the capitalistic process, as for instance during the world depression of the '30's, will almost immediately result in increased interest among the scientific community in technocracy, planned economy or, at least in Europe, Fascism. The tremendous impact of the Sput-niks upon the American mass-communication industry can, again, only be explained in terms of the ideology of corporate capi-talism which postulates, as an article of faith, that American—i.e., capitalist—"know-how" is supreme. The Sputnik became, therefore, a living symbol of the technical efficiency of a non-capitalistic system. This completely failed to impress rival non-materialistic philosophies—e.g., Scholasticism, Tory conservatism, or the romantic "New Left"—but was absolutely unbearable to the American business ideology. Ironically, both Soviet Russia and the United States have decided to make the purely mate-rialistic production efficiency of their respective systems the standard by which they wish to be judged!

Due to the revival of Jeffersonian sentiments, tactical considera-tion demanded a change in business pronouncements during the early 1900's. The public at large had to be convinced that there was no essential difference between finance capitalism and in-dustrial capitalism, that United States Steel and the corner grocery store were equally helpless in the grip of the market forces. Undoubtedly, there were many members of the business community—as we have already seen—who truly believed in the above statements. The sophisticated top echelon, however, had to change its public announcements, or at least become more circumspect.

The *Bankers' Magazine*, for instance, seemed to restrict its discussion more and more to financial and banking matters; from the year 1905/06 onward, there are less and less articles of social or economic significance. However, it is interesting to note that wherever the *Bankers Magazine* deals with contemporary topics, it still represents the Perkins-Gary wing of business and is hostile to both the "selfish interests" and the individualistic Wall Street speculators.

> What is to be the programme of "the interests" in the next Presidential campaign? They have evidently been greatly encouraged by the late financial revulsion, which they have ascribed to the activity of the President. The one event that probably did more than anything else to precipitate that catastrophe—the disclosures of the traction rottenness in New York—cannot be charged against the President. The doctors who reveal to us our diseases and tell us that safety can be assured only by a change of habits, do not bring a welcome message. . . .
>
> The American people know where lies the responsibility for the distrust of the high financiers, and whoever the Presidential candidate may be . . . the work of reformation inaugurated by Theodore Roosevelt will go on.[22]

Thus the years 1900–1915 can, perhaps, be considered as an ideological transition period. The business community as a whole did not share, or even know, the sentiments of either Gary and Perkins, or Morgan and Baker. So far as attitudes were expressed, beyond the pious and automatic restatements of the Protestant Ethic by Clews or Depew, they were essentially shaped to counter vehement attacks. First, in the initial merger and consolidation periods, business had to defend itself against the anti-trust sentiments of the Progressives and, later on, it was put very much on the defensive by the corruption charges. Although the economic and even the political position of corporate business was hardly affected by the muckrakers, the reputation of the businessman suffered a severe blow. Even the *Nation* and the *New York Evening Post,* the perennial exponents of classical liberalism and civil service reform, were forced to admit that business was as corrupt as politics. Under those conditions, it was surprising that not until World War I did the business community recover its élan sufficiently to formulate a coherent, unified ideology which seemed to express fully its actual opinion.

It is most significant, however, that the post-World War I, as well as the post-World War II ideology consisted essentially of a restatement of the Protestant Ethic of industrial capitalism,[23] with a healthy addition of Gary-Perkins paternalism. (The businessman's "social conscience" as preached by the *Harvard Business Review, Fortune, et al.,* seems to have its roots firmly in the paternalism of the early 1900's.) Whenever the reputation of the businessman was truly threatened, either by the muckrakers of the 1900's or by the depression of the 1930's, we find, however, that the business community returned quickly to the ideology of industrial captalism, which invariably seems to be the proper denominator of privately-held business opinion.

The separation of ownership and control proved itself to be a source of strength as well as weakness during the early 1900's. While, as pointed out above, the mass basis of private capitalism was significantly reduced, the individual embattled corporation, on the other hand, could easily assure its survival and improve its prestige simply by dropping the most malodorous executives from its ranks. In the wake of the Hughes (Armstrong) investigation, the Mutual Life Insurance Company, for instance, ran the following full page advertisement in the New York press, under the title "The Truth about the Mutual":

> People with the fairest minds—and that means most people —have been disturbed . . . by the developments and denunciations of the past few months. . . . To give them (the) truth is the object of this announcement. . . .
>
> We find that the Mutual Life is still the largest and staunchest Life Insurance Company in the world Without defendiing or in the least belittling the abuses and extravagances recently brought to light, everybody should keep in mind the fact that

the solvency of this Company has not for a moment been affected thereby. . . . Extravagance has been stopped, *and those
responsible for it have gone; a new management has been
installed and retrenchments have been effected.*[24]

Thus, under the separation of ownership and control, abuses
are committed by specific individuals while successes are won
by the corporation as an institution. Even if specific institutional characteristics should be held responsible for the existence
of abuses, then legal reforms automatically cleanse the organization, which is thereby enabled to start again with a clean
slate. The very reforms which were originally so strongly opposed—for example, the Sherman Act, the Hepburn bill, the
Armstrong reforms, and, later on, the Federal Deposit Insurance
and the Security Exchange Acts—become now an asset that
should convince every critic of the moral excellency of the re-
formed organization. In addition, the corporations are now able
to ask for similar restrictions for opposing institutions. Since the
Sherman Act "eliminated" monopolies, business can therefore
now ask for laws which will strike at the monopoly power of
unions, or, since private utilities are regulated and pay corporation taxes, they can now demand the same regulations for municipal or cooperative utilities.

The real ideological impact of the separation of ownership
and control, however, goes way beyond both the reduced mass
basis of capitalism and the increased ability of corporations to
avoid responsibility by shedding certain executives who have
become a liability. The separation of ownership and control
seriously undermined the entire justification for profits that
generations of economists and philosophers had developed.
Profit was a reward for risk-taking, saving, and the undertaking
of entrepreneurial activity. But, as bigness tended to reduce
risk, automated saving, and eliminated the role of the entrepreneur, the separation of ownership and control sharply separated
the receivers of profit from those who made the savings and
investment decisions.

It is doubtful whether today, any more than in the early

1900's, the public at large is greatly concerned over the consequences of this development. There existed two vital groups, however, that did recognize the consequence of this development. One was management, and the other the intellectual. It did not take long before management began to realize that there was essentially no difference between profits to be paid out to stockholders and interest payments to creditors. Both payments were essentially "out-of-pocket expenses," and modern accounting practice has finally begun to recognize it as such, just as the more conservative business organizations (e.g., A.T. & T.) have tried very hard to give their stock all the characteristics of a good bond.

It should be emphasized, of course, that since separation of ownership and control was essentially a consequence of bigness, the cleavage between managemnet and stockholder-owner must have already occurred in the period of industrial capitalism. The Hills, Vanderbilts, Harrimans and Rockefellers were able, however, to impress their personalities upon the corporations they controlled, no matter how little or how much of the outstanding stock they owned, while, on the other hand, the bureaucrats who managed the corporate combines for the financiers were generally not able to identify a particular organization with their personalities. There was never any doubt that a Perkins, Schwab or Archbold was a professional executive whose main interest and loyalty belonged to his own career or, at best, to his class, i.e., the managerial class. The interests of this class were not necessarily identical with those of the finance capitalists, and most certainly differed from the interests of the old middle class of small entrepreneurs and artisans. At least one articulate wing of this class, as represented by Gary-Perkins-*Bankers'* *Magazine*, and perhaps later by Gant, Gilbreth and Emerson, moved quite strongly away from the philosophy of individualistic capitalism toward some form of a planned corporate state. The managerial revolution in the United States was delayed, however, partly by the chain of events mentioned above and partly by the strong hold the ideology of industrial capitalism had on the minds of all classes. As long as the bureaucrats shared the opinions of the entire business community, the cleavage between management and stockholders was both delayed and concealed.

The intellectuals perceived the implications of the separation of ownership and control more clearly than did management; while some drew no apparent conclusions (especially writers and artists, such as the members of the Society of American Artists, who consciously withdrew from reality into an aesthetic dreamland), others (J.B. Clark, etc.) were able to persuade themselves that nothing had really changed. The previously commented upon notion of "workable competition" was one of the devices by which J.B. and J.M. Clark, among others, could convince themselves that the assumptions and techniques of neoclassical analysis were still valid. Intellectually, the "concept" of "workable competition" is rather similar to the dogma of the "survival of the fittest." Just as everyone who survives is *eo ipso* the "fittest," any competition for the consumer dollar, or any economic activity for that matter, is "workable," so long as chaos does not prevail. As long as people eat three meals a day, factories obtain raw materials, and the Long Island Railroad delivers its charges at their proper destinations in two out of three tries, we have obviously, "workable competition." It works, doesn't it? Beyond this descriptive virtue, there is little practical or theoretical content in this theory. Having neither rejected nor reaffirmed the classical notion that price competition maximizes welfare, the workable competition school, from the Clarks to Haney to Markham, has not been able to define its concepts of welfare or build a rigorous, theoretical model that could serve as a criterion.

The outstanding intellectuals of this period, however, such as Veblen, Lester Ward, Henry and William James, Holmes, Brandeis, Howell, Garland, Frank Morris and Dewey became more or less severe critics of the business society. Since the intellectuals of the 1890's and 1900's were recruited mainly from both the old middle class and the aristocracy, we might speculate that their economic interests as stock and property owners were threatened by the bureaucrats, and that thus their anta-

gonism has an economic basis. We can read into Veblen's attack
on absentee-owners the Populist views of the Germanic free-
holders of the West, and in the attitude of the James', the Boston
aristocracy's contempt and fear of a sprouting mass-society. It
was, of course, Veblen more than anyone else who analyzed the
consequences of the separation of ownership and control, and
it was he, above all, who shaped the attitude of the American
intellectual toward the business community for generations to
come.[25] To gain an understanding of Veblen's influence on the
young intellectuals one must go again to an artist rather than
to an economist or historian. I haven't found anything that even
approaches John Dos Passos' profile of Veblen in his *The Big
Money*[26] as an indication of Veblen's emotional impact upon
the intellectual youth of America. This influence seemed to gain
over the years—at least until the appearance of *The General
Theory*—rather than to diminish, as indicated, for instance, by
the attitude of the economist John Cummings, who reviewed
the *Theory of the Leisure Class* with vicious hostility in 1899,
and who wrote to Dorfman at the time of Veblen's death:

> I have often wondered how I could have been so blind. In
> the years since, we have all seen the accumulating evidence
> of the widespread influence of Veblen's analysis of social and
> economic behavior, as set forth in his *Theory of the Leisure
> Class*.[27]

Neither Veblen's influence nor the growing separation of ownership and control can be itself be held responsible for the
"anti-business mentality" of the American intellectual. Undoubtedly, other factors were as important or perhaps even more
important in producing this development.[28] The far-reaching
disenchantment with a business civilization that prevailed among
America's leading intellectuals during a period of prosperity,
stability and increasing national power, becomes only fully
understandable when we consider the alienating effects of corporate capitalism upon the property-holding classes.

Faced by the increasing hostility of the environment . . .

entrepreneurs and capitalists will eventually cease to function. Their standard aims are rapidly becoming unattainable, their efforts futile. The most glamorous of these bourgeois aims, the foundation of an industrial dynasty, has in most countries become unattainable already.[29]

THE ORGANIZATIONAL REVOLUTION

The increasing size of the various business organizations demanded not only new specialized skills in administering large organizations, but even led to the development of a discipline which concerned itself with the analysis of the internal structure and operation of an organization, the so-called theory of organization. Although the "scientific" pretensions of this discipline may be resented, it does provide a convenient introduction into a study, not of the operation of an organization, but into the sociological, political, and economic consequences that flow from the existence of the bureaucracy of large-scale organizations. The decline of individualism and the rise of collectivism were, in chapter 2, ascribed to the development of the giant corporation. We shall attempt now to look more closely into the organizational consequences of size and the socioeconomic effects of the decline of the old middle class and the rise of a new one.

One of America's leading management theorists attempted in 1952 to show how an increase in the number of employees not only forces the entrepreneur to delegate authority in general, but even compels him to delegate specific authorities at certain levels of growth.[30] Thus every finite increment in employment, according to Dale, reduces specific areas of the employer's overall authority and creates additional levels of organization and additional narrow specialists. Although I am quite sceptical whether an increase from eight to ten or from 750 to 1000 employees really would and should be accompanied by the change in the company organization structure postulated by Dale, I do think his emphasis on size as the determinant of the structure and personality of an organization is exceedingly important. The non-mathematical management theorists have generally neglected to follow Dale's lead and study the precise implications of size. Concerned mainly with the technical methods of assessing or "communicating" information, management theorists tend to take every organization as given, and proceed to "analyze" the situation by endless classifications. Perkins' comments on communication are much more in line with Dale's thinking:

> The basic cause of present business conditions (i.e., concentration) is . . . very largely the enormous development along practical lines of the methods of intercommunication in the last quarter of a century, . . . especially intercommunication as to thought and the ability of the mind to reach out and do business at enormous distances (especially telephone).[31]

Size and technology, together with the number and structure of business and non-profit organizations, hence determine the character and nature of a society even beyond its narrow class structure.

At least three major characteristics of large-scale organization have greatly modified the operational process of American capitalism and have changed the very nature and composition —but not necessarily the ideology—of American business. These characteristics are:

(1) The establishment of an elaborate hierarchy;
(2) The emergence of the new middle class; development of increased impersonal specialization and division of labor on the control, decision-making, and engineering levels;
(3) The emergence of an increasingly complex communication system reasonably efficient in the transmission of quantitative data but unable to digest qualitative information.[32]

The development of a bureaucratic hierarchy was essentially —but not exclusively—a function of the size and complexity, and especially the capital needs, of an organization.[33] Wherever large combinations of capital are required, the consequent corporate form of business requires a hierarchic bureaucracy to administer its affairs. Thus, a set hierarchy with all its status trappings and operating procedures appeared in the United

States as early as 1850 in railroad, banking and utility business. For our purpose, however, it is more advantageous to restrict our analysis to the industrial and service enterprises of industrial and finance capitalism where a large-scale organizational endeavor replaced the small individually or family-owned enterprise.[34]

The essentially aristocratic nature of a hierarchy, i.e., the "regular system of subordination and rank," with its status symbols and prvileges, should have been expected to have immediately the most severe impact upon the egalitarian world of radical post-Civil War America. Cochran, for instance, considers the notion that "the structure of nature is equalitarian rather than hierarchical" as one of the basic American assumptions.

> Not only are all men created equal, but all creatures and things are on an equal plane in the eyes of God. This assumption toward leadership which has led Americans to attack and belittle the leaders, while in power, that later became famous as symbols of American achievement . . . has also found expression in the cult of the average, and the belief that opportunities should be and in America are, open equally to all men.[35]

The fact that the large industrial combines relied so heavily upon foreign-born non-Germanic workers for their manual labor —the lowest level in the organization—and drew upon native labor for their primary and secondary supervisors, prevented immediate far-reaching cultural consequences. On the other hand, the antagonism of the old middle-class artisans and enterprisers toward the "trusts" rested not only on their economic interests, but upon the cultural and social threat to their status in society posed by the new middle class of salaried technicians, supervisors, bookkeepers and salesmen. The establishment of the large corporation as the basic and most important economic institution in America, and the adoption of the ideology of industrial capitalism by finance capital, thus brought about a severe contradiction between the hierarchical reality of the economic process and the egalitarian American tradition. Only during the last fifteen years has corporate management become aware of the essentially undemocratic nature of the modern business organization. Committee management, "flatter" organizational structures, and emphasis on "teamwork" seem to have been the answers to this dilemma. The "social management" doctrine of Mayo, Dubin, and Simon was a more sophisticated but hardly more convincing attempt to reconcile the contradiction between a hierarchical organization and an egalitarian tradition.

In emphasizing the aristocratic nature of a hierarchic organization one must not, of course, give the impresson that the simple organization of the small manager-owned firm was most democratic. The direct relationship, however, between employer and employee, the absence of a staff or additional supervisory levels, the production consciousness of every member of the firm, the absence of formal operating procedures, the lower degree of specialization and division of labor, and, last but most importantly, the very number of workers employed in a small plant made a much more democratic work situation possible.[36]

Culturally, the hierarchical organization of the corporate enterprise meant a return to the impersonal exploitation and sharp division of labor of the putting-out system.[37] Schumpeter mentions the fact that the putting-out system was the one system in which the capitalist played the narrow role assigned to him by classical theory.[37a] I should like to carry this point further by suggesting that the entrepreneur by replacing the putting-out system with factory operations, at least in the metal trades and basic industries, brought back some of the aspects of the guild system, only on the higher plane of capitalistic production, wherein he controlled—rather than owned—the tools of production. Corporate capitalism, in the same analysis, could thus represent the putting-out system on the "higher level" of finance capitalism.

The hierarchical nature of the large organization directed the ambition of an ever-increasing proportion of Americans toward the goal of attaining rewards within the hierarchy rather than embarking on an undertaking of their own. Regardless of how

rarely it might have been possible for a mechanic to become
an employer, and for a small employer to become wealthy, the
very fact that many a mechanic was now mainly concerned
with becoming a foreman, while the bureaucrats began to dream
of "making" vice-president, presaged a tremendous change for
the aims and culture of a society.[38] In order for a stable organization to exist, its members must be willing to accept the rewards
and punishments it can hand out. The success of the giant corporations during the latter part of the 19th and early part of
the 20th centuries demonstrated that its employees were eagerly
striving for andvancement in its hierarchy. This probably even
held true for significant sections of the manual workers among
the employees of the large organizations, especially for the skilled
craftsmen and foremen. Their frequent acceptance of hierarchic
goals was reflected, to a varying extent, in the labor views of
Hewitt, Gary, Perkins, *et al.* Hewitt, above all, saw in labor an
integral part of the giant organization:

> Most of the writers of the day have failed to comprehend
> the significance of the great movement which pervades all civil-
> ized people. It is toward concentration of management, accom-
> panied by diffusion of ownership. This is the keynote to the
> mighty wave of association which is passing over the world,
> and is particularly felt in this country, where the opportunities
> for development are greater than anywhere else. The harmony
> of capital and labor will be brought about by joint ownership
> in the instruments of production, and what are called "trusts"
> merely afford the machinery by which such ownership can be
> distributed among the workmen.[39]

Hewitt's views were hardly typical of either finance capital or
the hierarchical management, but are of interest mainly because
they were considered sufficiently enlightened to prompt leading
financiers and managers to associate themselves with them.
Tarbell claimed that Hewitt's views were "the philosophy which
Mr. Morgan and Judge Gary had accepted and which they particularly were anxious to see realized in the new venture"
(United States Steel).[40]

This was far from true, however; Hewitt was production-minded, Morgan and Gary finance-minded. It is doubtful whether "labor relations" ever concerned Morgan to any extent. As far as Gary was concerned, we have ample evidence to note that his approach was typical of the semi-paternalistic attitude which the large corporations were beginning to develop during the 1900's.[41] So long as labor accepted the values and goals of the organization, trusted top-management with its fate, and abstained from collective bargaining, Gary was perfectly willing to consider labor as a partner—a member of the team, in post-World War II management jargon—and even to include it in his profit-sharing plan.[42] Although Hewitt sincerely supported the aims and even the policy of the conservative AFL crafts unions,[43] Gary was opposed to all but company unions, even if he began his denunciation with the statement that he liked unions, "properly managed."[44] Before the Senate Committee investigating the steel strike, Gary defined his attitude toward labor unions, which epitomizes the point of view of the paternalistic management of a hierarchical organization:

> I think labor ought to be encouraged to deal collectively, and it ought not to be prohibited at any time from dealing collectively; but dealing collectively in the form of committee is one thing. . . . and dealing collectively as insisted upon by the labor union leaders, which means that the union labor leaders shall decide all these questions, and shall represent the men, whether they are asked or not, and will establish a basis for the closed shop which would shut out the individual voices of these men practically, is quite a different thing.[45]

Gary explained subsequently to Miss Tarbell how the worker could best "participate." It was simple; all he had to do was to advance his opinions, suggestions and/or complaints "through channels" via foreman, department head, etc., until they hit that last myth of an hierarchical organization which wants to maintain the fiction of mobility and democracy—the "always open door" to the boss.[46]

While Gary's views on labor relation and internal democracy

were perhaps typical, if not of the management of the 1900's, at least of the management of the 1920's, more sophisticated views were held by such representatives of "responsible" finance capitalism and management as the *Bankers' Magazine* and Perkins. The *Bankers' Magazine* had been taking a surprisingly pro-labor and pro-union point of view as far back as the 1880's.[47] Recognizing that the emerging collectivistic, hierarchical society had to accommodate its lowest echelons to obtain stability, it developed a labor philosophy that is quite similar in tone, perhaps, to the philosophy of both the *Quadragesimo Anno* and the *Rerum Novarum:*

> Strikes originate from antagonistic interests in productive industry, and seem to be unavoidable in our system. . . . The constant tendency of centralization of capital, and to a greater division of labor . . . is gradually but surely impairing the individuality of workmen, and forcing combinations to counteract the power of concentrated capital. . . . We see no reason why a number of persons should not do in concert what each may do for himself, especially as concentration of capital and subdivision of labor lessen the power of the individual workmen to redress grievances.[48]

The dual nature of the unionized worker employed by a large organization was recognized by Perkins. Anticipating Drucker and Barnard, he did not believe that the worker's role as a union member need necessarily conflict with his role of low-level employee of an hierarchical organization:

> Our labor troubles . . . can be made easier if we can introduce into our corporate methods profit-sharing plans, because I do not think that the question between labor and capital is so much the question of whether a man is paid $1.50 or $1.60 a day, as it is whether he thinks that he is getting his proper proportion of what is being earned.
>
> That being the principle, you never can satisfy the man by increasing him from $1.50 to $1.60 . . . so long as there is a secretive management there, and he does not know whether his proportion is right or not.[49]

It is not known whether Perkins thought that "profit-sharing" and "participation" might weaken the ideological holds of unionism and turn the worker into an organization man, more interested in advancement than in collective security. However, both the union leaders and the management of the 1920's seemed to have approached "profit-sharing" with this point of view. Essentially, Perkins' views, as well as the views of Gary and others, indicate that management might not have been opposed to unionism solely because it meant a restriction of their freedom of actions. Basically it presented a challenge to the paternalistic approach of the feudal management concepts of the 1900's, and perhaps even to the very existence of the large-scale organization, which cannot operate without the widespread acceptance by its members of the hierarchical values and status concepts.

A going hierarchical organization, be it the Army, the Standard Oil Company, or the Communist Party, must develop after a certain period an elitist philosophy among its leading members. A particular group of men—vice-presidents, generals, commissars, etc.,—cannot be endowed with privileges and power without, in turn, being convinced that the privilege and power due to their rank is actually due to them personally as a recognition of their superior talents. An elitist philosophy among people who hold actual organizational power must almost invariably lead to a manipulative "groupism," to use Riesman's term, characterized by "concern with the formation of group consensus through strong leadership."[50]

We find now at the top level of the hierarchy a rational basis for the merger of the individualism of the business ideology and the groupism of the successful, "going" hierarchy.[51] Individualism is for the survivors in the Darwinian struggle, while conformism to organizational standards is the lot of the multitude. In the writings of Mayo, Roethlisberger, Herbert Simon, and other proponents of the modern (social) management gospel, these views were at least implicit. They become explicit in the babbling of the contemporary "social engineers" and the social scientists turned hucksters and public relations men.[52] We must keep in mind, however, that the entire pseudo-science of human manipulation rests on the existence of a society composed of huge, hierarchical organizations. As Riesman points out, even Freud "thought that a strong elite, with a monopoly on the capacity for being reasonable, would have to compel the majority to cooperate in the tasks of civilization, at once demanding submission from the masses and providing them with consolation."[53]

In summary, we find that a large organization requires a complex hierarchy with all the "undemocratic" paraphernalia of rank, privilege, and etiquette. This hierarchy in turn must produce an elite skilled in the manipulation of human beings, which in turn leads, however, to the very negation of individuality and the systems of thought based upon it, such as Democracy and Christianity. In Professor Boulding's words:

> The iron law of size has a corollary: the iron law of hierarchy. The larger the organization, the more elaborate will be its hierarchical structure, the more grades there will be in it, and the greater is likely to be the difficulty of direct communication between the lower and upper grades. Hierarchy, however, conflicts with the ideal of equality. We cannot, therefore, achieve equality by establishing large, integrated organizations. The only hope for an egalitarian world is a world of small organizations held together in a network of contractual relationship.[54]

The point can and should be made, however, that in the United States giant organizations have played an increasingly important role for the last hundred years without weakening the democratic process in politics, and perhaps even without appreciably reducing the individuality of the average American. This fortunate state of affairs is, however, mainly due to the existence, initially, of a great number of large organizations with conflicting interests. Later on, we witnessed the development of countervailing organizations, and it is in this particular area that we have to look for the preservation and safeguarding of democratic institutions. In a world of giant, hierarchical organizations, only the existence of countervailing power and plural loyalties can

protect the individual and the nation from the *Brave New World*
of the manipulators.

The second characteristic of American business, the emergence
of the new middle class, equals in its sociological importance the
establishment of a hierarchical system. Marx predicted the rise
of monopolistic business enterprises and the concomitant slow
disappearance of the middle class of small entrepreneurs, artisans and merchants. He did not foresee, however, that the large-
scale enterprises would require an army of skilled or semi-skilled
technicians, clerks, and administrators to carry on the production
process. Although mere employees and wage earners, the members of this new bureaucracy, who were frequently recruited
from the disappearing old middle class,[55] quickly evolved a
unique *esprit de corps* which readily developed all the characteristics of a new class mentality. In spite of the differentia-
tions in salary, skill, and occupation, the various occupation-
strata identified their interests with that of top management and
the business community as a whole.

Their emulation of the modes of speech, living, and behavior
of the top hierarchy—so bitingly illustrated in Veblen's *Theory
of the Leisure Class*—perhaps was instrumental in producing the
impression that most Americans, regardless of income and status,
considered themselves "middle-class," and tenaciously adhered to
what they thought were "middle-class" standards. The conscious
adoption by the bulk of the finance and corporate business
community of the ideology of industrial capitalism—as pointed
out above—not only strengthened the democratic-egalitarian pretensions in the adopted ideology of the new middle class, but
made it even more difficult to discern that the organizational
revolution had produced a change in the structure of the American society and that the ideology of industrial capitalism had
no longer a rational basis in a society increasingly dominated
by giant organizations.[56] Perhaps one of the best examples of
this "mixed up ideology" was presented by Jacob Schiff's testimony before the "Pujo Committee." The senior partner of Kuhn,
Loeb and Co. was asked by the committee counsel whether he

objected to one banking firm owning another through stock ownership:

SCHIFF: Yes, I do see objections to it.

UNTERMYER: Does that objection apply even if the ownership is through the medium of a third company . . . that is owned by the bank?

SCHIFF: As a rule I am opposed to all holding companies.

UNTERMYER: Why?

SCHIFF: Because of concentration, which under our laws and tendencies should not exist.

UNTERMYER: You do not believe in concentration, do you?

SCHIFF: I do not believe in concentration through companies. . . . I believe in concentration through individuals.

UNTERMYER: You think that individuals should be permitted to get a monopoly of anything, but not through holding companies?

SCHIFF: I do not say a monopoly.

UNTERMYER: How near a monopoly would you let them get?

SCHIFF: I think individuals should have every possible freedom. I do not believe in anything that will limit individual freedom. . . . I would not limit the indvidual by law to buy whatever he pleases. . . . Even if it amounted to monopoly. . . .I would not limit, in any instance, individual freedom in anything, because I believe the law of nature governs that better than any man.[57]

Schiff's evident, irrational belief that individually owned firms are subject to "natural laws" while corporations are not, is an excellent example for the transitory and nonsensical ideology of industrial capitalism that still permeated the business opinion of the 1900's.

Although the ideology of industrial capitalism was patently unsuited for the needs of an emerging bureaucracy, until World War II the large-scale organization seemed to justify its existence in an almost Aesopian manner by expressing collectivistic aims and procedures in the language of the Protestant Ethic. Ideological differentiation seems to be absent in hierarchical organizations, so long as there is sufficient mobility to enable a small but steady number of lower-level bureaucrats to advance to the top level. It was not until the increasing educational requirements of the post-World War II period limited this mobility, that a split into a managerial class and a white collar class began to appear.[58]

This new middle class, however, was, and is, an "occupational" class and derives its status from the nature of its occupation. We have to analyze its occupational duties within the organization in order to appreciate the social evolution that took place in the United States between 1870 and World War I. This analysis is handicapped by the enthusiasm with which the bureaucrats adopted, at least formally, the morality and political ideology of the old, property-owning middle class.

Specialization and division of labor within a hierarchical structure was the one feature that more than any other determined the characteristics of the evolving bureaucracy. It led to an even greater dependence on the fellow bureaucrats in the production process—and provided thereby an opportunity to avoid individual responsibility—and, concomitantly, to a growing preoccupation with minutiae and techniques. A time study man, for example, will be first of all interested in the theory of time and motion study; secondly, in the need to demonstrate to his superiors the excellence of his applications, and lastly, in quantitative results that can demonstrate his achievements. Whether these concrete results really tend to improve the production process in the long run is frequently of no importance. The meritorious consequences of time study are, in other words, accepted on faith.

The larger the organization, the greater the degree of specialization, and the greater the formalization of decision-making and communication. This, again, must reduce the individuality of the bureaucrats at least at the lower levels, because the entire purpose of "standard operating procedures," budgets, policy handbooks, etc., lies precisely in the elimination of uncertainties that could be introduced into the production process by the variable which constitutes the human personality. Even more importantly, this impersonality of decision-making destroys human morality and creates the monster of impersonal organization morality.

The conflict engendered in a man's soul by the demands of his occupation or status, and the convictions of his "private" self, have been a stock in trade of Victorian literature. The over and over repeated phrase "I believe you as a man (father, friend, neighbor, etc.) but I can't believe you (or condemn you, sentence you, fire you, etc., etc.) as a judge (foreman, officer)" is by itself most characteristic of the impersonal morality that is the essential immorality of an organizational society. The Nürnberg and Eichmann trials, in actual life, and Kafka's *The Trial* and Moravia's *The Nonconformist*, in contemporary literature—just to name the two most depressing works in this genre—show to what extremes this dichotomy between private and organizational morals can be carried.

Conflicts between a status-determined role and the person who acts the role existed, of course, long before the predominance of large-scale organization. Large-scale economic organizations merely make it easier to hide oneself behind impersonal "company policy," and sharpen the conflict between the individual's role as a citizen and as an employee. An officer or a priest is always an officer or a priest. A department head, however, is a bureaucrat only from nine to five, and a father, lodge brother, citizen, etc., the rest of the time. Professor Boulding makes this comment:

> If we analyze a classic statement such as the Ten Commandments, for instance, we find that the last six, which deal with questions of morality involving relations with other people, contemplate no organization larger than a family. . . . The commandments are addressed in the second person singular, not the plural; they begin, "Thou shalt not" not "Ye shall not". . . . Acting "in name of,"—i.e., as representatives of others bound together in an organization—presents moral problems and dilemma additional to those which concern an individual acting solely on his own account.[59]

The entire development of "operating procedures," impersonal decision making, formalization of communications, and, above all, loyalty to an institution—the company—constitutes, in essence, a return to a form of feudal communal living, quite in line with the feudal beliefs of Morgan and Baker and the feudal sentiments of Durkheim and Mayo.

The rise of the organization has reduced the independence and individuality of the individual clerk or technician even outside the purely economic realm, at least if we compare his lot with the independent farmer or artisan of the pre-Civil War era.

The "jolly miller" who could sing "I care for nobody, no, not I, for nobody cares for me" is a relic of an age when a much larger proportion of people earned their living by selling the direct product of their labor to a lot of customers, and who therefore did not have to be particularly beholden to anyone of them.[60]

Thus conformity, at least outward conformity, to the standards of the group or the organization became one of the characteristics of the new middle class. Whether this conformity went beyond the regular and even necessary amount of conforming that any society requires from its members, is debatable. It is hardly debatable, however, that the sources of authority and punishment were more powerful and concentrated for the members of the new middle class. The village blacksmith who was an atheist, and the farmer who beat his wife were censured by their community. So long as their enterprises continued to perform their economic function, however, there was little economic pressure their neighbors could exert. The foreman who declared his sympathies for Bryan, however, and the clerk who was caught reading socialist literature, were much more open to economic reprisal and were, therefore, more apt to lose their individuality in a strenuous effort to conform.

This tendency to "organizational living," to conform, if coupled with an egalitarian tradition and Cochran's "cult of the average," can, within the trappings of a democratic ideology, give the impression of a "revolt of the masses," while basically the (middle class) masses are only emulating the organizational leaders with whom they vicariously identify themselves, at least in absence of depressions and national defeats.

If this view is adopted we find that the analyses of Ortega y Gasset and Professor Boulding—superficially contradictory—are quite compatible, and even supplement each other. Thus, the conformism and anti-intellectualism of the organization, or at least the manipulated lower levels of the organization, are identical with Ortega's distrust of the "select minorities" by the masses.

> The characteristic of the hour is that the commonplace mind, knowing itself to be commonplace, has the assurance to proclaim the rights of the commonplace and to impose them wherever it will. As they say in the United States: "to be different is to be indecent."[61]

Where Ortega sees the masses as the originators of action, Boulding sees essentially the various levels of a hierarchical organization conforming to the ideology of the business community, pretending to extol individualism, and practicing a highly developed form of groupism.

The third characteristic of the modern business system, the development of a complex communication system, has only received scant attention in contemporary historical analysis, although the nerve center of a large-scale organization is its communication system. Its effectiveness and peculiarities not only determine the economic and political efficiency of the organization, but also shape its institutional personality and may even select its top executives. It is customary among writers on organizational theory—from Boulding to Urwick and Simon —to carry the "nerve-center" simile even further and approach organizational analysis from a biological or cybernetic viewpoint, wherein the organization is treated as a living organism, stimulated by a communication-nerve system.[62] I should like to carry this approach even further and test the effectiveness of this nerve system by applying to it basic concepts from communication theory.

One of the major characteristics of an electronic communication system is its accuracy in the transmission of quantitative data and its difficulty of either transmitting qualitative data or translating qualitative into quantitative data. Similarly, large-scale (business) organizations have always been quite effective in transmitting and analyzing quantitative data such as production, costs and employment data. Quantitative data, in turn, make it easy to establish standard operating procedures and to delegate decision-making to lower levels of the hierarchy. Thus an important role which the organizational communication system plays is to shorten the communication circuit and prevent the overloading of the nerve center, top management.

The transmission of qualitative data presents, however, greater difficulty. First of all, by its very nature qualitative data do not lend themselves easily to symbolic or quantitative description, and therefore present a communication problem, even in electronic systems. This is magnified in human hierarchical systems by the variability of human nature. Such concepts, for instance, as shop morale, aggressiveness in sales organizations, cost-consciousness, etc., have different meanings to different individuals and will result in different action. The establishment of "company policy" attempts to reduce the action variability, and thus to establish a certain self-correcting information feed-back on the lower levels of the hierarchy. The problems in this area, however, are still sufficiently serious to constitute a real and serious limitation to future organizational expansion.

The property of organizations to handle quantitative data well and qualitative data poorly has several consequences. First of all it must result in an excessive concern with quantitative issues and a concomitant neglect of non-materialistic questions; the failure of the businessman of the 1900's, as well as of today, to develop a clear philosophy and to state his objectives concisely may well rest upon the difficulty organizations experience when dealing with non-quantitative material.

Secondly, the difficulty of developing operating and analytical procedures in the areas of qualitative judgments and information will prompt the lower levels of management to play it safe and either originate no information and take no action, or "pass the buck" of decision-making to ever higher echelons unless a crass and clear-cut case presents itself. The pronouncements of business leaders on labor relations during the 1900's, for instance, are good indications of the lack of information on this subject among the top hierarchy.[63]

The uncertainty of a bureaucracy in the face of qualitative problems—and such dynamic factors as changes in taste, public and government attitudes, and employee morale are highly qualitative—provides another impetus for a bureaucracy to play safe, do nothing, follow time-tested procedures, and regard with hostility all factors that may threaten the *status quo*.

The preference of the bureaucratic hierarchy for the present comfortable *status quo*—so frequently confused with conservatism—can thus be assumed to be at least partially based upon the inability of its communication system to process qualitative information. The spacious pragmatism, scientism, and admiration for the "practical man," found among the bureaucracy of large-scale organizations, is similarly deducible, at least in part, to the inability of the communication system to handle abstract concepts, and to the concomitant preference of the bureaucracy for "practical," vocationally trained members.[64]

SUMMARY

The increased scale of enterprises produced an organizational revolution that profoundly affected American society. As the Rockefellers, Morgans, and Perkins eliminated the independent entrepreneur, the employees of their trusts emerged as a new class, replacing the old middle class of artisans and small entrepreneurs. Though the new middle class adopted the ideology and vocabulary of the old middle class, we find that the very structure of the new organizations induced a collectivistic process of production, hostile to the individualistic tradition of the American society. The generally enthusiastic endorsement of the old Protestant virtues by the business leaders of the 1890's and 1900's disguised successfully this transition process. Only in the post-World War II period has it become obvious—thanks to Boulding,

Whyte, Riesman, *et al.*—that the individualistic ideology of the business community hides an increasingly hierarchical collectivistic and conformistic production process.

10. Summary and Conclusion

The history of the businessman during the Reform-Progressive era—a truly crucial transition period—betrays no evidence that he was the bearer of conservative thought. Essentially, the American businessman's greatest asset was his ability to adapt himself quickly to technological forces and, by the use of new or existing legal devices, create institutions capable of exploiting technological innovations. In his willingness to utilize technological change, the American businessman probably made his greatest contribution to the development of the American economy. In certain instances he even went beyond "utilizing innovation," but rather forced the nation to accelerate its rate of growth by anticipating it. The foremost examples of this development exist, of course, in the construction of the western railroad empires, and the organization of Standard Oil Company and United States Steel. The businessman, however, was (and is) not able to analyze the social and economic changes which were caused by his own economic institutions. The adherence to a business ideology, which has been highly anachronistic ever since 1870, not only evidenced the businessman's social and political inflexibility but, in turn, helped to increase this inflexibility by developing a host of ideologues—intellectuals who acted as spokesmen of business interests—who developed a vested interest in the intellectual content of the ideology.

The development of finance capitalism presented an opportunity for the businessman to break out of the confines of classical liberalism and Social Darwinism. The views of Morgan, Gary, Perkins, and Vanderlip were, at least, based upon a generally realistic assessment of the economic process. But these views were in the minority. Most entrepreneurs tried, as we have seen

198

in Chapters 7 and 8, to merge the ideologies of industrial and financial capitalism. This merger, however, was always a rather tenuous one. Certainly, the view that business was organically associated with the conduct of public affairs, and hence subject to both political analysis and public regulation, never became an integral part of business opinion; but, at least among certain segments of the business elite—i.e., the Gary, Perkins, Vanderlip group—the views of the *Bankers' Magazine*, rather than of the NAM, prevailed during the last decade before World War I.

It was during this comparatively short period that business began to play a politically and socially responsible role, responsible at least to the extent that men like Gary and Perkins considered the economic and social consequences of their actions. The promise of that period, the development of a politically responsible, intelligently conservative business community, never developed. The end of World War I saw an *en masse* return of business opinion to the ideology of industrial capitalism and to the politics of irresponsibility and "know-nothingism."[1] The very reason that the ideology fitted circumstances even less than before World War I might account for the increased anti-intellectualism of the business ideology of the inter-war period.[2]

The businessman's inflexibility and traditionalism in his dealings with social and political problems must, of course, not be confused with conservatism. Social Darwinism has already been analyzed as a highly radical doctrine. Although in the hands of the business ideologues the Spencerian concept of slow, eternal change became a powerful tool for the preservation of the *status quo*, the anti-authoritarian, a-political, a-historical, even anti-intellectual concept of Social Darwinism impressed its radical imprint on those business groups that adhered to the ideology of industrial capitalism.[3]

This combination of flexibility and daring in the economic area, traditionalism and inflexibility in the socio-political sphere, and radicalism in the philosophical outlook, explains the difficulties in the ordinary assessment of the role and thought of the businessman. The difficulties which an anachronistic ideology of the most vital economic class imposed upon the economic development of the country were minimized by the businessman's ingenious development of the corporation. This institution provided sufficient continuity and large-scale planning to furnish a setting for continued economic activity and progress. Under the influence of Morgan, Baker, Gary, and Perkins the management of the large financial and industrial organizations even developed a certain sense of moral responsibility for the consequences of its action. This feeling of personal responsibility must not be confused with the vague concept of "social responsibility" which is currently so freely bandied about by management spokesmen. Responsibility meant to Morgan and Perkins essentially an awareness of the vast powers inherent in their own persons or, respectively, in the management of the giant corporation. It meant, secondly, a conscious use of these powers consistent with their own value system.

The collective nature of the giant corporation, influenced by the feudal, conservative philosophy of the Morgan-Baker, Gary-Perkins wings of finance and managerial capitalism, developed into the status-conscious, hierarchical organization which has become the dominant feature of modern society. The modern corporation has emerged today as the very antithesis of the individually owned enterprise of the classical model. Its management promises to become the first truly conservative force in American history since the demise of the Whigs. In order for contemporary management to play the intelligent, conservative role even Liberals would welcome, it must divorce itself completely from the obsolete and stifling ideology of industrial capitalism. Except for its ideology, corporate management has little in common with the entrepreneurs of industrial capitalism, as this book, it is hoped, has demonstrated.

STATISTICAL APPENDIX TO CHAPTER 2

TABLE I

Total and Per Capita National Income
(1869–1913)
Based on 1929 prices

	AVERAGE PER YEAR			% CHANGE FROM DECADE TO OVERLAPPING DECADE		
DECADE	National Income ($ bill.) (1)	Population (mill.) (2)	Per Capita ($) (1)÷(2) (3)	National Income (4)	Population (5)	Per Capita (6)
1869-78	9.3	43.5	215			
1874-83	13.6	48.8	278	+45.6	+12.2	+29.3
1879-88	17.9	54.8	326	+31.4	+12.1	+17.3
1884-93	21.0	61.2	344	+17.7	+11.7	+ 5.5
1889-98	24.2	67.6	357	+14.9	+10.6	+ 3.8
1894-03	29.8	74.3	401	+23.1	+ 9.8	+12.3
1899-08	37.3	81.5	458	+25.5	+ 9.8	+14.2
1904-13	45.0	89.6	502	+20.5	+ 9.9	+ 9.6

Source: Simon Kuznets, *National Income, A Summary of Findings* (National Bureau of Economic Research, New York, 1946), table x, p. 32.

TABLE II

Percentage Distribution of National Income by Origin
(1870–1910)

	Employee Compensation (1)	Entrep. Net Income (2)	Service Income (3)	Dividends & Interest (4)	Rent (5)	Property Income Incl. Rent (6)
Average of						
1870 & 1880	50.0	26.4	76.5	15.8	7.8	23.6
1880 & 1890	52.5	23.0	75.4	16.5	8.2	24.6
1890 & 1900	50.4	27.3	77.7	14.7	7.7	22.4
1900 & 1910	47.1	28.8	75.8	15.9	8.3	24.2

Source: W.I. King, *The Wealth and Income of the People of the United States* (The Macmillan Company, New York, 1919), table xxi, p. 160.

TABLE III

National Income, Percentage Distribution between
Flow of Goods to Consumers and Net Capital Formation*
(1869–1913)

	Flow of Goods to Consumers	Net Capital Formation
1869-78	$7.9	12.1
1874-83	$7.0	13.0
1879-88	$6.8	13.2
1884-93	$5.9	14.1
1889-98	$5.9	14.1
1894-03	$6.4	13.6
1899-08	$7.4	12.6
1904-13	$7.9	12.1

*In current prices.

Source: Kuznets, *op. cit.*, table xvi, p. 53.

NOTES

CHAPTER 1

1. Miriam Beard, *A History of the Business Man* (The Macmillan Company, New York, 1938), p. 6.

2. cf. Richard Hofstadter, *The American Political Tradition* (Vintage Books, New York, 1954), chapters iii, iv; James Bryce, *The American Commonwealth* (Macmillan & Co. Ltd., London, The Macmillan Company, New York, 1897), Vol. II, Part III, chapters lvii, lxvii, Part IV, chapters lxxvi-lxxv.

3. Miriam Beard, *op. cit.*, p. 60.

4. Russell Kirk, *The Conservative Mind* (Henry Regnery & Co., Chicago, 1953), William H. Chamberlin, *The World's Iron Age* (The Macmillan Company, New York, 1941); John Chamberlin, *The American Stakes* (Carrick & Evans, New York, 1940).

5. See Erick Goldman, *Rendezvous with Destiny* (Alfred A. Knopf, Inc., New Nork, 1952), chapter iii-vi for a friendly though critical study of America's radical third parties. The discontent in the 1880's and 1890's is vividly rerflected in Arthur M. Schlesinger, *The Rise of the City*, 1878-1898 (The Macmillan Company, New York, 1933); John D. Hicks, *The Populist Revolt* (University of Minnesota Press, Minneapolis, 1931); and Chester M. Dester, *American Radicalism*, 1865-1901 (Collegiate Press, Menasha, Wisc., 1946).

6. cf. C. Wright Mills, *White Collar* (Oxford University Press, New York, 1953), *passim;* Karl Mannheim, *Man and Society in an Age of Reconstruction* (Harcourt Brace Company, New York 1940), *passim.*

7. Typically, traditionalist groups reached in 1967 for the weapon of "direct democracy," the recall, in an attempt to get rid of the leftist Senators Church and Morse in Idaho and Oregon.

CHAPTER 2

1. Charles Beard, *An Economic Interpretation of the Constitution of the United States* (The Macmillan Company, New York, 1935).

2. James Madison, *The Writings of James Madison*, ed. Gaillard Hunt (G. P. Putnam's Sons, New York, 1900–1910), pp. 351–3.

3. Bray Hammond, *Banks and Politics in America* (Princeton University Press, Princeton, 1957) pp. 328–9.

4. Arthur M. Schlesinger, *The Age of Jackson* (Little, Brown & Company, Boston, 1945), *passim*, esp. chapters ii and iii.

5. cf. Thurman Arnold, *The Folklore of Capitalism* (Yale University Press, New Haven, 1937), *passim*.

6. Lewis Mumford, *The Golden Day* (W. W. Norton & Company, Inc., New York, 1926), pp. 158–9. It should be added that the suddenness of this transformation was exaggerated by Mumford. See also Henry Adams, *The Education of Henry Adams* (Houghton Mifflin Co., Boston, 1930); Ralph H. Gabriel, *The Course of American Democratic Thought* (The Ronald Press Company, New York, 1940); Merle Curti, *The Growth of American Thought* (Harper Brothers, New York, 1943).

7. "The peculiar condition of American society has made your writings far more fruitful and quickening here than in Europe." Henry Ward Beecher in a letter to Herbert Spencer in 1866. (David Duncan, *The Life and Letters of Herbert Spencer* (D. Appleton and Company, New York, 1908, p. 66.

8. Edward Youmans to Herbert Spencer, quoted in Richard Hofstadter, *Social Darwinism in American Thought* (The Beacon Press, Boston, 1955), p. 31.

9. Emmett John Hughes, *The Church and the Liberal Society* (Princeton University Press, Princeton, 1947), pp. 188–9.

10. Charles Francis Adams in the *North American Review* (April, 1871), p. 243.

11. See Arthur Meir Schlesinger, *The Rise of the City* (The Macmillan Company, New York, 1933), pp. 84, 109, 110 for a vivid description of these tenements.

12. Robert H. Bork, "Antitrust in Dubious Battle, *Fortune*, Sept., 1969, p. 103ff.

13. For a precise account see F. Doody and R. Clemence, *The Schumpeterian System* (Addison-Wesley Publishing Company, Cambridge, 1948).

14. cf. N.S.B. Gras, *Business and Capitalism* (Crofts & Co., New York, 1933), chapter v; Krooss, *American Economic Development*, chart 3, p. 20.

15. See appendix to Chapter I, Tables I.1–I.4.

16. Andrew Carnegie in the *North American Review*, CXLVIII, (February 1889), pp. 141–2.

17. John von Neumann and Oscar Morgenstern, *Theory of Games and Economic Behavior* (Princeton University Press, Princeton, 1947), *passim*, esp. pp. 555–84.

18. *The American Individual Enterprise System*, Economics Principle Commission of the National Association of Manufacturers (McGraw-Hill, New York, 1946) Volume II, pp. 592, 597; for a similar view see the editorial on "administered prices" in the *New York Times*, Wednesday, July 10, 1957. A somewhat more sophisticated version of post World War II business ideology can be found in Henry Hazlet, *Economics in One Lesson*, (Pocket Books, New York, 1946) and E. M. Quesney, *The Spirit of Enterprise* (Scribner's Sons, New York, 1943).

19. Another author who might be mentioned in this connection is John B. Jervis whose *Railway Property* (Phinney, Blakeman & Mason, New York, 1861), seems to consist of the first body of thought that resembled modern management theory.

20. Henry Steele Commager, *The American Mind* (Yale University Press, New Haven, 1950), p. 18.

21. (Rev.) William Channing, *Works* (American Unitarian Association, Boston, 1875), p. 46.

22. Charles Francis Adams, *North American Review*, April 1871, p. 243.

23. cf. Carl R. Fish, *The Rise of the Common Man* (The Macmillan Company (New York, 1927), esp. chapters i, ii and v; Bryce, *The American Commonwealth*, esp. pp. 258–60. Also note William Dean Howells, *A Traveler from Altruria* (Harper & Brothers, New York, 1894), where, five years before the publication of *The Theory of the Leisure Class* and fifteen years before the appearance of *The Instinct of Workmanship*, the acquisitive, money-making spirit of his contemporary America is satirized in terms of the production-consciousness of old.

24. Andrew Carnegie thus epitomized the spirit of industrial capitalism: "Put all your eggs in one basket, then watch the basket; compete with rivals, drive your men, make and sell; finance takes second place. Your firm is your monument, a corporation your exit."

25. Significantly, the census of 1889 was the last one to include "Hand and Neighborhood Industries" in its census of factory establishments. Unfortunately the Census of Manufacture up until 1910

does not provide us with clear-cut data of the socioeconomic composition of the work force, especially in regard to the ratio of skilled and unskilled workers. Also see Robert and Helen Lynd's *Middletown* (Harcourt, Brace and Company, New York, 1929), pp. 73ff., for comments on the disappearance of the mechanic in 1890.

26. *Andrew Carnegie* is an address to workmen at the dedication of Carnegie Library, Braddock, Pennsylvania, January 1887. Reprinted in his *The Empire of Business* (Doubleday Page & Co., New York, 1902), p. 71.

27. *The Nation,* XLII, 1886, p. 419.

28. W. J. Ghent, *Our Benevolent Feudalism* (The Macmillan Company, New York, 1902), p. 58. For a more detailed discussion of this point see Ghent's *Mass and Class* (The Macmillan Company, New York, 1904).

29. "The laborer appears to be less worthy of his hire than heretofore, and to have lost his interest in his work." Special Commission of the Revenue, *Report for 1869,* p. xxxiii.

30. "The Tyranny of Labor Organizations," *North American Review,* July 1889, pp. 412–18.

31. Henry Clews, *Twenty-Eight Years in Wall Street* (Irving Publishing Co., New York, 1888), pp. 491–2.

32. Special Commission of the Revenue, *Report for 1868,* pp. 14–15; the *Scientific American,* XVI, January 3, 1867, p. 3, found that the weekly wage of an unskilled laborer was $12 compared with $25 a week for a skilled mechanic.

33. "Census Bulletin, No. 150, gives the increase in men working in manufacturing pursuits at 23.9%, of women at 28.4%, of children at 39.5%." (Ghent, op. cit., p. 74.) Also see Victor S. Clark, *History of Manufacture in the United States,* Volume II, 1860–1893 (Carnegie Institute of Washington, 1909), chapter xiv, "Technical Education."

34. Discussing conditions in 1871 an engineer wrote: "[It is difficult] to receive from the employer the slightest consideration for the educated professional; while the so-called 'practical man' was attempting to lead as a general the industrial armies of the nation." (New England Cotton Manufacturer's Association, *Transactions* [n.p., September, 1901], p. 112.

CHAPTER 3

1. Claude Bowers, *Jefferson and Hamilton* (Houghton Mifflin Co., Boston and New York, 1933), *passim,* and *Beveridge and the Pro-*

gressive Era (The Literary Guild, New York, 1932), *passim;* A. J. Simons, *Social Forces in American History* (The Macmillan Company, New York, 1911), *passim;* Henry Adams, *The Degradation of the Democratic Dogma* (The Macmillan Company, New York, 1919), chapter i.

2. The existence of vertical as well as horizontal class conflicts, e.g. alliance of planters with western farmers against industrialists and artisans, does not conflict with our analysis. Farmers as well as mechanics mainly played the role of auxiliaries, leaving the essence of political combat to the gentlemen who always united when "property" itself seemed to be threatened. (cf. W. E. Binkley, *American Political Parties* [Alfred A. Knopf, New York, 1954], e.g. pp. 162–5; Henry Adams *Education of Henry Adams* [Houghton Mifflin Co., Boston, 1918], pp. 140–50.)

3. Veblen, *Absentee Ownership & Business Enterprise in Recent Times,* pp. 114–16.

4. These characteristiics were aggressiveness, individualism, a strong interest in production and efficiency, and the drive to excel and to command; to wit Havemeyer's statement in 1889: "Business is not a philanthropy. . . . I do not care two cents for your ethics. I do not know enough of them to apply them. . . . *As a business proposition it is right to get all out of a business that you can possibly get"* (Gras, *op. cit.,* p. 44.) (Italics mine.)

5. People of the State of New York versus The North River Sugar Refining Company, Supreme Court of New York—at Circuit, January 9, 1889, *Investigation of Trusts,* New York Senate, 1889, p. 278.

6. Even relatively recent studies of industrial concentration invariably start with the merger movements of the 1890's, thereby completely ignoring the invaluable lessons of the preceding period of industrial capitalism. (To wit: George Stigler, *Five Lectures on Economic Problems* [the Macmillan Company, New York, 1950]; Corwin Edwards, *Maintaining Competition* [McGraw-Hill Book Company, New York, 1949]; George J. Stigler, "Monopoly and Oligopoly by Merger"; *American Economic Review,* Proceedings, XL, May 1950.)

7. *Chicago Conference on Trusts* (n.p., Chicago, 1899); William Ripley, editor, *Trusts, Pools and Corporations* (Ginn & Co., Boston, 1905); John Moody, *The Truth About the Trusts* (Moody Publishing Company, New York, 1904).

8. "The Bugaboo of Trusts," *North American Review,* CXLVII

(February 1889), pp. 141ff. If we ignore Carnegie's naive faith in "survival of the fittest" and the "great laws of economics, (which) like nature remain unchanged" (*ibid.*, p. 141), we can find a surprisingly large number of similarities between him, Drucker, and other contemporary exponents of the new "managerial" economy.

9. *Ibid.*, pp. 142–3.

10. Once the unique Rockefeller was no longer the head of the enterprise, Carnegie was willing to bet 100 to 1 that the combination would break up. On many other occasions, however, Carnegie emphasized that business is an art and not a science obeying set laws (e.g. "The Road to Business Success," an address delivered at the Curry Commercial College, Pittsburg, June 23, 1885, and "Business," a lecture delivered at Cornell University, January 11, 1896. Both are reprinted in Carnegie's *The Empire of Business*.)

11. Carnegie Steel's Henry Frick seemed to have had some notion of the determinism of modern technology. "The demand of modern life called for such works as ours, and if we had not met the demands others would have done so. Even without us the steel industry of the country would be just as great as it is." (James H. Bridge. *The Inside History of the Carnegie Steel Company* [The Aldine Book Company, New York, 1903], p. viii.)

12. *Banker's Magazine*, XLII, 1887–88, pp. 729–35.

13. *Ibid.*, p. 731.

14. *Ibid.*, p. 278.

15. e.g., cattle and meat monopolies. *Report of United States Senate Committee on Meat Products*, 51st Congress, first session, 1890, No. 829, p. 18ff.

16. "Take away our money, our great works, ore-mines, coke ovens, but leave our organization, and in four years I shall have reestablished myself." (Andrew Carnegie, quoted by James Bridge, in *The Inside History of the Carnegie Steel Company*, [The Aldine Book Company, New York, 1903], p. vii.

17. For example, note The Michigan Salt Association, an early example of pooling agreements, the Addison Pipe and Steel Company pool, the Anthracite Coal pool, Wire-Nail pool, etc. For judicious combination of the trustee device with political corruption, note the Sugar Trust, and the Distillers and Cattle Feeders Trust.

18. cf. Charles Beard, Jr., "Facts About the Trusts," *The Forum*, Sept. 1889.

19. J. D. Clark, *The Federal Trust Policy* (Johns Hopkins Press, Baltimore, 1931), p. 31.

20. (From the report of the National Association of Stove Manufacturers, 1884.) (Italics mine.)

21. *Bulletin of the American Iron and Steel Association,* XVIII, 1884, p. 140.

22. The *Banker's Magazine,* XLII, 1887–88, p. 5.

23. *The Commercial and Financial Chronicle,* XLIII, July-December 1886, p. 257.

24. cf. Gardner Means, "Industrial Prices and Their Relative Inflexibility," *Senate Document #13,* 74th Congress, First Session, 1940.

25. *Final Report of the Industrial Commission,* XIX (Washington, D.C., Govt. Printing Office, 1902), p. 596.

26. *Forum,* V, 1888, p. 655.

27. *Forum,* VIII, 1889, p. 68.

28. Arthur J. Eddy, *The New Competition* (A. G. McClurg & Co., Chicago, 1904), p. 52.

29. Thus salaried officials, officers, and clerks increased by 133% in the period 1880–1890. (*Census of Manufacture, 1905* [Gov't. Printing Office, Washington, D.C., 1907], Volume 1, p. xxxvi, table II.

30. As a matter of fact sufficient evidence seems to exist (David Riesman, *Thorstein Veblen; A Critical Interpretation* [Charles Scribner's Sons, New York, 1953]; Joseph Dorfman, *Thorstein Veblen and His America* [The Viking Press, New York, 1934]; Lewis Atherton, *The Pioneer Merchant in Mid-America* [The Universty of Missouri, Columbia, Mo., 1939]; Kenneth W. Porter, *John Jacob Astor* [Harvard University Press, Cambridge, 1931]), that the pre-Civil War merchants and traders depended primarily upon geographic monopoly, price, tenacity, and opportunism to make their fortunes. Their personality seemed to have fitted rather well into Riesman's "inner-directed" category, and I doubt very much whether a John Jacob Astor could even pass the first battery of salesman aptitude tests General Electric, for instance, would throw at him. The Yankee traders and merchants seem to have been hated as much by their rural customers as were the Jews by the East European farmers, the East Indians by the South African Negroes, and the Chinese by the Malayans.

CHAPTER 4

1. cf. Francis Sutton, Seymour Harris, Carl Kaysen, James Tobin,

The American Business Creed (Harvard University Press, Cambridge, 1956), for a masterful analysis of post-World War II business ideology.

2. The charge that big business is beyond the scope of supply and demand was not made explicitly until the 1890's and 1900's, although it was implicit in Lloyd's sensational *Wealth v. Commonwealth* and in the attacks of specific interest groups such as Grangers and Oil Producers Association against their monopolistic adversaries.

3. Bryce, *op. cit.*, Volume II, pp. 408–9.

4. Andrew Carnegie in the *North American Review*, February 1889, as quoted in his *The Empire of Business*, p. 153.

5. Quoted in Henry Clews *The Wall Street Point of View* (Silver Burdett & Co., New York, 1900), p. 37. Note that the above can be interpreted as an exposition of Marshall's "long run equilibrium."

6. *Commercial and Financial Chronicle*, XLIV, Jan.-June 1887, p. 639.

7. In reading some of Gunton's and Wood's articles that appeared in *Gunton's Magazine*, one is struck by the modern flavor of the rhetoric. Professor Gunton first attracted attention by advocating the eight hour day in the article "Shall an Eight Hour System Be Adopted?" (*Forum*, I, 1886, p. 136ff.) in which he brilliantly anticipated some rather Keynesian notions of a stimulated "consumption function" due to elimination of unemployment and more leisure. The ridicule which the orthodox press heaped upon him consequently (cf. *Nation*, XLII, 1886, p. 147) seemed to have discouraged him, because his subsequent articles adhered to established doctrine. In 1894 Gunton again attracted attention in an article in the *Social Economist*. "Attacking Llloyd's exposés of the Standard Oil Company, he wrote as one who was profoundly concerned for the integrity of economic literature because of this irresponsible performance. He quoted a letter from Professor John A. Hobson . . . corroborating Gunton's views. Lloyd wrote Hobson, who promptly replied that he had written Gunton, but that he had written exactly the opposite. Lloyd denounced Gunton for this distortion and Gunton remained silent. Later he appeared as the editor of *Gunton's Magazine* which functioned for many years, a persistent defender of almost everything Rockefeller and the oil trust did. In 1908 it came out that he who had 'trembled for the integrity of economic literature' had been getting money regularly from John D. Archbold." (John T. Flynn, *God's Gold* [Harcourt, Brace and Company, New York, 1932,] p. 329.) Gunton was

thus the first academic economist who found a lucrative position as spokesman and ideologist for vested interests. (For a more sympathetic appraisal of Gunton, see Jack Blacksilver's "George Gunton: Pioneer Spokesman for a Labor–Big Business Entente" *The Business History Review*, XXI, Spring '57, p. 61.)

8. *Forum*, V, 1888, pp. 588–9.

9. Andrew Carnegie, *North American Review*, *op. cit.;* John B. Clark, *The Philosophy of Wealth* (Ginn & Co., Boston, 1886); Francis Bowen, *American Political Economy* (C. Scribner & Co., New York, 1870); Francis A. Walker, *Political Economy* (H. Holt and Company, New York 1883); James L. Laughlin, *The Elements of Political Economy* (D. Appleton & Company, New York, 1887).

10. "Feudalism or Commonwealth," *Independent*, May 1902, pp. 1 276–9). It should be added, however, that J. B. Clark changed his mind later an and became a strong critic of trusts. (cf. his *The Control of Trusts* [The Macmillan Company, New York, 1910.])

11. National Association of Manufacturers, Economic Principles Association, *op. cit.* Volume II, chapter xii.

12. *Report of the Industrial Commission*, Volume XIII, p. 372ff., especially pp. 442–50.

12a. F. A. Fetter, *op. cit.*, p. 106.

13 John Maurice Clark in a letter of Joseph Dorfman, November 8, 1947, quoted by Dorfman in *The Economic Mind in American Civilization* (The Viking Press, New York, 1949, Volume III,) pp. 204–5. (Italics mine.)

14. C. E. Perkins to Atkinson, June 15, 1881, Atkinson papers quoted by Dorfman, *ibid.*, p. 118.

15. It must be noted that Carnegie was not the only one who combined classical concepts with the above points one and two. Only those who like Gunton or Eddy fully embraced the concept of the "New Economics" rejected classical concepts completely.

16. Allan Nevins, *John D. Rockefeller* (C. Scribner's Sons, New York, 1940), Volume I, p. 622.

17. *Ibid.*, pp. 434–5.

18. L. Coolidge, *An Oldfashioned Senator; Orville H. Platt* (G. P. Putnam's Sons, New York, 1910), p. 72.

19. Quoted by Moses Y. Beach in his "In Defense of Trusts," *Forum*, September 1889.

20. *Forum*, VII, 1889, pp. 62, 63, 64. The *Nation*, the spokesman for the classical liberalism of the (non-business) upper classes, com-

mented in an editorial, "Mr. Beach on Trusts": ". . . general overproduction is a flat absurdity and an impossibility," thus indicating that
Say's law had a firm foothold even outside the academic journals.
(The *Nation*, XLIX, September 5, 1889.) The *Nation*, incidentally,
opposed trusts in a rather ambivalent manner, distinguishing between
"natural trusts," i.e. trusts that are the result of modern communication, and "artificial" ones. (cf. the editorial, "The Competition of
Trusts," December 20, 1888, p. 491.) The major preoccupation of
Nation was, of course, the tariff and only the monopoly practices of
"protected trusts," i.e. "artificial trusts," would arouse the antagonism
of the editors. (e.g. XLIX, 1889, p. 104.) Especially the editor, Horace White, seemed to believe that the removal of tariffs would also
solve the trust problem. (cf. editorial, "Trusts," *Commercial and
Financial Chronicle*, July 28, 1888; editorial, "The Competition of
Trusts," *Nation*, December 20. 1888.)

21. *Forum*, VII, 1889, pp. 68, 69.

22. *Forum*, VIII, 1889, p. 77.

23. *Commercial and Financial Chronicle*, XLV, 1887, pp. 227–8.

24. Assembly of the State of New York, Trust Investigating Committee, *Report and Proceedings*, March 9, 1897, p. 45; hereafter referred to as "Hepburn" Report.

25. Burton J. Hendrick, *The Life of Andrew Carnegie, 1835–1919)*
Doubleday, Doran & Company, Garden City, New York, 1932), Volume I, p. 183.

26. *Nation*, XLVII, August 23, 1888. In an editorial the paper compared Blaine's speech with the Republican party platform on trusts:
"We declare our opposition to all combinations of capital organized in
trusts or otherwise, to control arbitrarily the condition of trade among
our citizens and we recommend such legigslation as will prevent the
execution of all schemes to oppress the people." The *Tribune* of June
23, 1888, commented editorially upon this platform: "It is a good platform, because it utters plainly the hostility of the Republican party
to those trusts and combinations by which the best fruits of the protective systems are in *some* cases denied to consumers." (Italics mine.)
Significant for the scant regard given party platforms in American
political life is the fact that hardly anyone seemed to have related the
passage of the Sherman Act to this plank in the party platform.

27. Matthew Josephson, *The Robber Barons* (Harcourt, Brace and
Company, New York, 1936), p. 166.

28. Shelby Cullom, *Fifty Years of Public Service* (A. C. McClurg & Co., Chicago, 1911), p. 235.

29. Brooks Adams, "Natural Selection in Literature," *American Economic Supremacy* (The Macmillan Company, New York, 1900, p. 165.)

30. Quoted in Merle Curti, *The Social Ideas of American Educators* (C. Scribner's Sons, New York, 1935, p. 322.)

31. E. L. Youman, ed., *The Correlation and Conservation of Forces* (D. Appleton and Company, New York, 1871), p. ii.

32. John B. Clark and Franklin H. Giddings, *The Modern Distributive Process* (Ginn and Co., Boston, 1888).

33. *Commercial and Financial Chronicle*, XLVII, July-December 1888, pp. 128–29.

34. *New York Assembly of 1879, Hepburn Report*, p. 1, 566.

35. *Ibid.*

36. *Report of the Executive Committee*, Petroleum Producers Union, (n.p., 1872).

37. Testimony, Commonwealth of Pennsylvania vs. Pennsylvania Railroad et al., 1879, pp. 656–57.

38. John T. Flynn, *op. cit.*, p. 219. It is to John Flynn's credit that he refused to portray the independent oil producers as innocent victims of a predatory trust. His picture of a suspicious, greedy, conniving, cowardly mob of selfish businessmen who were as amoral as the Standard Oil gang and as equally opposed to competition seems historically valid, but is rarely found in critical accounts of the Standard Oil Company.

39. *Ibid.*, p. 340.

40. Caro Lloyd, *Henry Demarest Lloyd* (G. P. Putnam's Sons, New York, 1912), Volume I, pp. 128–9.

41. Senator Orville Platt, quoted by L.A. Coolidge, *op. cit.*, p. 29. This interpretation is also in agreement with the theory explicit and implicit in Krooss, *op. cit.*, pp. 171–3, that the Sherman Act helped rather than hindered the merger movement. A law passed to satisfy inarticulate discontent rather than specific demands for reform is quite likely to be as general and vague as the plan to enforce it.

42. Grover Cleveland, "Fourth Annual Message," December 7, 1896, *Messages and Papers of the Presidents*, (1782–1907), James D. Richardson, editor (Bureau of National Literature and Art, n.p., 1907), Volume IX, pp. 744–5. (Italics mine.)

CHAPTER 5

1. *Forum*, VIII, 1889, p. 77.

2. *Ibid.*

3. Defendant before the Circuit Court in Johnson vs. Milburn, 173 Fed. Rep. 177, pp. 170–71.

4. Malthus, the only classicist who saw in mild poverty a necessary and positive force, had appreciable influence on Darwin, and indirectly upon the entire development of Social Darwinism. This impact of Malthus is frequently overlooked.

5. Andrew Carnegie in a speech at Union College, January 1895. Reprinted in his *The Empire of Business*, pp. 125–6. At the time of Morgan's death the newspapers did not rely on Carnegie's notion that the son of a wealthy man is especially worthy if he overcomes his "handicap" and amasses additional wealth. On the contrary, they rather tried to fit Morgan forcibly into the "self-made man" mold by pointing out that "relatively" Morgan started out as a poor man. (cf. Diamond, *The Reputation of the American Businessman*, chapter iv.)

6. Clews, *The Wall Street Point of View*, p. 51.

7. *Outlook*, LXXV, 1903, p. 932.

8. Max Weber, "Social Psychology of World Religions," *Essays in Sociology* (Oxford University Press, New York, 1946), pp. 271, 276.

9. *Nation*, XLII, 1886, p. 5, 377.

10. It is, of course, of great importance for a materialistic philosophy to be "scientific." Hence the great emphasis of Social Darwinism, Marxism and Taylorism ("Scientific" Management) on being "scientific." The truly "scientific" basis of these materialistic philosophies is clearly indicated by the incessant use of the adjective "scientific."

11. Above all, this seems to hold true of Richard Hofstadter's *Social Darwinism in American Thought* (The Beacon Press, Boston, 1955). In the following pages I shall try to take issue with his interpretation.

12. cf. Giorgio de Santillana, *The Crime of Galileo* (University of Chicago Press, Chicago, 1955), for an excellent analysis of the considerable intellectual freedom granted to scholars and universities by the Catholic Church during the Middle Ages. Galileo's major crime seems to have been his publication of his heresy rather than the "heretical" *Dialogue* itself.

13. Auguste Comte, *Cours de Philosophie Positive*, second edition, (E. Littre, Paris, 1864) Volume III, pp. 188-9.

14. William Graham Sumner, *What Social Classes Owe to Each Other* (Harper and Brothers, New York, 1883), p. 34.

15. This absence of sentimentality in the practice and ideology of the industrial capitalists can be contrasted with the sentimental image of a 19th century small-town businessman which is again and again invoked by the business ideologyy of managerial capitalism as the picture of the "typical" American. (cf. Sutton et al., *American Business Creed.*)

16. *Autobiography of Andreww Carnegie* (Houghton Mifflin and Co., Boston, 1920), p. 327.

17. Andrew Carnegie, "How to Win Fortune," *New York Tribune,* April 13, 1890; reprinted in *The Bulletin,* XXIV, 1890, p. 121. It should be added that at least one businessman, Abram S. Hewitt, publicly disagreed with Carnegie's views. (*New York Tribune,* May 4, 1890.) Judging by the "letters to the ediitor" that appeared in the Tribune and the Evening Post, Hewitt was not representative of the New York businessman of his period. As a matter of fact he resembled more the paternalistic pre-Civil War captain of industry than the businessman of his own period. We shall see later on that he anticipated and influenced the development of the "socially responsible" wing of business opinion as expressed by Gary, Perkins, and the *Banker's Magazine.*

18. The term "survival of the fittest" was originally coined by Spencer about two years *before* the appearance of *The Origin of Species.* For Darwin this term meant essentially the adjustability of biological specimens to the chance variation of nature. It did not imply a technological development. Neither did Sumner share Spencer's optimiistic interpretation of the "survival of the fittest." Sumner's essential pessimism seems to have escaped the attention of the general (business) public as well as the scrutiny of most critics.

19. *The Commercial and Financial Chronicle,* XLIV, January-June, 1887, p. 639.

20. *The Commercial and Financial Chronicle,* XLV, July-December, 1887, p. 227.

21. *American Industries,* May 1, 1909, pp. 5–6.

22. *The Commercial and Financial Chronicle,* XVIII, January-June 1889, p. 780.

23. Quoted in Ghent, *Our Benevolent Feudalism,* p. 29.

24. *North American Review,* CXLVIII, February 1889, pp. 141ff. Compare this with Spencer's brutal statement: "Not simply do we see that in the competition among individuals of the same kind,

survival of the fittest has from the beginning furthered production of a higher type; but we see that to the increasing warfare between species is mainly due both growth and organization. Without universal conflict there would have been no development of the active powers." (Dynamic Sociology, *The Principles of Sociology* [D. Appleton and Co., New York, 1876-97], Volume I, p. 142.) Spencer, perhaps motivated by his anti-militarism, tried to soften the brutal implication of his theory by forecasting a future state of peaceful cooperation. This aspect of Spencerism has, however, never penetrated into business opinion and thus cannot be considered in our analysis.

25. John T. Flynn, op. cit., p. 406.

26. Allan Nevins, *Selected Writings of Abram S. Hewitt* (Columbia Uniiversity Press, XXI, 1887, p. 12.

27. *The Bulletin*, XXI, 1887, p. 12.

28. United States Strike Commission, *Report and Testimony on the Chicago Strike of 1894* (Government Printing Office, Washington, D.C., 1895), pp. 621–2.

29. *The Bulletin*, XXII, 1888, p. 329.

30. *The Detroit News*, November 1892, (n.d.) quoted by Allan Nevins in *American Press Opinion* (Heath and Company, New York, 1928), p. 406.

31. *The Bulleltin of the American Iron and Steel Association,* XXI, 1887, p. 153.

32. *The Bulletin*, 1890, p. 324.

33. *Autobiography of Andrew Carnegie*, p. 327.

34. Albert Keller and Maurice Davies, editors, *Essays of William Graham Sumner* (Yale University Press,, New Haven, 1934), p. 87.

35. *What Social Classes Owe to Each Other*, p. 135.

36. Quoted in Josephson, *The Robber Barons*, p. 321.

37. This seems to have been mainly the optimistic interpretation of Spencer. Sumner, and the more sophisticated Ward, held more pessimistic opinions. The businessman, knowingly or unknowingly, however, accepted Spencer's views—it is doubtful whether even a handful were familiar with Sumner or Ward—and it is with this businessman that we are concerned.

38. Youmans, *The Correlation and Conservation of Forces*, p. iv.

39. Curti, *The Social Ideas of American Educators*, p. 325.

40. Kenneth S. Lynn in *The Dream of Success* (Little Brown and Company, Boston, 1955), shows very well how the "success" motive has not only influenced our pseudo-Marxian writers, Dreiser and

London, but how characteristic this motive is of post revolutionary Russian society where the "Darwinian Marxists," Dreiser and especially London, have become exceedingly popular. (cf. pp. 69-72, 75-7.) An analysis of Social Darwinism, rather than of the influence of Social Darwinism on the American businessman, ought to consider the impact of Darwin, Nietzsche, and London on Soviet Communism.

CHAPTER 6

1. cf. Bryce, *The American Commonwealth,* especially pp. 100–170.

2. James Bryce, *ibid.;* Cochran and Miller, *op. cit.,* chapter viii.

3. Charles and Mary Beard, *op. cit.,* especially pp. 29-7; Eric F. Goldman, *Rendezvous with Destiny* (Alfred A. Knopf, New York, 1952), chapters i–iii.

4. Like most folklore, there was good reason for its development. cf. Teddy Roosevelt's letter to Lodge in 1897: "The really ugly feature of the Republican canvass is that it *does* represent what the populists say, that is, corrupt wealth." (Quoted in Beard, *op. cit.,* p. 425.)

5. "The source of power and the cohesive force in American political parties is the desire for office and for office as a means of gain." (James Bryce, *op. cit.,* Volume II, p. 102.)

6. "In fact, the record of orations delivered in the House of Representatives shows a continuous division over economic issues along the lines of the cleavage which existed in Jackson's day." (Beard, *op. cit.,* p. 324.)

7. For a different opinion see Matthew Josephson's *The Politicos* (Harcourt Brace and Company, New York, 1938). Implicit in chapters iv–vi is the view that the politicos consciously interjected irrelevant issues to detract the "have-nots" from the class struggle (especially pp. 255, 256, 321).

8. "In a metropolis each year thousands of immigrants arrived who did not know the language or the laws of the country, (to whom) Tammany could render innumerable services. From the moment of the immigrant's arrival the machine guided him in his undertakings, helped him to become naturalized, and asked nothing in return except his vote. The system had its advantages, for the aid thus given to these unfortunates was useful and genuine. The small services of the machine resembled those that a French deputy used to render his constituents. But there were abuses. In cities that were growing

constantly and rapidly, electric light, transportation, and police
services had to be developed. Too often this was an occasion for the
friends of the machine to enrich themselves. Politics became for many
adventurers a high road to wealth. In the name of one or the other
of the two great parties one man would seek a well-paid position;
another a streetcar concession; a third, a contract for paving or for
the construction of some municipal building. Too often the electoral
machine was made the agent of private interests." (André Maurois,
The Miracle of America [Harper & Brothers, New York, 1944], p.
320. In this charming but superficial study of America, Maurois'
account of the Gilded Age lacks the tone of moral outrage American
historians seem to reserve for their accounts of this period. Perhaps
it takes the eyes of a Gallic novelist, reared upon accounts of the
Panama and Stavinsky scandals, to see the corruption of the Gilded
Age in its proper perspective.

9. This is what Roscoe Conkling had to say about machines: "We
are told the Republican party is a machine. Yes. A government is
a machine; a church is a machine; an army is a machine . . . the
common-school system of the State of New York is a machine; a
political party is a machine." (Donald B. Chidsey, *The Gentleman
from New York* [Yale University Press, New Haven, 1935], p. 74.
Conkling is, of course, correct. The word "machine" has been over-
used, and a machine is not necessarily corrupt *per se*. It is also an
oversimplification to portray a corrupt political machine solely as
the product of the big cities, supported by immigrants.

10. William Allen White, *Masks in a Pageant* (The Macmillan
Company, New York, 1938), p. 79.

11. The above statement is meant only to apply to the period
1867–1896. We shall have to modify it somewhat when we discuss
the period 1900–1913. Note the remarks of an observer of this
period, Frederick Townsend Martin: "The class I represent [the
grande bourgeoisie] cares nothing for politics. Among my people I
hear seldom purely political discussions. . . . We care absolutely
nothing about . . . political questions, save in as much as it threatens
or fortifies existing conditions. [But] touch the question of the tariff,
touch the issue of the income tax, touch the problem of railroad
legislation or touch the most vital of all business matters, the question of general federal regulation of industrial corporations, and the
people amongst whom I live my life become immediately rabid
partisans. . . . It matters not one iota what political party is in

power or what President holds the rein of office. We are not politicians or public thinkers; we are the rich; we own America; we got it, God knows how, but we intend to keep it if we can by throwing all the tremendous weight of our support, our influence, our money, our political connections, our purchased senators, our hungry Congressmen, our public-speaking demagogues into the scale against any legislature, and political platform, any presidential campaign that threatens the integrity of our estate. . . . The class I represent cares nothing for politics. In a single season a plutocratic leader hurled his influence and his money into the scale to elect a Republican governor on the Pacific and a Democrat governor on the Atlantic coast." (Frederic T. Martin, *The Passing of the Idle Rich* [Doubleday, Page & Company, Garden City, N.Y., 1911], pp. 148–9.)

12. Paul Studenski and Herman Krooss, *Financial History of the United States* (The McGraw Hill Book Company, New York, 1952), p. 200.

13. New York *World*, October 30, 1884.

14. "Reform as an unbusiness, almost antibusiness assertion of aristocracy, reform as the program of a business-minded man like Tilden—the dissidence within the Best People started from a different basis and aimed toward different goals, but it joined in a drive against what both groups abhorred as 'Grantism.'" (Eric Goldman, *op. cit.*, p. 19) Of course, there were many, such as the editors of *The Springfield Republican*, who objected to Grantism but remained loyal Republicans.

15. e.g. Hamilton Fish, Ray Hamilton, C. Crosley, D. Manning, C. Fairchild, William Endicott, etc.

16. Hofstadter, *The American Political Tradition*, p. 174.

17. Hofstadter, *The American Political Tradition*, p. 167.

18. They accomplished this task much more successfully than is ordinarily assumed. Thus, between 1870—the restoration of the last Southern state—and 1896, the Democrats won eight out of twelve Congressional elections!

19. "[The public wants] men in office who will not steal but who will not interfere with those who do." Horatio Seymour in a letter to Tilden in 1871. (De Alva S. Alexander, *Political History of the State of New York* [Henry Holt & Co., New York, 1906], Volume III, p. 311.)

20. Henry Adams, *Letters*, 1858–1891, edited by W.C. Ford (Houghton Mifflin Co., Boston, 1930), p. 360. (Italics mine.)

Beard disagreed. "Thus it happened that, except on sound money and correct banking, capitalism was divided against itself." (*op. cit.*, p. 297.) There is little evidence though, that would support Beard's view, unless the election battles are taken seriously.

21. The anti-business sentiment during the Grant administration and the depression of the 70's is, I believe, vastly exaggerated by some historians (Hofstadter, Goldman, perhaps even Beard). Grant himself seemed to assess the mood of the American people best by recognizing that behind the loud clamor of the reformers only a handful of intellectuals and patricians were hiding. (Helen Todd, *A Man Named Grant* [Houghton Mifflin Co., Boston, 1940], pp. 446–8. Grant, incidentally, expressed his opinion much more forcefully and picturesquely than the above exceedingly loose paraphrasing might indicate.) It might be similarly advisable to discount the importance of the Farmer Alliances and other agrarian movements during the 70's. Perhaps the fact that such a long drawn out depression did *not* create any major anti-business movements, nor even dislodge the party in power, is the most significant feature of the 70's.

22. Lloyd, *op. cit.*, p. 403.

23. Senate Report #485, 53rd Congress, Second Session, June 21, 1894. p. 68.

24. United States Senate, 53rd Congress, Second Session, Report #606, pp. 351–2.

25. *Ibid.*

26. Josephson, *Politicos*, p. 488.

27. Ida M. Tarbell, *The History of the Standard Oil Company* (The Macmillan Company, New York, 1904), Volume II, p. 290.

28. Josephson, *Politicos*, p. 345.

29. Oliver Morton (1877), Zach Chandler (1879), and John Logan (1886) died; Simon Cameron (1877), Roscoe Conkling, and Thomas Platt (1881) retired; Ben Butler moved to the left into the Greenback Party; Sherman, Arthur, and Depew became respectable and "conservative."

30. Such as the railroad tycoon Leland Stanford, the Michigan millionaire industrialist Russell Alger, the shipping magnate William Grace, the ironmongers Peter Cooper and Abram Hewitt, the merchant John Wanamaker, the Vermont marble king Redfield Proctor, the Michigan lumber barons James McMillan and Francis Stockbridge, and the Wisconsin lumber dealer Philetus Sawyer, the

bankers Levi Morton and Calvin Brice, the Nevada mine owners James Fair and John Jones, the newspaper owner George Hearst, the Pennsylvania metal manufacturers Joseph Wharton and Daniel Morrell, etc.

31. Senators Allison, Aldrich, and Depew, the lobbyists Hayes and Swank, Justin Morrill, William Folger, etc. (cf. G.F. Hoar, *Autobiography of Seventy Years* [Charles Scribner's Sons, New York, 1903], *passim;* Lloyd, *op. cit., passim;* Charles Beard, The American Party *Battle* [The Macmillan Company, New York, 1928] chapter viii; *The Nation,* 1888, XLVI, p. 358.)

32. Gould, Hill, Huntington; the leaders of the New York "reform"—Republicans, Stewart, Dodge, Sloan, etc.

33. The term "leisure class," as used in this work, most emphatically does not have a disapproving, Veblenian connotation. It simply means that the art of government in a civilized society has required the existence of a group of men who do not have to work in order to survive. Professional politicians do not comprise a leisure class because they exchange their political skills for the necessities of life. The professional politician must look for another line of endeavor when he loses an election, while a Teddy Roosevelt, a Wilkie, a DeGaulle, a Stevenson, or a Churchill can afford "to broaden" themselves through travel, study, and artistic pursuits in such an eventuality.

34. The only non-lawyer in the cabinet was Thomas James, the Postmaster General, who was a newspaper owner and journalist.

35. Such as the scions of old American families Bayard, Endicott, Whitney, Lamar (later Senator from Mississippi).

36. G.F. Howe, *Chester A. Arthur, A Quarter-Century of Machine Politics* (Dodd, Mead & Company, New York, 1934), p. 211.

37. Royal Cortissoz, *The Life of Whitelaw Reid* (Charles Scribner's Sons, New York, 1921), pp. 80–82.

38. C. Wright Mills showed in his "The American Business Elite," *Journal of Economic History,* Volume V, (Supplement, 1945), pp. 20–40, that "only" some 40% (his figure, 43.0%) of business leaders of this period included in the *Dictionary of American Biography* came from "lower" classes.

39. *op. cit.,* pp. 53, 54. There were many similar comments. James Gordon Bennett's *Herald* wrote: "He had no advantages in his battle—no political, social, educational aid. . . . In time the world came to his feet." (p. 57) The New York *Evening Telegram* wrote:

"His life is more important to us than his death, because *it is a typical career*, illustrating one of the principles by means of which a man may make progress in a country like the United States." (p. 66; italics mine.) At a memorial mass meeting at Vanderbilt University, Judge James Whitworth emphasized: "He rose from the humble ranks of society by honest effort and perseverance." (New York American, April 1, 1913.)

40. "American Historians and the Business Elite," *The Journal of Economic History*, IX, 1949, p. 204. Mills' figures agree essentially with the data presented for the same period by Francis Gregory and Irene Neu in *Men in Business*, pp. 202–3, tables VI and VII.

41. C. Wright Mills, "The American Business Elite," *Journal of Economic History*, Volume V, Supplement, 1945, pp. 20–40); Frank W. Taussig and Carl S. Joslyn, *American Business Leaders* (The Macmillan Company, New York, 1932); William Miller, "American Historians and the Business Elite," *Journal of Economic History*, IX, 1949, pp. 196–200; William Miller, "The Recruitment of the American Business Elite," *Quarterly Journal of Economics*, LXIV, 1950, pp. 242–53; William Miller, ed., *Men in Business* (Harvard University Press, Cambridge, 1953); Mabel Newcomer, "The Chief Executives of Large Business Corporations," *Explorations in Entrepreneurial History*, Volume V, Harvard University Press, Cambridge, 1952–53); Mabel Newcomer, *The Big Business Executive* (Columbia University Press, New York, 1955), chapter v., especially tables XVII, XVIII, pp. 53–5; Chester M. Destler, "Entrepreneurial Leadership Among the Robber Barons," *Journal of Economic History*, Supplement VI, 1946, pp. 28–49.

42. For an excellent account of the social intermingling of the "new" captains of industry with the old classes of "inherited wealth" see Miriam Beard, *A History of the Business Men*, pp. 640ff. Edward C. Kirkland covers the same subject matter in *Dream and Thought in the Business Community, 1860–1900*, chapter ii. For a sarcastic and critical comment on this period cf. Charles Beard, *The Rise of American Civilization*, chapter xxv, especially pp. 383-93.

43. Stuart Daggett, *Chapters on the History of the Southern Pacific* (The Ronald Press Company, New York, 1922), p. 212.

44. Howe, *op. cit.*, p. 226.

45. Nathaniel W. Stephenson, *Nelson W. Aldrich* (Charles Scrib-

ner's Sons, New York, 1930), p. 431ff. Also Josephson, *Politicos*, p. 327.

46. Miriam Beard, *op. cit.*, p. 61.

47. *Report of the United States Pacific Railway Commission*, 1887, on the Expenditures of the Pacific Railroads, quoted in *Government and the American Economy, 1870–Present*, Manning, Potter and Davies, editors (Henry Holt & Co., New York, 1950), p. 63.

48. Stuart Daggett, *op. cit.*, p. 211. For an excellent and well documented account of the corrupting activities of Archbold and the Standard Oil crowd, see J.T. Flynn, *God's Gold*, Part VII, chapters iii, iv, v.

49. *Harper's*, LXII, December 1880-May 1881, p. 307.

50. Diamond, *op. cit.*, p. 61.

51. *World's Work*, Volume I, 1900, p. 286–7.

52. Clews, *The Wall Street Point of View*, p. 217.

53. Sir James Bryce, *op. cit.*, Volume II, p. 653. Bryce's chapter on the railroads (pp. 643–54) is a masterpiece of concise descriptive writing.

54. *Forum*, LV, pp. 83–4.

55. *Ibid.*, p. 712.

56. Stuart Daggett, *op. cit.*, p. 184

57. Hofstadter, *The American Political Tradition*, p. 167.

58. John Bigelow, *The Life of Samuel J. Tilden* (Harper and Brothers, New York, 1895), Volume II, p. 21.

59. J.T. Flynn, *op. cit.*, p. 355

60. cf. Carl R. Fisk's authoritative study, *The Civil Service Reform and Patronage* (Longman and Green, New York, 1905).

61. "There are few offices, with the duties of which a person can, till after a considerable length of time, [have] so far familiarized himself, as to perform with accuracy all the necessary details" (William Coleman, expressing Hamilton's view, in the *New York Evening Post*, 1788, quoted by Fisk, *ibid.*, p. 36.)

62. *Ibid.*, chapters iii–v.

63. The tendency to see in a single legislation either a panacea or, respectively, the "end of democracy" is a characteristic that has been common to both classical and welfare liberals. It reenforces my belief that the current welfare liberals are the intellectual and emotional heirs of the classical liberals.

64. Nevins, *Abram S. Hewitt*, p. 463.

65. *New York Evening Post*, November 2, 1888. Significantly,

the New York Republicans proceeded to make a successful deal with Tammany, whereby they would sell out their local nominee if Tammany in turn would stab Cleveland in the back. The result was the election of a Tammany mayor and of Harrison. (cf. *New York Mail and Express,* Nov. 22, 1888; *New York Evening Post,* Dec. 6, 1888; also see Nevins' *Hewitt,* pp. 5200–27.)

66. Lincoln Steffens, *The Autobiography of Lincoln Steffens* (Harcourt, Brace and Company, New York, 1931), pp. 255, 257.

67. Curiously enough Lenin held a similar opinion not only of civil service but of all managerial and bureaucratic jobs. These egalitarian traits in the bolshevist make-up cause problems quite similar to the consequences of the Jacksonian spoils system. (cf. Barrington Moore, Jr., *Soviet Politics, The Dilemma of Power* (Harvard University Press, Cambridge, 1950), chapter ii, especially pp. 39–50).

68. New York *Sun,* August 13, 1889 (A Dana editorial).

69. cf. Max Weber, *Wirtschaft und Gesellschaft* (J.C.B. Mohr, Tubingen, 1922), especially Volume I, pp. 660–80. I have always believed that Weber's analysis of the relationship between capitalism and civil-service bureaucracy is much more applicable to American conditions than European. While there existed corruption and a form of spoils system in the German petty-principalities prior to capitalist development, Prussia and Austria had an efficient and honest bureaucracy long before the advent of capitalism. As a matter of fact, in these countries the civil-service has constituted until this day a reservoir of rightwing anti-capitalism.

70. Quoted in the *Nation,* November 13, 1890, on the occasion of Ingalls' defeat in the election. The *Nation* commented further that although Ingalls' conspicuous corruption was widely known, he was repeatedly elected to the Senate presidency by the Republicans and only lost in 1890 after a Kansas legislature was elected that held too large an anti-Ingalls majority to be bought by the Senator.

71. The *Nation,* July 23, 1908.

72. Note that by 1888, both parties have strong civil-service reform planks in their platforms, and that, moreover, Harrison appointed Theodore Roosevelt to the Civil Service Commission!

73. Blaine at a pre-election dinner at Delmonico's before two hundred business leaders: "I am sure, gentlemen, that the Republican party is not arrogant nor over-confident when it claims to itself the credit of organizing and maintaining the industrial system which

gives to you and your associates the equal and just laws which enabled you to make this marvelous progress." (*New York World*, October 2, 1884.) Note the Hamiltonian vision of an imperial America ruled for its own good by the industrial interest, Blaine developed during his terms as Secretary of State! (Charles Edward Russell, *Blaine of Maine* [Farrar & Rinehart, New York, 1931], p. 380ff.)

74. *Messages and Papers of the Presidents*, Volume VIII, pp. 584, 585, 774.

75. Nation, XLVI, 1888, p. 358.

76. "American Lawyers in Business and Politics," *Yale Law Journal*, January 1951, p. 68n.

77. Quay and Platt are good examples of state bosses who ran their own show while developing strong, permanent ties with businessmen in their states ánd in the Senate. As a matter of fact it was the machine-controlled state legislatures of the Quays and Platts that enabled individual businessmen to join this most exclusive club—the Senate.

78. Aldrich, Gorman, Allison, O.H. Platt, Spooner, Depew. "One senator . . . represented the Union Pacific System, another the New York Central, still another the insurance interests of New York and New Jersey. . . . Coal and iron owned a coterie from the Midddle and Eastern seaport states. Cotton has half a dozen senators. And so it went." (William Allen White, *op. cit.*, p. 79.)

79. *The American Political Tradition*, p. 178.

80. For such an interpretation of the Senate's role see Charles and Mary Beard, *The Rise of American Civilization*, and *American Government and Politics;* Cochran and Miller, *op. cit.;* Hofstadter, *The American Political Tradition*, and *The Age of Reform;* Lincoln Steffens, *op. cit.;* Harold Laski, *op. cit.;* Robert LaFollette, *Autobiography* (LaFollette Company, Madison, 1913.)

81. Senator Aldrich, quoted in Stephenson, *op. cit.*, p. 68.

82. Senator Orville Platt in Coolidge's *An Old Fashioned Senator: Orville H. Platt*, p. 444.

83.Adams, *The Education of Henry Adams*, p. 344.

84. Thus Hoar rejected vehemently the suggestion that Coxey's petition be received by Congress. (*Nation*, May 3, 1894, p. 319.) Edmunds directed the attack upon the income tax together with Senator Choate, who was "wholly inspired by the impulse of the patriot.'" (E.S. Martin, *The Life of Joseph Hodges Choate* [Charles

Scribner's Sons, New York, 1920], Volume II, p. 1.) Both Hoar and Edmunds specialized later on in advising corporations how to utilize the loopholes in the Sherman Act. (Joseph B. Foracker, *Notes of a Busy Life* [Stewart and Kidd, Cincinnati, 1916] Volume II, p. 345.)

Chapter 7

1. Simon S. Kuznets, *National Income: A Summary of Findings,* (National Bureau of Economic Research, New York, 1946), p. 32; Krooss, *op. cit.,* p. 222. The actual decrease in capital formation as a percentage of national income is comparatively small. (The period 1899–1908 showed a decline of 9.2% from the period 1889–1898.)

2. Wright, *Economic History of the United States,* p. 60, Fig. 54; Paul Douglas, *Real Wages in the United States 1890–1926* (Houghton Mifflin Company, Boston, 1930), chs. vi and xiii; Alvin Hansen, *Business Cycles and National Income* (W.W. Norton & Co., New York, 1951), Part III, *passim;* Harold Moulton, *Income and Economic Progress* (The Brookings Institution, Washington, D.C., 1935), *passim.*

3. Wright, *op. cit.,* p. 562.

4. Henry Seager and Charles Gulick, drawing freely on previous studies, confirmed Moody's data. They found that the 300 combinations controlled fully two-fifths of the manufacturing capital of the country. Henry Seager and Charles Gulick, *Trust and Corporation Problems,* 1929, quoted in J. Keith Butters, John Lintner, and William Carey, *Effects of Taxation: Corporate Mergers* [Harvard University Press, Cambridge, 1951], p. 278. Other early studies presenting corroborating data are: Arthur Dewing, *Corporate Promotions and Reorganization* (Harvard University Press, Cambridge, 1914); Jeremiah Jenks, *op. cit.,* perhaps the classic in this field; Eliot Jones, *The Trust Problem in the United States* (The Macmillan Company, New York, 1921); Charles Van Hise, *Concentration and Control* (The Macmillan Company, New York, 1912). During the 50's an attempt was made by several quantitative economists to question the conclusion of the earlier studies. (cf. Universities-National Bureau of Economic Research, *Business Concentration and Price Policy* [Princeton University Press, Princeton, 1955], especially Jesse Markham's "Survey of the Evidence and Findings on Mergers" and Weston's *The Role of Mergers in the Growth of Large Firms.*) On the basis of, in my opinion, pedantic definitions, they come to the conclusion that

there is insufficient evidence for condemning mergers as breeders of monopoly.

5. John Moody, *The Truth About the Trusts* (Moody Publishing Company, New York, 1904), p. 453ff. Undoubtedly, these capitalization figures contain a good deal of "water and air."

6. cf. Charles Francis Adams, *Autobiography* (Houghton Mifflin Company, Boston and New York, 1916), *passim;* Steffens, *op. cit., passim,* especially chapter viii.

7. *Theory of Capitalistic Development* (Oxford University Press, New York, 1944.)

8. In the period 1888–1905, 328 combinations or mergers were carried out, of which 156 were sufficiently successful to produce a degree of monopoly control in their general industries. cf. Shaw Livermore, "The Success of Industrial Mergers," *Quarterly Journal of Economics,* L, p. 68ff.

9. cf. Sutton, Harris, Kayson, Tobin, *The American Business Creed, passim,* esp. pp. 33, 36, 39, 54.

10. James J. Hill stated: "A starving man will usually get bread if it is to be had, and a starving railroad will not maintain rates." (William Z. Ripley, ed. *Trusts, Pools and Corporations* [Ginn and Co., New York, 1955], p. 42.) Similarly, "Distillers, when they have an accumulation of goods on hand, will not hesitate to cut prices to make a sale." (*Ibid.,* p. 29.)

11. Cleona Lewis, *America's Stake in International Investments,* (The Brookings Institution, Washington, 1938). Though important, foreign investment never again was as essential to America's economic development as it was in the pre-Civil War period, especially in the 1830's and 1850's. In 1869 Europeans owned one billion American government bonds (out of a total of two and three-quarter billion) and almost one-half billion of American securities. (*New York World,* December 21, 1869.)

12. The National City Bank (the "Standard Oil" bank) and the First National Bank (the "Morgan" bank) were the two commercial banks most involved in investment banking and "reorganization" of industry. (cf. Lewis Corey, *The House of Morgan* [G. Howard Watt, New York, 1933], esp. pp. 227, 256, 259, 261–295, 359–453.) Two of the most important life insurance companies, The New York Life Assurance Society and the Equitable Life Insurance Company, both closely allied with the Morgan combine, were an important source of financial resources in most of the corporate organization activity of

the Morgans, (cf. *Bankers' Magazine,* September 1901, p. 438; *Commercial and Financial Chronicle,* February 8, 1902, p. 309; Lewis Corey, *op. cit.,* p. 257ff.) Also (cf. Krooss, *op. cit.,* p. 252ff)

13. *Bankers' Magazine* (September 1879, p. 189), estimating the loss of European investors between 1873–79 at $600,000,000, declared: "This despoiling of European investors has been going on for more than a generation."

14. "The Government and the Theory of Competition," *American Economic Review,* XV, p. 446.

15. *Iron Age,* February 6, 1908, p. 442 (italics mine).

16. U.S. vs. United States Steel Corporation, *et al.* Fed 55 (1915), 251 U.S. 417 (1920), *Brief for U.S.,* Vol. II, p. 149.

17. Gary quoted in *Iron Age,* Feb. 6, 1908, p. 443 (italics mine).

18. Quoted in Krooss, *op. cit.,* p. 296 (italics mine). A formal exposition of Gary's views on the subject matters of price competition and government regulation is contained in a bill drafted by Gary and submitted to the Senate Committee on Interstate Commerce. (cf. Hearings before the Senate Committee on Interstate Commerce on the Control of Corporations . . . engaged in Interstate Commerce, 62 Cong. 2nd Sess., 1911–1912, pp. 2407–2412.) Gary's bill contained proposals for the issue of federal corporation licenses, and federal supervision of the behavior of the corporation, especially in respect to capital market transactions and conspiracies in restraint of trade.

19. American Iron and Steel Institute, *Basing Point and Competition in Steel,* New York, 1925.

20. "Our theory is that mergers for monopoly (were) profitable . . . in many industries well before the mergers occurred. The only persuasive reason for their late occurrence is the development of the modern capital market." (George Stigler, "Monopoly and Oligopoly by Merger," *American Economic Review,* XL, May, 1950, p. 28.)

21. As a matter of fact, Poor, *op. cit.,* complains about the bureaucratization in the railroad management of the 50's, which was later to become typical of the finance capitalism of the 1900's. It is amazing, though, how little railroad management has changed in the last hundred years. Poor's complaints of the 1850's were echoed by Brandeis in the early 1900's; and a recent study by John Carroll *et al.* (University of Michigan Press, to be published), repeats exactly the same criticism!

23. "Instead of peace [the Carnegie dominated] consolidation in

the steel industry produced the threat of more dangerous competition as the competitors disposed of larger resources." (Lewis Corey, *op. cit.*, p. 263.

24. *Commercial and Financial Chronicle*, March 2, 1901, p. 416.

25. Lewis Corey, *op. cit.*, pp. 135–6.

26. *New York Tribune*, January 19, 1901.

27. *Commercial and Financial Chronicle*, March 2, 1901, p. 416.

28. *North American Review*, May 1901, No. 534, p. 650.

29. *New York Times*, January 7, 1903.

30. *Commercial and Financial Chronicle*, November 1907, p. 1109.

31. Josephson, *The Robber Barons*, p. 447.

32. Morgan defined "community-of-interests" as the concept "that a certain number of men owning property should do what they like with it . . . and act toward mutual harmony." (*New York Tribune*, March 27, 1902, italics mine.)

33. "Practically all the railroad and industrial development of this country has taken place initially through the medium of the great banking houses." (J.P. Morgan & Company, in a letter to the Pujo Committee, quoted in Louis Brandeis' *Other People's Money* [National Home Library Foundation, Washington, 1933], p. 91.)

35. Louis Brandeis, *The Curse of Bigness* (The Viking Press, New York), 1935, pp. 116–7, reprinted; originally appeared in the *American Legal News*, XLIV, January 1913, pp. 5–14.

36. *New York Times*, June 5, 1902. The huge promotional profits of organization and reorganization of large enterprises attracted also many industrialists. Hill himself became an integral part of the Morgan group, Carnegie made a huge profit on the organization of U.S. Steel, and Rogers and Archbold, who started out as industrialists, became highly effective Wall Street operators. (cf. Thomas W. Lawson, *Frenzied Finance* [The Ridgeway-Thayer Company, New York, 1905].

37. *Bankers' Magazine*, April 1901, p. 498. (Italics mine.)

38. *New York Tribune*, March 27, 1902.

39. Josephson, *The Robber Barons*, p. 434.

40. J.J. Hill, among others, was well aware of the consequences of the closing of the frontier. He anticipated the severe depression of the 90's because "everything was built up," America was "no longer a frontier country." (Joseph Gilpin Pyle, *Life of James Hill* [P. Smith, New York, 1936], Volume II, p. 234.)

41. cf. Wilford J. King, *The Wealth and Income of the People of*

the United States (The Macmillan Company, New York, 1923), pp. 13, 129; "The Natoinal Income and its Purchasing Power," *National Bureau of Economic Research,* New York, 1930, p. 74. This writer approaches wealth estimates at any time with a good deal of scepticism. Wealth estimates for the pre-World War I period are received with boundless incredulity. However, for our purposes, these data may give an indication of the relative growth and rate of growth of income and wealth.

43. *New York Tribune,* March 27, 1902.

44. *Report of the Industrial Commission on the Relations and Conditions of Capital and Labor Employed in Manufactures and General Business;* 19 volumes. (Government Printing Office, Washington, 1900, Volume I, p. 39.) Hereafter referred to as the *Report of the Industrial Commission.*

45. James J. Hill quoted by Josephson, *The Robber Barons,* p. 416.

46. Pyle, *The Life of James J. Hill,* Volume II, p. 12.

47. *Journal of Commerce,* April 1, 1913.

48. Just as frequently did it conflict with the overt action of businessmen. The NAM—the guardian of the ideology of individualism—became a very efficient lobby for the solicitation of government support for industry. "The Association through its leaders seeks the aid of government and asks for legislation favorable to the interests of manufacturers. It asks for aid in building up foreign commerce . . . wishes liberal appropriations for the Bureau of Manufacturers. . . . It favors ship subsidies . . . waterway developments. . . . It advocates a strong militia, and a large army and navy, not only for war but 'to squelch the rebellion that springs into existence with every strike.' " (Clarence Bennett, *Employers' 'Associations in the United States* [The Macmillan Companyy, New York, 1922], p. 318.)

49. *Bankers' Monthly,* July 1900, p. 15.

50. *Investigation of Financial and Monetary Concentration in the United States* ("Pujo Committee"), United States Congress, 62nd Congr. 3rd Sess., House Committee on Banking and Currency, 1913, p. 1855. Hereafter referred to as Money Trust Investigation.

51. Morgan, taking the unfortunately worded questions of Untermyer literally, was, of course, right, but Untermyer was talking about investment funds, while Morgan was thinking—or pretending to be thinking—of money as a commodity.

52. *Ibid.,* pp. 1052–53. In this instance Morgan was obviously

consciously not telling the truth. He was fully aware and proud of his influence.

53. *Ibid.*, p. 1050.

54. George Stigler, *op. cit.*, pp. 330–31.

55. *Nation*, July 20,, 1899, p. 46. This unsigned editorial was quite representative of the arch-conservative editorial policy of the *Nation* during the post 1896 period. In its avid anti-Bryan stand, the *Nation* sacrificed most of its classical-liberal ideas but for the retention of free trade, civil-service and anti-imperialist editorials.

56. *Forum*, XXX, September 1900–February 1901, pp. 286ff.

57. *Ibid.*, p. 288.

58. *Ibid.*

59. *Ibid.*

60. *Ibid.* Thus while trusts and small manufacturing companies are equal, the trusts are merely "more equal."

61. *Ibid.*

62. Forum, XXX, 1900, p. 104.

63. Mr. C. Cochran, unidentified delegate, quoted by the *Nation*. September 21, 1899, p. 219.

64. *Bankers' Monthly*, July 1900, pp. 13–14. For a lengthier expression of essentially the same point of view note Charles Stevenson's "Economic Meaning of Consolidated Corporations" in the August, 1900 issue of the *Bankers' Monthly*.

65. *North American Review*, CLXXII, May 1901, pp. 641–700.

66. Andrew Carnegie, "The Bugaboo of Trusts," *op. cit.*

67. This is, of course, rather ironic if Russel Sage's colorful Wall Street history is considered. "There is no more disgraceful chapter in the history of stock jobbing than that which records the operations of Jay Gould, *Russell Sage*, Cyrus W. Field and their associates in securing control of the system of elevated rairoads in New York City." (*New York Times*, quoted in Josephson's *The Robber Barons*, *op. cit.*, p. 210, italics mine.)

68. The banker and successful fund-raiser for the Republican Party, Henry Clews, expressed surprisingly similar sentiments: "With them (the Standard Oil Company) manipulation has ceased to be speculation. Their resources are so vast that they need only to concentrate on any given property in order to do with it what they please. . . . There is an utter absence of chance that is terrible to contemplate. This combination controls Wall Street almost absolutely." Clews, *Fifty Years in Wall Street*, p. 702.) Clews, the great recep-

tacle of the prejudices and folklores of his day, seemed to have been overly impressed by the singlemindedness of the Standard Oil crowd. Without in any way discounting the skill and resources of the Archbolds and Rogers, we can tell from even so flamboyant a description as Lawson's *Frenzied Finance* that this single-mindedness was pure fiction, hiding predatory, self-centered men who, in their Wall Street escapades had, above all, their own individual interests at heart.

69. Russell Sage, "A Grave Danger to the Community," *North American Review*, CLXXII, May 1901, pp. 641–6. (Italics mine.)

70. cf. Woodrow Wilson's campaign speeches in 1912: "When we undertake the strategy which is going to be necessary to overcome and destroy this system of monopoly we are rescuing the business of the country, we are not injuring it." (Quoted by Arthur M. Schlesinger, *The Crisis of the Old Order* [Houghton Mifflin Company, Boston, 1957], p. 27.

71. James J. Hill, *ibid*, pp. 646–55. (Italics mine.) Compare the last paragraphs with the views of Taylor, Gant and Urwick, the fathers of professional management.

72. *North American Review*, CLXXII, May 1901, pp. 655–64.

73. *North American Review*, CLXXII, May 1901, pp. 655–64. (Italics mine.)

74. *North American Review*, CLXXII, May 1901, pp. 664–77.

75. cf. Drucker, *The Practice of Management, passim*, and *The New Society, passim*.

76. *North American Review*, CLXXII, May 1901, pp. 686–700.

77. The reader should note the implicit assumption of an existing "just price" that permeates Logan's thinking, just as the notion of a "reasonable," i.e. "just" profit was implicit in the thinking of Schwab, Flint, Morgan, etc. This return to medieval Thomistic economics is an exceedingly important facet of finance capitalism and shall be examined below (especially in chapter 9).

78. It is noteworthy, again, to what extent the above paragraph expresses current business opinion about oligopolistic industries. (cf. Sutton, Harris *et al.*, *op. cit.*, especially chapter viii.)

79. *North American Review*, CLXXII, May 1901, pp. 686–700.

CHAPTER 8

1. The term "Protestant Ethic" as used by Whyte (*The Organization Man*) and Riesman (*The Lonely Crowd*) connotes essentially the ideology of industrial capitalism, i.e. Social Darwinism, too frequently

expressed in the unsophisticated vocabulary of *Poor Richard*. However, to the extent that the concept of the "survival of the fittest" does not seem to be included in Whyte's and Riesman's definition of the "Protestant Ethic" it is not quite synonymous with my usage of this term as defined in chapters 3 and 4.

2. cf. his address at Yale, Nov. 1, 1907, which is the purest expression of Social Darwinism and Protestant Ethics. (Clews, *Fifty Years in Wall Street*, pp. 1001ff.)

3. This is probably not quite correct. The Chamber of Commerce and the N.A.M. seem frequently more representative of small than of big business.

4. *America Comes of Age* (Harcourt Brace and Company, New York, 1927, p. 30.)

5. For a view that deprecates the qualitative nature of this change, see Herman Maurer, *Great Enterprise; Growth and Behavior of the Big Corporation* (The Macmillan Company, New York, 1955).

6. *Money Trust Investigation*, p. 130.

7. Moody, *The Truth About the Trusts*, p. 493.

8. The supposed risklessness of the manipulation of finance capitalism was well described by Henry Clews. "They (the Standard Oil crowd) are the greatest operators the world has ever seen, and the beauty of their method is the quietness and lack of ostentation with which they carry on . . . there is an utter absence of chance that is terrible to contemplate." (Henry Clews, *op. cit.*, p. 73.) Thanks to Clews and Lawson the "risklessness" with which the Standard Oil crowd operated has been exaggerated. John D. Rockefeller, who did not gamble, was by far the wealthiest of them all. He believed, interestingly enough, that his brother William was not nearly as rich because "he speculated." Without discounting the advantages huge financial resources bestow upon insiders, as long as Standard Oil or any other giant had not complete control over the business cycle or over technological innovations, the speculations of its executives bore a certain amount of risk.

9. *Money Trust Investigation*, pp. 1070–72.

10. *Money Trust Investigation*, pp. 1020–21.

11. *Ibid.*

12. Corey, *The House of Morgan*, p. 213. This quotation has become a classic and seems to appear in virtually every work that deals with this particular period.

13. *Bankers' Monthly*, XX, July 1900, pp. 13–14. Note the com-

plete absence of any Darwinian sentiment. There is no "change" possible in the world of the *Bankers' Monthly*.

14. *The Social Problems of an Industrial Civilization* (Harvard University Press, Cambridge, 1945), and *The Human Problems of an Industrial Civilization* (Harvard University Press, 1933).

15. *Money Trust Investigation*, p. 1568.

16. The Equitable Life Assurance Society scandal brought the following comment from the *Nation:* "That [graft] is at least much more prevalent than they have been ready to admit, we think the most wide-eyed optimist must now concede. . . . It is probably true today that the United States is regarded abroad as crowding Russia and Turkey hard for the championship in corruption." (The *Nation*, LXXXI, July–December 1905, p. 48.)

17. "Corporation Absolutism," *Nation*, LXXXI, July–December 1905, pp. 252–253. Incidentally, the general "poor memory" displayed by insurance and bank executives before the Armstrong and Pujo committees would force even the most sympathic contemporary congressional investigator to demand a "contempt of Congress" citation.

18. *Ibid.* (Italics mine.)

19. cf. Frederick Townsend Martin, *The Passage of the Idle Rich*, for a caustic view of the would-be Louis XIV's and Marie Antoinettes. For a more gentle criticism, note Lloyd Morris, *Postscript to Yesterday* (Random House, New York, 1947), chapters i and ii.

20. Henry Adams, *The Education of Henry Adams*, p. 347.

21. Charles F. Adams, *Autobiography*, p. 196.

22. For an excellent summary of most of the muckraking literature see chapters iii and iv, "The New Democracy," and "The Decline of Laissez-Faire" in H.V. Faulkner's *The Quest for Social Justice* (The Macmillan Company, New York, 1931). The two classics in the field are, of course, Lincoln Steffens' *Autobiography* and *Shame of the Cities* (McClure, Phillips & Company, New York, 1904). Steffens' latter work is, above all, notable because it shatters the myth that municipal corruption was the consequence of corrupt Irish-Italian political machines who depended upon illiterate immigrants for support. In San Francisco, St. Louis, Minneapolis, Philadelphia, and Providence the powerful and corrupt local machines were headed by impeccable Nordics with very excellent ties to the Yankee or Southern aristocracy of their respective towns. Even in New York, Boston, and New Jersey, however, the Irish supplied mainly the

bribe-takers while the upstanding businessmen of these cities were the bribe-givers. This rather nice distinction between bribe-givers and bribe-takers has been a characteristic of American business opinion until today (cf. *National Observer*, Nov. 22, 1970, p. 1).

23. See Faulkner, *The Quest for Social Justice*, *op. cit.*, pp. 3, 24, 111, 126.

24. George W. Perkins on December 13, 1911, before the Senate Committee on Interstate Commerce; *Report of Hearings*, 1911, p. 1091.

25. *Ibid.*, p. 1091–2. Perkins distinguished between such a regulatory commission and the enforcement of the Sherman Act, which "put brakes on business expansion."

26. William Temple, November 24, 1911, at a Hearing Before the Special Committee on Investigation of the U.S. Steel Corporation; House of Representatives ("Stanley Committee"), *House Office Report #22*, 1911, p. 1744.

27. *Ibid.*, pp. 100, 1744. (Italics mine.)

28. *Ibid.*, pp. 2696–8.

29. *Hearings*, Senate Committee on Interstate Commerce, *op. cit.*, pp. 1134, 1135.

30. Quoted in Hofstadter, *The American Political Tradition*, p. 200.

31. *Ibid.*

32. *Ibid.*

33. "Competition under present methods . . . is too destructive to be tolerated" (Perkins before the Special Committee of the U.S. Steel Corp., *op. cit.*, p. 1552).

34. Frank A. Vanderlip, "The Views of Frank A. Vanderlip," *Outlook*, 1911, pp. 858–62. Roosevelt, in a previous editorial in the *Outlook*, "The Trusts, the People and the Square Deal" (*Ibid.*, pp. 649ff.) expressed similar views; he especially opposed indiscriminate enforcement of the Sherman Act. Also note the similarity between the views of Vanderlip and Galbraith, and Vanderlip and Hamilton for that matter.

35. It is interesting to follow the controversies between real conservatives and "libertarians" (i.e. classical liberals) in the *National Review;* equally interesting is the wide area of agreement that seems to exist between the "New Left" and the right wing "libertarians" which already has resulted in joint SDS and YAF membership by "libertarian" students and the cooperation of Karl Hesse, Goldwater's speechwriter in 1964, with the New Left.

36. Kenneth E. Boulding, *The Organizational Revolution* (Harper & Brothers, New York, 1953), p. 132.

CHAPTER 9

1. *Money Trust Investigation,* p. 1025. (Italics mine.)

2. Gary was especially fond of emphasizing U.S. Steel's "enlightened policy" of voluntarily increasing wages. (Tarbell, *The Life of Elbert H. Gary,* p. 176.) Gary forgot to mention, however, that these wage increases consistently lagged behind price increases. In 1915 the average real wage for all workers was the same as in 1895, while the relative position of the steelworkers had slightly deteriorated. In terms of purchasing power, steelworkers' wages were 5% lower in 1912 than in 1895. (Douglas, *Real Wages in the United States, 1890–1926,* pp. 271. 391–2.)

As far as working conditions were concerned, the long twelve hour day and the prevailing company town conditions probably made the steelworker one of the most exploited workers in the United States. (John A. Fitch, *The Steel Workers,* Pittsburgh Survey, Russell Sage Foundation, pp. 171–6.) It was in answer to the criticism of these very conditions that Morgan made his famous comment: "Men owning propertyy should do what they like with it." (*New York Tribune,* March 29, 1902.) Years later Morgan's son made a very similar reply when questioned whether he thought that $10 a week for a workingman was the proper wage. "If that's all he can get and takes it," he answered, "I should say that it is enough." (*New York Times,* February 2, 1915.)

3. How smooth Schwab, the first president of United States Steel, really was can be seen by his "success" as organizer of the United States Shipbuilding Company. This organization venture brought a $55,000,000 profit to Schwab and his group, and bankruptcy to the company. Ex-United States Senator J.M. Smith, the court-appointed receiver, referred to Schwab's activity as an "artistic swindle." (*Receiver's Report to United States District Court,* Newark, New Jersey, November 2, 1903.)

4. In 1927 a General Motors director said, "Bankers regard research as most dangerous and a thing that makes banking hazardous, due to the rapid changes it brings about in industry." (Edward C. Kirkland, *A History of American Economic Life* [Appleton-Century, Crofts, Inc., New York, 1939], p. 647.

5. Cochran and Miller, *op. cit.,* p. 298.

6. cf. Simon Kuznets, *National Income: A Summary of Findings*

(National Bureau of Economic Research, New York, 1946), pp. 31–3.

7. Joseph Schumpeter, *op. cit.*, p. 156.

8. "The most successful corporations in the United States today are those in which the merit system is most faithfully observed. Take the Pennsylvania Railroad, for instance. A compilation of records of the 160 principal officers shows that 150 of them started with the company as beginners." (Similar statements are made by the author for the Standard Oil Company and Marshall Field's.) (Henry Licht-feld West in the Aegis of Civil Service Reform," *Forum*, XLI, Jan.–June 1909, p. 519.)

9. As an example for lieutenants possessing vast authority, Carnegie's top executives, Henry Frick and Charles Schwab, may be cited.

10. Carl D. Thompson, *Confessions of the Power Trust* (Dutton & Co., New York, 1932), p. 14.

11. Frederick W. Taylor, *The Principles of Scientific Management* (Harper & Brothers, New York, 1915), pp. 6–7.

12. *Bankers' Magazine*, LXV, July–December 1902, pp. 274– . . . (Italics mine.) This editorial was written to comment upon an unspecified exchange between Sage and Depew regarding "combinations and trusts."

13. Note in this sentence, and in those to follow, the development of a definite "countervailing power theory."

14. *Bankers' Magazine*, LXV, July–December 1902, pp. 19–20. (Italics mine.)

15. E.C. Machen, a banker and contributor to Progressive magazines, in the June 1901 *Cosmopolitan*, condensed for *Public Opinion*, XXX, 1901, pp. 741–2. (Italics mine.)

16. Perkins, before Senate Committee on Interstate Commerce, *op. cit.*, p. 1139.

17. *Ibid.*, p. 1140.

18. Charles J. Bullock, *Atlantic Monthly*, June 1901, excerpted in *Public Opinion*, XXX, June 15, 1901, p. 741.

19. *Small Business and General Motors* (Detroit, no date), p. 1, has the following typical preface: "Curiously enough, some people seem to believe that the large business and the small business are antagonists. Nothing could be further from the truth.

"The small supplier and the large manufacturer are partners in production. Each is dependent on the other and together they form a team. "To help explain this aspect of our competitive free enterprise economy, we have been carrying on a national advertising campaign for the past several months in which we tell the General Motors supplier story."

20. cf. Edward H. Carr, *The New Society* (Beacon Press, Boston, 1957), esp. chs. i and iv.

21. Brandeis, *Other People's Money*, pp. 91–2.

22. *Bankers' Magazine*, LXXVI, January 1908, p. 13.

23. Two studies of post-World War I and post-World War II business opinion and ideology (Krooss, *Business Opinion Between Two Wars* and Sutton, Harris, *et al., op. cit.*) clearly show the amazingly static nature of the American business ideology during the last forty years.

24. *Public Opinion*, XL, June 30, 1906, p. 781 (Italics mine.)

25. cf. *Theory of Business Enterprise* (Charles Scribner's Sons, New York, 1904); *The Engineer and the Price System* (Viking Press, New York, 1921); *Absentee Ownership and Business Enterprise in Recent Times: The Case of America* (Viking Press, New York, 1923).

26. Harcourt Brace and Company, New York, 1936, p. 93ff.

27. Quoted in Riesman's *Thorstein Veblen* (Charles Scribner's Son's, New York, 1953), p. 79.

28. In his thoughtful, previously cited study, *The Dream of Success, op. cit.*, Kenneth Lynn seems to hold the somewhat contrary opinion that America's emergence as a success society—rather than a status society—and the consequent all-pervading materialism were the real causes of the anti-business sentiment of the intellectuals. (See especially pp. 241ff.) I wonder if there really was an *emerging* success society in the 1880-1914 period? If anything, it was a transition from a comparatively undifferentiated society into a hierarchical society, but I doubt that America was less materialistic during the post-Civil War period than during the 1970's.

29. Schumpeter, *op. cit.*, p. 156.

30. Ernest Dale, *Planning and Developing the Company Organizational Structure* (American Management Association, New York, 1952), chapter i, esp. pp. 4–6.

31. Perkins, before the Senate Committee on Interstate Commerce, *op. cit.*, p. 1089.

32. Boulding, *op. cit.*, pp. 133ff., as a matter of fact, almost defines organization as a system of communication. Similarly Forrester (*Industrial Dynamics*, MIT Press, 1962) and S. Beer (*Decision and Control*, Wiley, 1967) see the firm as an information center.

33. Speaker Thomas Reed, in the *North American Review,*
December 1902, p. 771: "These unions of capital have been forced
upon the capitalist. Perhaps you think that men were glad to get into
these unions and went cheerfully into combinations. Such was not
the fact. Men hated to give up their independence. They and their
fathers had built up their business. They were proud of their success, and meant to leave their establishment to their children. In the
new combinations only one could be the head; the others must . . .
take rear seats."

34. Berle and Means, R. H. Gordon, O. Knauth, and especially
James Burnham give mistakenly the impression that a corporate
bureaucracy—and the concomitant separation of ownership and con-
trol—did not develop until after 1910. (cf. Adolf Berle and Gardner
Means, *The Modern Corporation and Private Property* [The Macmillan
Company, New York, 1932]; Robert A. Gordon, *Business Leadership
in the Large Corporation* [Brookings Institute, Washington, 1945];
Oswald Knauth, *Managerial Enterprise* [W.W. Norton & Co., New
York, 1948]; James Burnham, *The Managerial Revolution* [The John
Day Company, New York, 1941].)

35. Thomas C. Cochran, "Role and Sanction in American Entrepreneurial History" in *Change and the Entrepreneur* (Harvard University Press, Cambridge, 1949), p. 172.

36. The last point is easily the most important one. The West Point
platoon leader, for instance, or the new ensign as a P.T. boat skipper,
rather quickly became "Joe" or "Bill" to their units, once they were
isolated for a sufficiently long period of time.

37. Blanche Hazard's *The Organization of the Boot and Shoe
Industry in Massachusetts before 1875* (Harvard University Press,
Cambridge, no date), presents a case in which the transition from
handicraft stage, to the putting-out system, to capitalistic production,
was accompanied by continuously increasing division of labor and
specialization. However, this was not a process typical of American
industry in the post-Civil War era. Judging by the works of Taylor
and Towne, division of labor in the steel industry was promoted by
functional factors only, and specialization was absent to the degree
that each worker determined his own production plan and operating
schedule.

37a. "Economic Theory and Entrepreneurial History" in *Change
and the Entrepreneur, op. cit.*

38. In this respect we might also consider the different attitudes

induced into employees by the very fact of absentee-ownership. Robert Michels draws attention to this fact in his "Psychologie Der Antikapitalistischen Massenbewegung." *Grundriss Der Social Ökonomie* (A. Kroner, Leipzig, 1926), Volume II, Part II, pp. 244ff.)

39. Quoted by Ida Tarbell in *The Life of Elbert Gary*, p. 163.

40. *Ibid.*

41. True "paternalism" was a characteristic of the old Schumpeterian entrepreneur, and of the small or, at the most, medium-sized firm.

42. Gary's profit-sharing plan, possibly well-meant, never seemed really to get started. Especially John Fitch *(The Steel Workers)* was rather doubtful of its impact. Tarbell, however, seems to produce pretty solid evidence that, at least in some plants, a good many steelworkers bought their share of U.S.Steel stock. Tarbell implies that is was the coincidence of a few dividend-less years immediately after the start of the program that impaired its effectiveness. However, the wage statistics produced by Fitch would indicate that only a few highly skilled craftsmen would have had a sufficient income to buy U.S. Steel stock.

43. Nevins, *Abram S. Hewitt,* pp. 465, 596, etc.

44. Tarbell, *Gary,* pp. 222–3. Also see Gary's comments on the occasion of his refusal to meet the union leaders during the strike in 1918, *ibid.,* pp. 282–3.

45. This nice distinction between the "good union member" and the "bad leader" has been a permanent stock in trade of management. William H. Whyte, in his amusing *Is Anybody Listening?*, provided abundant evidence that "trade-union-wise" management's sophistication has not progressed beyond Judge Gary:

> An institutional ad prepared for a trade association is evidence in point. Pictured at the lathe is a patently oaken-hearted man . . . 'I AM A WORKER, MY CREED' goes the caption. There follows a set of quite unexceptionable aphorisms, at the end of which is tucked in a little snapper that almost anyone would correctly sense was the rationale of the ad: *'I believe in the right of every union man to question the conduct and motives of his union bosses.'* (Italics mine.)
>
> Recently the man responsible for this item explained the theory that was behind it. It was just a matter of practical between the worker and those union bastards. We tell him what a hell of a fine guy he is and he likes that. That part at

the end is a little subtle for him, of course. But he'll see it every day.' Workers would like the ad so much, he explained, that many would frame it and put it up in their living rooms. (*Ibid.*, p. 33.)

46. cf. Tarbell, *Gary*, pp. 299–300.

47. cf. the editorial attack on Corbin's conduct during the anthracite strike in the *Bankers' Magazine* of 1887–1888, XLII, pp. 576–80.

48. *Bankers' Magazine*, XXXIX, 1884-1885, p. 370.

49. Perkins before the Senate Committee on Interstate Commerce, *op. cit.*, p. 1135.

50. cf. David Riesman, *Individualism Reconsidered* (Doubleday & Company, Garden City, 1954), p. 17.

51. In *Academic Freedom, an Essay in Definition* (Henry Regnery, Chicago, 1955), Russell Kirk, quite properly, distinguishes sharply between indivdualism—the philosophy of classical liberalism and Social Darwinism, and individuality—the awareness and emphasis of one's self. The term "individualism" as used in this chapter, will carry Kirk's connotation.

52. "The supposed evils of [communist] materialism and atheism are insignificant compared with the cruelties which follow inevitably from the communist pretension that its elite has taken the leap from the realm of necessity to the realm of freedom and is therefore no longer subject to the limitations of nature and history which have hitherto bound the actions of men." (Reinhold Niebuhr, *op. cit.*, p. 65) Niebuhr's comments about the communist elite are equally fitting if applied to the unholy, and I hope ineffective, alliance of personnel experts, psychotherapists, psychologists, motivation researchers, and sociologists.

53. Riesman, *Individualism Reconsidered*, p. 17.

54. Boulding, *op. cit.*, p. 79.

55. C. Wright Mills provides the following data in his *White Collar* (Oxford University Press, New York, 1953), p. 63.

	1870	1940
The Labor Force		
Old middle class	33%	20% •
New middle class	6%	25%
Wage workers	61%	55%

56. One important difference in the opinions and beliefs of the old and the new middle class, between industrial and finance capitalism, may have been what Karl Polanyi calls the increasing "market mentality" of the latter period. For an excellent discussion of the

"market mentality" and its neglect by purely materialistic analysis, note Polanyi's "Our Obsolete Market Mentality," *Commentary*, Februrary 1947, pp. 109–116.

57. Money Trust Investigation, pp. 226ff.

58. This differentiation occurred much earlier in Europe due, I believe, to the more rigid nature of the continental hierarchies. Even there, however, it took wars and depression before the low-paid clerical workers—the lumpen-bourgeoisie—began to join anti-capitalistic, Marxist or Fascist movements. The complete insignificance in these class alignments of the absence or possession of property again characterizes the 19th century fetish role that the concept of property has played in the Marxian system. (cf. Robert Michel's "Psychologie der Antikapitalistischen Massenbewegung," *op. cit.*)

59. Boulding, *op. cit.*, p. 9.

60. Boulding, *op. cit.*, p. 53.

61. Ortega y Gasset, *The Revolt of the Masses*, (W.W. Norton, New York 1932), p. 18.

62. The German geopolitical school, very much like contemporary organization theory, had also taken an "organic" approach to the study of the life-cycle of the state. As a matter of fact, the similarity in the respective treatment of the "State" as an organism by Haushofer, Rietz, Sven Hedin, *et al.*, and business as an organism by Ashby, Urwick, Simon, *et al.*, is quite impressive. If, as most Anglo-Saxon political scientists claimed, this organic approach is mythical nonsense in the case of the Haushofer school, then most contemporary organizational theory is similarly based upon nonsense.

63. Thus, in spite of the fact that, at the turn of the century, more than 500,000 workers were either killed or maimed every year, and most of them in the basic industries, the large corporations for a long time refused even to consider this problem. In Bridge's *Inside History of the Carnegie Steel Company*, there is not a single indication that anyone from Carnegie to Frick to Schwab considered it his responsibility to deal with industrial accidents or their consequences. An inventor is quoted by E.A. Ross (*Sin and Sanity* [Houghton Mifflin Company, Boston, 1907], p. 95) as declaring that he could sell labor-saving devices in twenty places, but nowhere a life-saving invention. At the convention of the National Association of Manufacturers in 1909, the president, Mr. Kirby, reported in glowing terms that the NAM, thanks to the services of its chief lobbyist Emery, was able to defeat all "bad bills" before state and federal

legislatures. And what were those bad bills? The Indiana NAM representative, Hauch, explained: "In the recent legislative session in Indiana we had both houses in the hands of the opposing party, and I think the largest list of *malicious class bills* ever presented . . . (such as) employer's liability, master and servant, assumption of risks, fellow servants . . . aesthetics and hygiene in factories, and everything of that kind, and we thought we were up against it; but through the insistent persistence of Mr. Emery we were able to prevent every one of those bills from getting to the Governor." (*Annual Convention of the National Association of Manufacturers*, 1909), p. 228. (Italics mine.)

It should be added, however, that on the other hand U.S. Steel saw the handwriting on the wall and began, voluntarily, to pay sizable death benefits after 1910 (Fitch, *The Steelworkers*, p. 197), and formalized a safety program at the same time.

64. cf. W.H. Whyte's comments on the training of the organization man, *op. cit.*, Part II, esp. Chapter VIII. See, also, F. A. von Hayek's *The Counter-Revolution of Science* (The Free Press, Glencoe, Illinois, 1952), chapter ii, "The Collectivism of the Scientistic Approach."

CHAPTER 10

1. cf. Herman Krooss, *Business Opinion Between Two Wars*.
2. Sutton *et al.*, *op. cit.*, pp. 177–83, chapter ix.
3. cf. chapter 4.

BIBLIOGRAPHY

Books

Adamic, Louis, *Dynamite*. New York, The Viking Press, 1935.

Adams, Brooks, *American Economic Supremacy*. New York, The Macmillan Company, 1900.

Adams, Charles Francis, *Charles Francis Adams*. Boston, New York, Houghton Mifflin Company, 1916.

Adams, Henry, *The Degradation of the Democratic Dogma*. New York, The Macmillan Company, 1919.

———, *The Education of Henry Adams*. Boston, New York, Houghton Mifflin Company, 1918.

———, *Letters of Henry Adams 1858–1891*, edited by W. C. Ford, Boston, New York, Houghton Mifflin Company, 1930.

Alexander, De Alva S., *Political History of the State of New York*. New York, Henry Holt & Co., 1906.

Allen, Frederick L., *The Lords of Creation*. New York, Harper & Brothers, 1935.

Arnold, Thurman, *The Folklore of Capitalism*. New Haven, Yale University Press, 1937.

———, *The Symbols of Government*. New Haven, Yale University Press, 1935.

Atherton, Lewis, *The Pioneer Merchant in Mid America*. Columbia, Mo., The University of Missouri Studies, Volume XIV, No. 2, 1939.

Beard, Charles A., *An Economic Interpretation of the Constitution of the United States*. New York, The Macmillan Company, 1948; revised edition.

——— and Beard, Mary R., *The Rise of American Civilization*. New York, The Macmillan Company, 1941.

Beard, Miriam, *A History of the Business Man*. New York, The Macmillan Company, 1938.

Beer, Thomas, *Hanna*. New York, Alfred A. Knopf, 1929.

244

———, *The Mauve Decade.* New York, Alfred A. Knopf, 1926.

Berle, Adolf A., and Means, Gardner C., *The Modern Corporation and Private Property.* New York, The Macmillan Company, 1933.

Bigelow, John, *The Life of Samuel Tilden.* New York, Harper & Brothers, 1895.

Billington, Ray A., *The Protestant Crusade.* New York, The Macmillan Company, 1939.

Binkley, Wilfred E., *American Political Parties.* New York, Alfred A. Knopf, 1954.

Bennett, Clarence, *Employers' Associations in the United States.* New York, The Macmillan Company, 1922.

Boulding, Kenneth, *The Organizational Revolution.* New York, The & Brothers, 1953.

Bowers, Claude, *Beveridge and the Progressive Era.* New York, The Literary Guild, 1932.

———, *Jefferson and Hamilton.* Boston, New York, Houghton Mifflin Company, 1933.

Brandeis, Louis D., *The Curse of Bigness.* New York, The Viking Press, 1935.

———, *Other People's Money.* Washington, National Home Library Foundation, 1933.

Bridge, James, *The Inside History of the Carnegie Steel Company.* New York, The Aldine Book Company, 1923.

Brogan, Denis William, *The American Character.* New York, Alfred A. Knopf, 1941.

Bryce, James, *The American Commonwealth.* New York, The Macmillan Company, 1897; 2 volumes.

Burnham, James, *The Managerial Revolution.* New York, The John Day Company, 1941.

Burns, Arthur Roberts, *The Decline of Competition.* New York, McGraw Hill Book Company, 1936.

Butters, Keith J., and Lintner, John, and Carey, William, *Effects of Taxation: Corporate Mergers.* Cambridge, Harvard University Press, 1951.

Carnegie, Andrew, *Autobiography of Andrew Carnegie.* Boston, Houghton Mifflin Company, 1920.

———, *The Empire of Business.* New York, Doubleday, Page, 1902.

Chamberlain, John, *Farewell to Reform,* New York, Liveright Publinhers, Inc., 1932.

Channing, William E., *Works*. Boston, American Unitarian Association, 1875.

Chidsey, Donald B., *The Gentleman from New York*. New Haven, Yale University Press, 1935.

Clark, John D., *The Federal Trust Policy*. Baltimore, Johns Hopkins Press, 1931.

Clark, Victor S., *History of Manufacture in the United States*. Carnegie Institute of Washington, 1929.

Clews, Henry, *Fifty Years in Wall Street*. New York, Irving Publishing Company, 1928.

———, *Twenty-Eight Years in Wall Street*. New York, Irving Publishing Company, 1888.

———, *The Wall Street Point of View*. New York, Silver Burdett and Co., 1900.

Cochran, Thomas, *The American Business System 1900–1955*. Cambridge, Harvard University Press, 1957.

———, "Role and Sanction in American Entrepreneurial History" in *Change and the Entrepreneur*. Cambridge, Harvard University Press, 1949.

———, and Miller, William, *The Age of Enterprise*. New York, The Macmillan Company, 1942.

Commager, Henry Steele, *The American Mind*. New Haven, Yale University Press, 1950.

Comte, Auguste, *Cours de Philosophie Positive*. Paris, E. Littre, 1864; 3 volumes.

Coolidge, Louis A., *An Oldfashioned Senator: Orville H. Platt of Connecticut*. London, New York, G.P. Putnam's Sons, 1910.

Corey, Lewis, *The House of Morgan*. New York, G. Howard Watt, 1930.

Cortissoz, Royal, *The Life of Whitelaw Reid*. New York, Charles Scribner's Sons, 1921; 2 volumes.

Cullom, Shelby, *Fifty Years of Public Service*. New York, A.C. McClurg, 1911.

Curti, Merle, *The Growth of American Thought*. New York, Harper & Brothers, 1943.

———, *The Social Ideas of American Educators*. New York, Charles Scribner's Sons, 1935.

Daggett, Stuart, *Chapters on the History of the Southern Pacific*. New York, The Ronald Press Company, 1922.

Dale, Ernest, *Planning and Developing the Company Organization*

Structure. New York, American Management Association, 1952.

Dean, Joel, *Managerial Economics.* New York, Prentice-Hall, Inc., 1951.

Depew, Chauncey, *My Memories of Eighty Years.* New York, Charles Scribner's Sons, 1922.

―――, editor, *One Hundred Years of Commerce 1795–1895.* New York, D.O. Haynes & Co., 1895; 2 volumes.

Destler, Chester M.,*American Radicalism, 1865–1901.* Menasha, Wisc., Collegiate Press, 1946.

Dewing, Arthur, *Corporate Promotions and Reorganization.* Cambridge, Harvard University Press, 1914.

Diamond, Sigmund, *The Reputation of the American Businessman.* Cambridge, Harvard University Press, 1955.

Dixon, Frank Haigh, *Railroads and Government.* New York, Charles Scribner's Sons, 1922.

Dooly, Francis S., and Clemence, Richard V., *The Schumpeterian System.* Cambridge, Addison-Wesley Press, 1948.

Dorfman, Joseph, *The Economic Mind in American Civilization.* New York, The Viking Press, 1946; 3 volumes.

Douglas, Paul, *Real Wages in the United States.* Boston, Houghton Mifflin Company, 1930.

Drucker, Peter, *The New Society.* New York, Harper & Brothers, 1950.

―――, *The Practice of Management.* New York, Harper & Brothers, 1954.

Duncan, David, *The Life and Letters of Herbert Spencer.* New York, D. Appleton & Co., 1908.

Dunne, Peter Finley, *Mr. Doolys Now and Forever,* Stanford, California, Selected by Louis Filler, Academic Reprints, 1954.

Eddy, Arthur J., *The New Competition.* New York, London, D. Appleton & Co., 1912. (A previous edition, also referred to in the text was published by McClurg & Co., Chicago, 1904.)

Edwards, A.M., *Comparative Occupation Statistics 1870–1940.* Washington, U.S. Bureau of the Census, 1943.

Edwards, Corin, *Maintaining Competition.* New York, McGraw Hill Book Company, 1949.

Edwards, George, *The Evolution of Finance Capitalism.* New York, London, Longmans Green & Co., 1938.

Facts and Factors in Economic History. Articles by former students of Edwin F. Gay. Cambridge, Harvard University Press, 1932.

Faulkner, Harold Underwood, *The Quest for Social Justice.* New

York, The Macmillan Company, 1931.

Fetter, Frank Albert, *The Masquerade of Monopoly.* New York, Harcourt, Brace and Company, 1931.

Fish, Carl R., *The Civil Service Reform and Patronage.* New York, London, Longmans Green & Co., 1905.

———, *The Rise of the Common Man.* New York, The Macmillan Company, 1927.

Fiske, John, *American Political Ideas.* New York, Harper & Brothers, 1885.

Fitch, John A., *The Steel Workers.* New York, Russell Sage Foundation, The Pittsburg Survey, Charities Publication Committee, 1911.

Flynn, John T., *God's Gold.* New York, Harcourt, Brace and Company, 1932.

Foraker, Joseph B., *Notes of a Busy Life.* Cincinnati, Stewart and Kidd, 1920.

Frickey, Edwin, *Production in the United States, 1860–1914.* Cambridge, Harvard University Press, 1947.

Gabriel, Ralph H., *The Course of American Democratic Thought.* New York, The Ronald Press Company, 1940.

Ghent, W.J., *Our Benevolent Feudalism.* New York, The Macmillan Company, 1902.

———, *Mass and Class.* New York, The Macmillan Company, 1904.

Gibbons, Herbert Adams, *John Wanamaker.* New York, London, Harper & Brothers, 1926; 2 volumes.

Goldman, Eric F., *Rendezvous with Destiny.* New York, Alfred A. Knopf, 1952.

Gordon, Robert A., *Business Leadership in the Large Corporations.* Washington, The Brookings Institution, 1945.

Gras, N.S.B., *Business and Capitalism.* New York, Crofts, 1939.

———, and Larson, Henrietta M., *Casebook in American Business History.* New York, Crofts, 1939.

Hacker, Louis M., *The Triumph of American Capitalism.* New York, Simon & Schuster, 1940.

Hamilton, Walton, *The Politics of Industry.* New York, Allfred A. Knopf, 1957.

Hammond, Bray, *Banks and Politics in America.* Princeton, Princeton University Press, 1957.

Haney, Lewis H., *A Congressional History of Railroads in the United States.* Madison, Democratic Printing Company, 1910; 2 volumes.

————, *History of Economic Thought*. New York, The Macmillan Company, 1936.

Hansen, Alvin, *Business Cycles and National Income*. New York, W.W. Norton & Co., 1957.

Hazard, Blanche, *The Organization of the Boot and Shoe Industry in Massachusetts Before 1895*. Cambridge, Harvard University Press, 1921.

Hazlitt, Henry, *Economics in One Lesson*. New York, Pocket Books, 1946.

Hendrick, Burton J., *The Life of Andrew Carnegie*. Garden City, N.Y., Doubleday, Doran & Company, Inc., 1932; 2 volumes.

Hicks, John D., *The Populist Revolt*. Minneapolis, University of Minnesota Press, 1931.

Hidy, Ralph, and Hidy, Muriel, *Pioneering in Big Business, 1882–1915*. New York, Harper & Brothers, 1955.

Hoar, George F., *Autobiography of Seventy Years*. New York, Charles Scribner's Sons, 1903.

Hofstadter, Richard, *The Age of Reform*. New York, Alfred A. Knopf, 1955.

————, *The American Political Tradition*. New York, Alfred A. Knopf, 1948.

————, *Social Darwinism in American Thought*. Boston, The Beacon Press, 1945.

Howe, George Frederick, *Chester A. Arthur, A Quarter Century of Machine Politics*. New York, Dodd, Mead & Company, 1934.

Howells, William Dean, *A Traveller from Altruria*. New York, Harper & Brothers, 1894.

Hughes, Emmett John, *The Church and the Liberal Society*. Princeton, Princeton University Press, 1944.

Jaffee, A.C., and Stewart, C.D., *Manpower Resources and Utilization*. New York, John Wiley & Sons, Inc., 1901.

Jenks, Jeremiah W., *The Trust Problem*. New York, McClure, Phillips & Co., 1900.

Jervis, John B., *Railway Property*. New York, Phinney, Blakeman & Mason, 1861.

Jones, Eliot, *The Trust Problem in the United States*. New York, The Macmillan Company, 1921.

Josephson, Matthew, *The Politicos*. New York, Harcourt, Brace and Company, 1938.

———, *The President Makers.* New York, Harcourt, Brace and Company, 1940.

———, *The Robber Barons.* New York, Harcourt, Brace and Company, 1934

King, Wilford J., *The National Income and its Purchasing Power.* New York, National Bureau of Economic Research, 1930.

Kirk, Russell, *Academic Freedom.* Chicago, Henry Regnery, 1955.

———, *The Conservative Mind.* Chicago, Henry Regnery, 1953.

Kirkland, Edward C., *Business in the Gilded Age.* Madison, University of Wisconsin Press, 1952.

———, *Dream and Thought in the Business Community 1860–1900.* Ithaca, Cornell University Press, 1950.

———, *A History of American Economic Life.* New York, Appleton-Century-Crofts, Inc., 1939.

Krooss, Herman E., *American Economic Development.* Englewood Cliffs, Prentice-Hall, Inc., 1955.

———, *Business Opinion Between Two Wars.* Unpublished Ph.D. dissertation, New York University, 1947.

Kuznets, Simon, *National Income: A Summary of Findings.* New York, National Bureau of Economic Research, 1946.

LaFollette, Robert, *Autobiography.* Madison, R.M. LaFollette Publishing Company, 1913.

Larson, Henrietta M., *Guide to Business History.* Cambridge, Harvard University Press, 1948.

Larson, Thomas W., *Frenzied Finance.* New York, The Ridgeway-Thayer Company, 1905.

Lewis, Cleona, *America's Stake in International Investment.* Washington, The Brookings Institution, 1938.

Lloyd, Henry Demarest, *Wealth Against Commonwealth.* New York, Harper & Brothers, 1894.

Lynd, Robert and Lynd, Helen, *Middletown.* New York, Harcourt, Brace and Company, 1929.

Lynes, Russelll, *A Surfeit of Honey.* New York, Harper & Brothers, 1956.

Lynn, Kenneth S., *The Dream of Success.* Boston, Little Brown and Company, 1955.

McCloskey, Robert Green, *American Conservativism in the Age of Enterprise.* Cambridge, Harvard University Press, 1957.

Mackinder, Sir Halford J., *Democratic Ideas and Reality.* London, Constable Company, Ltd., 1919.

Madison, James, *The Writings of James Madison.* Edited by Gaillard Hunt. London, New York, G.P. Putnam's Sons, 1900–1910.

Mannheim, Karl, *Ideology and Utopia.* New York, Harcourt, Brace and Company, 1940.

———, *Man and Society in an Age of Reconstruction.* New York, Harcourt, Brace and Company, 1940.

Maurois, André, *The Miracle of America.* New York, Harper & Brothers, 1949.

Martin, Edward Sanford, *The Life of Joseph Hodges Choate.* New York, Charles Scribner's Sons, 1920; 2 volumes.

Martin, Frederick Townsend, *The Passinig of the Idle Rich.* Garden City, N.Y., Doubleday, Page & Company, 1934.

Maurer, Herman, *Great Enterprise: Growth and Behavior of the Big Corporation.* New York, The Macmillan Company, 1955.

Mayo, Elton, *The Human Problems of an Industrial Civilization.* Cambridge, Harvard University Press, 1935.

———, *The Social Problems of an Industrial Civilization.* Cambridge, Harvard University Press, 1945.

Messages and Papers of the Presidents. James Richardson, editor. Bureau of National Literature and Art, n.p., 1907, 10 volumes.

Michels, Robert, *Grundriss der Social Ökonomie.* Leipzig, A. Kroner, 1925.

———, *Political Parties.* New York, Hearst's International Library, 1915.

Miller, William, editor, *Men in Business.* Cambridge, Harvard University Press, 1952.

Mills, C. Wright, *The Power Elite.* New York, Oxford University Press, 1956.

———, *White Collar.* New York, Oxford University Press, 1953.

Moody, John, *The Truth About the Trusts.* New York, Moody Publishing Company, 1904.

Morris, Lloyd, *Postscript to Yesterday.* New York, Random House, 1947.

Moulton, Harold, *Income and Economic Progress.* Washington, The Brookings Institution, 1935.

Mumford, Lewis, *The Golden Day.* New York, W. W. Norton & Co., 1926.

Myers, Gustavus, *History of the Great American Fortunes.* New York, Random House, n.d., Modern Library edition.

National Association of Manufacturers, Economic Principles Commission, *The American Individual Enterprise System.* New York,

McGraw-Hill Publishing Company, 1951; 2 volumes.

Neil, Thomas P., *The Rise and Decline of Liberalism*. Milwaukee, Bruce Publishing Company, 1953.

Nevins, Allan, *American Press Opinion*. New York, Heath & Company, 1928.

———, *Abram S. Hewitt*. New York, Harper & Brothers, 1935.

———, *Hamilton Fish*. New York, Dodd, Mead & Co., 1932.

———, *John D. Rockefeller*. New York, Charles Scribner's Sons, 1940.

———, *Selected Writings of Abram S. Hewitt*. New York, Columbia University Press, 1937.

Newcomber, Mabel, *The Big Business Executive*. New York, Columbia University Press, 1935.

New England Cotton Manufacturer's Association, *Transactions*. n.p., September 1901.

Newmann, John von, and Morgenstern, Oskar, *Theory of Games and Economic Behavior*. Princeton, Princeton University Press, 1947.

Newman, William, *Administrative Action*. New York, Prentice-Hall, Inc., 1947.

Niebuhr, Reinhold, *The Irony of American History*. New York, Charles Scribner's Sons, 1955.

Ortega y Gasset, Jose, *Revolt of the Masses*. New York, W.W. Norton & Co., 1932.

Parrington, Vernon Louis, *Main Currents in American Thought*. New York, Harcourt, Brace & Company, 1927, 1939.

Pigou, Arthur C., *The Economics of Welfare*. London, The Macmillan Company, 1920.

Porter, Kenneth W., *John Jacob Astor*. Cambridge, Harvard University Press, 1941.

Pyle, Joseph G., *Life of James Hill*. New York, P. Smith, 1936, 2 volumes.

Queeney, Edgar M., *The Spirit of Enterprise*. New York, Charles Scribner's Sons, 1943.

Riesman, David, *Individualism Reconsidered*. Garden City, N.Y., Doubleday Anchor Book, Doubleday & Company, Inc., 1955.

———, *Thorstein Veblen*. New York, Charles Scribner's Sons, 1953.

———, with Nathan Glazer and Reuel Denney, *The Lonely Crowd*. New Haven, Yale University Presn, 1950.

Ripley, William Z., editor, *Trusts, Pools and Combinations*. Boston, New York, etc., Ginn & Co., 1905.

Ross, E.A., *Sin and Sanity*. Boston, Houghton Mifflin Company, 1907.

Russell, Charles Edward, *Blaine of Maine*. New York, Farrar & Rinehart, 1931.

Schlesinger, Arthur M., *The Rise of the City 1878–1898*. New York, The Macmillan Company, 1933.

Schlesinger, Arthur M., Jr., *The Age of Jackson*. Boston, Little, Brown & Co., 1945.

———, *The Crisis of the Old Order*. Boston, Houghton Mifflin Company, 1957.

———, *Paths to the Present*. New York, The Macmillan Company, 1949.

Schumpeter, Joseph A., *Capitalism, Socialism and Democracy*. New York, Harper & Brothers, 1950.

Siegfried, André, *America Comes of Age*. New York, Harcourt, Brace & Company, 1927.

Simon, Herbert A., *Administrative Behavior*. New York, The Macmillan Company, 1947.

Simons, A. M., *Social Forces in American History*. New York, The Macmillan Company, 1911.

Spencer, Herbert, *Dynamic Sociology*. New York, D. Appleton & Company, 1876-97; 2 volumes.

Stephenson, Nathaniel W., *Nelson W. Aldrich*. New York, Charles Scribner's Sons, 1930.

Steffens, Lincoln, *The Autobiography of Lincoln Steffens*. New York, Harcourt, Brace & Company, 1931.

———, *The Shame of the Cities*. New York, McClure, Phillips & Co., 1904.

Studenski, Paul, and Krooss, Herman, *Financial History of the United States*. New York, McGraw-Hill Book Company, 1952.

Sumner, William Graham, *What Social Classes Owe to Each Other*. New York, Harper & Brothers, 1883.

Sutton, Francis; Harris, Seymour; Kaysen, Karl, and Tobin, James, *The American Business Creed*. Cambridge, Harvard University Press, 1956.

Sweezey, Paul M., *Theory of Capitalist Development*. New York, Oxford University Press, 1944.

Tarbell, Ida M., *The History of the Standard Oil Company*. New York, The Macmillan Company, 1904.

———, *The Life of Elbert Gary*. New York, London, D. Appleton & Company, 1925.

———, *The Nationalizing of Business*, *1878–1898*. New York, The Macmillan Company, 1936.

Taussig, Frank W., and Joslyn, Carl S., *American Business Leaders*. New York, The Macmillan Company, 1932.

Todd, Helen, *A Man Named Grant*, Boston, Houghton Mifflin Company, 1940.

Towne, Henry, *The Engineer as Economist*. American Society of Mechanical Engineers, n.p., 1886.

Universities—National Bureau of Economic Research, *Business Concentration and Price Policy*. Princeton, Princeton University Press, 1958.

Van Hise, Charles, *Concentration and Control*. New York, The Macmillan Company, 1912.

Veblen, Thorstein, *Absentee Ownership and Business Enterprise in Recent Times*. New York, B.W. Huebsch, 1933. (The edition published by Viking Press, New York, 1938, is also referred to in the text.)

———, *The Theory of Business Enterprise*. New York, Charles Scribner's Sons, 1904.

———, *The Theory of the Leisure Class*. New York, The Macmillan Company, 1893.

Von Hayek, Fredrich A., *The Counter-Revolution of Science*. Glencoe, Ill., The Free Press, 1952.

Ware, Caroline F., *The Cultural Approach to History*. New York, Columbia University Press, 1940.

Watson, James B., *As I Knew Them*. Indianapolis, Bobbs Merrill Co., 1936.

Weber, Max, *Essays in Sociology*. New York, Oxford University Press, 1946.

———, *Wirtschaft und Gesellschaft*. Tübingen, J.C.B. Mohr, 1922.

Weston, Fred J., *The Role of Mergers in the Growth of Large Firms*. Berkeley, University of California Press, 1953.

White, William Allen, *Masks in a Pageant*. New York, The Macmillan Company, 1938.

Whyte, William S., *Is Anybody Listening?* New York, Simon & Schuster, 1952.

———, *The Organization Man*. New York, Simon & Schuster, 1956.

Williamson, Harold, editor, *The Growth of the American Economy*. New York, Prentice-Hall, Inc., 1944.

Wish, Harvey, *Society and Thought in Modern America*. New York, Longmans, Green & Co., 1952.

Wright, Chester, *Economic History of the United States*. New York,

McGraw-Hill Book Company, 1949.

Youman, Edward L., editor, *The Correlation and Conservation of Forces*. New York, D. Appleton & Company, 1871.

PUBLIC DOCUMENTS

Assembly of the State of New York, Trust Investigating Committee, ("Hepburn Committee"), *Report and Proceedings*, March 9, 1879.

Census of Manufacture of 1905. Washington, Government Printing Office, 1907; 4 volumes.

Commissioner of Corporations, *The International Harvester Company*. Washington, Government Printing Office, 1913.

———, *The Petroleum Industry*. Washington, Government Printing Office, 1907; 2 volumes.

———, *The Steel Industry*. Washington, Government Printing Office, 1911–1914.

Committee on Banking and Currency ("Pujo Committee"), *Investigation of Finance and Monetary Concentration in the United States*. Washington, House of Representatives, 63rd Congress, 1913; 3 volumes.

Committee on Interstate Commerce, *Hearings on the Control of Corporations*. Washington, Senate Resolution 98, 63rd Congress, 2nd Session, 1912–14.

Special Committee on Investigation of the United States Steel Corporation ("Stanley Committee"), *Hearings, House Office Report 22*. Washington, Government Printing Office, 1911.

State of New York, Trust Investigating Committee, *Report and Proceedings*. March 9, 1897.

U.S. Industrial Commission, *Report on the Relations and Conditions of Capital and Labor*. Washington, Government Printing Office, 1900; 19 volumes.

———, *Report on Industrial Combinations*. Washington, Government Printing Office, 1900; Volumes 1, 4, 13.

———, *Final Report of Industrial Commission*. Washington, Government Printing Office, 1902; Volume XIX.

U.S. Strike Commission, *Report and Testimony on the Chicago Strike*. Washington, Government Printing Office, 1895.

MAGAZINE AND JOURNAL ARTICLES OF
SPECIAL INTEREST

Beach, Moses Y., "In Defense of Trusts." *Forum*, VIII, September, 1889.

Blicksilver, Jack, "George Gunton, Pioneer Spokesman for a Labor-Big Business Entente." *The Business History Review*, XXXI, Spring, 1957, pp. 1ff.

Bork, Robert H., "Antitrust in Dubious Battle." *Fortune*, September, 1969, pp. 103ff.

Carnegie, Andrew, "The Bugaboo of Trusts." *North American Review*, CXLVIII, February 1889, pp. 141ff.

Clark, John B., "Feudalism or Commonwealth." *Independent*, May 1902, pp. 1276–9.

Chandler, Alfred D., "Management Decentralization: An Historical Analysis." *The Business History Review*, XXX, June 1956, pp. 111ff.

Fortune, "The Moral History of United States Business," an editorial, XL, December 1949, pp. 143ff.

Haney, Lewis H., "Price Fixing in a Competitive Industry." *American Economic Review*, IX, 1919, pp. 47ff.

Klyce, E.D.H., "Scientific Management and the Moral Law." *Outlook*, 1911, pp. 660ff.

Means, Gardner C., "The Growth in the Relative Importance of the Large Corporation in American Economic Life." *American Economic Review*, XXI, March 1931, pp. 10–37.

———, "Industrial Prices and their Relative Inflexibility." *Senate Document #13*, 74th Congress, First Session, 1940.

Miller, William, "American Historians and the Business Elite." *The Journal of Economic History*, IX, 1949, pp. 196-200.

———, "The Recruitment of the American Business Elite." *Quarterly Journal of Economics*, LXIV, 1950, pp. 242–253.

Mills, C. Wright, "The American Business Elite." *Journal of Economic History*, Volume V, Supplement, 1945, pp. 20–40.

The Nation, "The Competition of Trusts," an editorial, XLVIII, December 20, 1888.

———, "Corporate Absolutism," an editorial. LXXXI, July-December 1905, pp. 252ff.

Peterson, Shorey, "Antitrust and the Classical Model." *American Economic Review*, March 1957, pp. 60ff.

Polanyi, Karl, "Our Obsolete Market Mentality." *Commentary*, February, 1947, pp. 109–117.
Roberts, George E., "Can There Be a Good Trust?" *Forum*, XXX, Sept. 1900-Feb. 1901, pp. 286ff.
Roosevelt, Theodore, "The Trusts, the People and the Square Deal." *Outlook*, pp. 649ff.
Sage, Russell, "A Grave Danger to the Community." *North American*
Schwab, Charles, "What may be Expected in the Steel and Iron Industry." North American Review, CLXXII, May 1901, pp. 655–64. *Review*, CLXXII, May 1901, pp. 641–6.
Stigler, George, "Monopoly and Oligopoly by Merger." *American Economics Review*, Proceedings, XL, May 1950.
Vanderlip, Frank A., "The Views of Frank A. Vanderlip." *Outlook*, 1911, pp. 858-62.
White, Horace, "Trusts." *The Commercial and Financial Chronicle*, XLVI, July 28, 1888.
White, William S., "The Misunderstood Conservative." *Harper's*, September 1958, pp. 77ff.

PERIODICALS

American Industries (NAM publication), 1902–13.
Bankers' Magazine, 1882–1913.
Bankers' Monthly, 1883–1910.
Bulletin of the American Iron and Steel Association, 1867–1913.
The Commercial and Financial Chronicle, 1880–1913.
Fortune, 1949–1970.
Forum, 1886–1914.
Literary Digest (merged with *Public Opinion* 1906), 1906–1914.
The Nation, 1878–1913.
Outlook, 1910–1913.
Political Science Quarterly, January 1889.
Public Opinion, 1886–1906.
Scientific American, XVI, 1867.
World's Work, 1900–1914.
Yale Law Journal, January 1951.

NEWSPAPERS

New York Evening Post, 1885–1905.
New York Tribune, 1898–1902.

INDEXES

NAME INDEX

SUBJECT INDEX